GIVING IS THE GOOD LIFE

Randy Alcorn

GIVING
IS THE
GOOD
LIFE

The Unexpected Path to
Purpose and Joy

Tyndale House Publishers, Inc.
Carol Stream, Illinois

Visit Tyndale online at www.tyndale.com.

Visit Tyndale Momentum online at www.tyndalemomentum.com.

Visit Randy Alcorn's website at www.epm.org.

TYNDALE and Tyndale's quill logo are registered trademarks of Tyndale House Publishers, Inc.

Giving Is the Good Life: The Unexpected Path to Purpose and Joy

Designed by Dean H. Renninger

Edited by Stephanie Rische

The author is grateful for the helpful counsel of the literary agency, WTA Services LLC, Franklin, TN.

For information about special discounts for bulk purchases, please contact Tyndale House
Publishers at csresponse@tyndale.com, or call 1-800-323-9400.

ISBN 978-1-4964-2593-5

Printed in the United States of America

25   24   23   22   21   20   19
7   6   5   4   3   2   1

To Paul and Michele Norquist and their wonderful children,
for making our personal lives and our church a much richer place; for serving and
honoring Jesus and shepherding God's people with pure and humble hearts.

To Linda Jeffries,
for your many years of faithful, excellent, and kindhearted service to all our EPM
staff, to Nanci and me, and to everyone around the world you've touched through
our ministry.

To Bobby and Tanya Atkins,
for your amazing servants' hearts as you have cheerfully labored behind the scenes
over the decades for our beloved Good Shepherd Community Church.

To Karen Stout Coleman,
a great and happy-in-Jesus servant of God, in Cameroon and in Gresham and
Boring and Sandy, Oregon, with EPM and in every other place she ever set foot.
Now with Jesus, Karen's presence has made Heaven richer and her absence has
made Earth poorer. The grand reunion awaits. We can't wait to see you again,
precious sister.

Contents

CHAPTER 1

WHAT IS THE GOOD LIFE?

....

Not life, but a good life, is to be chiefly valued.
SOCRATES

The good life is reserved for the person who fears God,
who lives reverently in his presence.
ECCLESIASTES 8:12, MSG

Are you living the good life? If not, I know you wish you were.

People define the good life in different ways, but *everybody* wants to live it. After all, what's the alternative? Living a bad life? A pointless, guilt-ridden, or miserable life?

We'd all choose the good life any day, and yet we often don't understand how to make it happen.

A quick online search reveals that most people's idea of the good life includes happiness. That makes sense—nobody wants to be unhappy. Most of us also want to make other people happy and help them if we can. But when it comes down to it, even Christ-followers suspect that spending our lives serving God and others might cost us our happiness.

Wouldn't it be great if we could do what pleases God *and* what's best for others, while at the same time enjoying happiness and deep satisfaction?

But that's not possible, you may think.

Or is it?

What if we really can live the good life without being selfish? What if God not only wants us to live life more abundantly, as Jesus put it (John 10:10), but also provides clear instructions for how to actually experience it? What if it's possible to discover what to embrace and what to avoid so we can live a meaningful and fulfilling life—*the good life*—even in this broken world?

Does that sound too good to be true?

Actually, it's both "too good" *and* true.

That's what this book is about.

The Good Life Is Countercultural

We live in a world that screams, "Make lots of money and spend it on yourself, and you'll be happy. *That's* the good life!"

There's just one problem. It's a lie.

Throughout his ministry, Jesus repeatedly turned our definition of the good life on its head. For instance, he said, "There is more happiness in giving than in receiving" (Acts 20:35, GNT).

Jesus told us that parting with money to help others will bring us more joy than hanging on to that money. Counterintuitive as it may seem, our greatest good, and the happiness that accompanies it, is found in giving, not receiving.

In other words, generosity is the good life.

This idea that giving away money and possessions equals happiness is a paradox. Human reasoning says that spending money on ourselves is in our best interest—and to a degree, that's true. We all need food to eat, a place to live, clothes to wear. But once our basic needs are met, money can easily stop helping us and start hurting us.

According to CreditCards.com, the average American has nearly $16,000 in credit card debt. The average college student graduates with $40,000 in student loans, and some with far more. Almost 40 percent of Americans carry credit card debt month to month, continuing to spend more than they have and remaining in financial bondage. Debt is routinely incurred in pursuing the good life, yet psychologists attest that the debt-funded lifestyle leads to depression, anxiety, resentment, stress, denial, anger, frustration, regret, shame, embarrassment, and fear.[1] This is the very opposite of the good life. It's the terrible life!

Here's a truth that can set us free: "living large" actually makes us smaller. Living "the good life" (as our culture defines it) results in *missing* the best life.

Deep down, we all know it's true: you can spend every last cent you own on yourself—and, through credit, far more—and still end up miserable. In fact, if you want to be miserable, greed and stinginess are the perfect recipe. Those who hoard their money, like those who spend it all on themselves, are the unhappiest people on the planet. Jesus calls us to do something radical: love others by giving away our money and time. That sounds like loss, not gain. Yet in God's economy, that's exactly how we can expand and enhance our own lives.

Generosity Pays Off

This book really *is* about living the good life. I say this because you may wonder if I'm trying to make the generous Christian life sound easier and happier than it really is.

First, I'm not suggesting that giving always comes easily or without sacrifice. What I *am* saying is that in God's providence, the payoff far outweighs the sacrifice. Generosity is God's best, designed just for us. This is always true in the long run, and usually it's true in the short run too.

Suppose I give up some vanilla lattes and two lunches out each month in order to support a child in Haiti. There's nothing wrong with lattes or meals out, and I may miss them, but thoughts of how the money helps a needy child flood me with happiness greater and far more enduring than twenty minutes of pleasure from a drink or eating out. My life has a purpose beyond myself, and as I say no to that small thing, my day is put in perspective. That gladness and perspective don't disappear when I finish the meal or toss the coffee cup in the recycle bin.

This book is about that kind of joy-filled, openhanded adventure of following Jesus, which brings us lasting pleasure and reaches far beyond this life to the next.

So what's ahead? In part 1 we'll explore the good life as God defines it and discover what Jesus meant when he said, "I have come that they may have life, and that they may have it more abundantly" (John 10:10, NKJV). The first step to finding life is clear: we need to place our trust in Christ. That's where eternal life—the ultimate good life—begins. Jesus said, "If anyone thirsts, let him come to me and drink. Whoever believes in me, as the Scripture has said, 'Out of his heart will flow rivers of living water'" (John 7:37-38).

Once we believe in Christ, what can we do to experience the abundant life—a life overflowing with vibrancy, satisfaction, and contentment?

Though we've been granted eternal life, many Christians don't fully experience what Jesus came to give us. The stresses

THE BEST CHRISTMAS EVER

While shopping online for a bike as a present for her dad, ten-year-old Riley and her mom followed a video link about an organization that provides specially engineered bicycles for individuals with disabilities. Seeing the happy faces of people riding the bikes, Riley told her mom, "I'm going to buy a bike for one of those kids."

Riley's mom loved her daughter's heart, but the cost of just one special bike was a few thousand dollars. Two days later, Riley showed her mom a letter she'd written explaining how the bikes could help those in need and requesting donations.

After Riley sent the letter to seventy-five relatives and friends, money started pouring in. Word spread, and as Christmas neared, more donations came. On Christmas, Riley donned a Santa hat and delivered bicycles to three girls: thirteen-year-old Ava, who has spina bifida; fifteen-year-old Jenny, who has cerebral palsy; and four-year-old Rose, who has a rare genetic disorder.

"This is the best Christmas I ever had," Riley declared.

She ultimately raised enough to pay for seven bikes, each given to a grateful recipient.

Riley says that when she rides her bicycle with one of the girls she gave a bike to, "I like to go fast, get sweaty, and feel the breeze. . . . So does Ava. She pumps with her arms, not her feet, but she really flies."

Riley plans to continue raising funds for bicycles every Christmas. She says, "I want kids to feel the wind in their faces."*

* "Project Mobility Cycles for Life Riley Christensen 2010 Adaptive Cycle Giveaway," YouTube video, 1:46, posted by Project Mobility, December 16, 2011, https://www.youtube.com/watch?v=RbuhnHXXoF8. See also Gary Sledge, "5 Stories That Celebrate the Spirit of Giving," *Reader's Digest*, accessed January 27, 2019, https://www.rd.com /true-stories/inspiring/5-stories-that-celebrate-the-spirit-of-giving/.

and pressures of life weigh us down and leave us feeling like we're missing something. We lose both joy and purpose. Life becomes a drudgery, not an adventure. It's a shrunken life, not a flourishing one.

If that's where you find yourself, take heart. True, it's not possible to eliminate difficulties and challenges until we're living at last in the world we were made for (the New Earth, not this one). But we certainly don't have to wait until we die to experience the abundant life Jesus promised.

Part 2 of this book delivers the bad news and the very good news about money, as described in 1 Timothy 6. The bad news is that loving and serving money will destroy us and rob us of life and happiness. The good news is that if we recognize God's ownership of everything, we'll steward our resources to help meet physical and spiritual needs. Our reward will be both future rewards and present contentment, purpose, and what Scripture calls "the life that is truly life" (1 Timothy 6:19, NIV).

Giving Is an Eternal Investment

Okay, you might be thinking, *I understand that giving to others can bring me happiness. But is there really any benefit beyond that initial good feeling I get when I help someone?*

One of the biggest misconceptions about giving is that the money we part with to help the needy or to spread the gospel just disappears and is gone forever. While we hope others will benefit from it, we're quite sure *we* won't. We even buy into the devil's lie that giving will rob us of the good life.

We couldn't be more wrong.

Jesus told his disciples that when they gave money away, their hearts would follow the treasures they were storing in Heaven (Matthew 6:19-21). He also said that at the Resurrection, God would reward them for helping the needy (Luke 14:14). Somehow we're forever connected to what we give and the people we give it to. Martin Luther has been credited with saying, "I have held many things in my hands and I have lost them all. But whatever I have placed in God's hands, that I still possess."

The Bible shows that anything we put in God's hands is an investment in eternity. But that doesn't just mean that *someday* our giving will bring us good. It will actually do us good here and now—at the same time it does good for others. That's why the good life is inseparable from generosity.

I once heard a longtime Christian say, "I always used to tithe, checking off the box of spiritual duties. I never got excited about it. Then, as my wife and I learned about generosity, suddenly giving became fun. My wife told me that until then she'd never seen me write a check with a smile on my face!"

Does this seem too good to be true? Keep reading, because as we'll discover, the truth is far better than we could ever imagine.

Generosity Is Good for Everyone, Not Just Christians

Even outside the Christian world, there's a great deal of emphasis on philanthropy. Bill Gates, Warren Buffett, and various actors, musicians, and athletes have championed giving to various causes. It's not uncommon for people who don't profess Christ to believe in helping the poor and advocating for the oppressed.

In fact, modern research has much to say about the benefits of generosity. In their book *The Paradox of Generosity: Giving We Receive, Grasping We Lose*, sociologists Christian Smith and Hilary Davidson write about Smith's findings on giving, which are based on years of careful studies. His conclusions may seem unexpected, but they shouldn't be at all surprising to those who understand we're created in the image of a generous God. They write, "Those who give, receive back in turn. By spending ourselves for others' well-being, we enhance our own standing. . . . This is not only a philosophical or religious teaching; it is a sociological fact."[2]

Smith's extensive research, which included more than two thousand surveys of American adults and many personal interviews, reveals this:

> Giving money, volunteering, being relationally generous, being a generous neighbor and friend, and personally valuing the importance of being a generous person are all significantly, positively correlated with greater personal happiness, physical health, a stronger sense of purpose in life, avoidance of symptoms of depression, and a greater interest in personal growth.[3]

In her book *The Giving Way to Happiness: Stories and Science behind the Life-Changing Power of Giving*, Jenny Santi shares the results of a 2008 study by Professor Elizabeth Dunn of the University of British Columbia. Participants received an envelope with either five dollars or twenty dollars. Some were instructed to spend the money by the end of the day; others were told to give it away. "Participants who were instructed to spend the money on a gift for someone else or for a charitable donation reported greater happiness than those who were instructed to spend the money on themselves."[4]

These are not isolated examples. Scientific studies back up what God's Word has been saying for thousands of years: generosity pays immeasurable dividends. God rewards people for generosity in this life as well as in the life to come. He does this because he is a God of grace and a lavish giver himself.

Generosity Benefits Recipients *and* Givers

Surprisingly, the Bible doesn't talk that much about how giving changes the lives of its recipients. More often, it talks about what giving does for *the one who gives*.

I could have filled this book with stories of how the hungry are fed, how clean water saves children, and how people weep for joy when they receive God's Word in their heart language. While I've included some of those vital stories, I'm following the example of Scripture by focusing on the giver's happiness and spiritual transformation.

GOD'S BONUS

Jack Alexander says, "Our giving went to a whole 'nother level when one day I got my first bonus ever. It was $5,000. I organized a dinner at Wendy's with Lisa and my two little boys to tell them."

When he shared the news with his family, Lisa responded, "You won't believe what happened today." She said they had received a letter from a nurse in Sudan who needed to buy a Jeep. The cost of that vehicle? Five thousand dollars!

Jack's initial response was, "Noooooo . . ."

But Lisa said these fateful words: "Will you pray about it?"

"God met me in that prayer, and he showed me two things," Jack says. "First, he showed me . . . the value of probably hundreds of kids who could get inoculations, and people [who] could be helped. I was just overwhelmed with what a great investment it was to give that money away. The second thing I really knew was from the Holy Spirit because I got this overwhelming sense . . . that this was a privilege, that God . . . had chosen us to do it and join his work. And we gave the money away."*

* "Jack and Lisa Alexander: 2015 Celebration of Generosity," Vimeo video, 20:25, Generous Giving, April 25, 2015, https://vimeo.com/126023293.

This small book isn't big enough to explore the extent of the world's needs. While I briefly summarize the facts of poverty, injustice, and unreached people groups, you are probably aware of those needs already or you can learn about them elsewhere. I believe the best way I can serve the needy is to show God's people the wonder and joy, as well as the present and future rewards, of generous giving.

This book is full of stories of people who have put into practice the life-changing biblical principles of generosity. Each story is a practical example that can help stimulate your imagination and expand your dreams of serving Jesus in fresh ways. These real-life models give you not just words to remember but footprints to follow. In turn, as you apply these principles in your own unique way and place, you will become an example to others, "a letter from Christ . . . written not with pen and ink, but with the Spirit of the living God . . . carved not on tablets of stone, but on human hearts" (2 Corinthians 3:3, NLT).

I'm excited about how we can change others' lives through our giving. But I'm also excited about how giving can change *our* lives, for God's glory and our good.

I pray that this book will give you a bigger view of God and of generosity—one that stretches far beyond this present life. And in the process, I pray that you will understand more than ever what the good life is really all about.

PART 1

THE GOOD LIFE

I have come that they may have life, and
that they may have it more abundantly.

JOHN 10:10, NKJV

CHAPTER 2

HAVING MONEY IS NOT THE GOOD LIFE

....

He who hath never led a good life, cannot die a good death.
ROBERT BELLARMINE

*The good life begins in the fear of GOD—do that and
you'll know the blessing of GOD. His Hallelujah lasts forever!*
PSALM 111:10, MSG

In 2007, actor Owen Wilson slashed his wrists in an unsuccessful
suicide attempt. *People* magazine's cover story about the "funny
man who had it all" implied that his material abundance gave
him every reason to live. Public shock over his actions unveiled
the widespread belief that money, fame, cars, sex, a second home
on the shores of Maui, and the whole celebrity package really
do buy happiness. After all, wasn't Owen Wilson living the
good life?[1]

In a subsequent issue of *People*, one letter to the editor astutely
asked, "If a red-hot career, traveling the globe, a Malibu mansion
and million-dollar paychecks didn't prevent Owen's 'demons' from
rearing their ugly heads before the August incident, why would
they do the trick now?"[2]

The irony is inescapable: most of Owen Wilson's fans would have, in a heartbeat, exchanged their mundane, commonplace lives for that of their idol. But the trade would have given them the life Wilson desperately wanted out of.

Most of us don't have access to the amount of money and possessions celebrities do, but a similar story plays out in countless lives. If money were enough to constitute the good life, why does the prosperity-driven United States have a higher per capita suicide rate than war-torn, tragedy-plagued, poverty-riddled Sudan?[3]

One thing is clear: what's relentlessly advertised and sold to us as the good life is *not* the abundant life Jesus promised.

Exchanging Good Things for Great Things

A few years ago, my wife, Nanci, and I spent five days aboard a ship that belongs to Operation Mobilization. The *Logos Hope* goes from port to port, bringing the gospel message all over the world. The volunteer teams use street dramas and music to share the Good News; other crew members distribute Bibles and Christian books to people visiting the ship's huge bookstore.

While docked in Jamaica, we watched a crew of four hundred young people from sixty different nations welcome and serve thousands of visitors. Some also left the ship for the day to serve the poor in surrounding communities.

As we talked late into the night with crew members, we heard laughter and stories of God's life-giving grace. These young people, many with little cash in their pockets and without credit cards, could have been making much more money doing something else. We might have felt sorry for them, since

THE HAPPIEST PLACE ON EARTH

Angel Williams tells this story: "My best friend's family took me in after my parents split up. That same year, our senior class was going to Disneyland. Through fundraising, the cost was down to forty dollars, but I had no financial support and didn't want to ask for help. A teacher reminded me that the money was due, but I just didn't have it. The next day I saw my name on the list of paid students. When I went to the office to let them know of the error, I was told my payment had been made. I knew my teacher had done this for me, and that has stuck with me all my life. He wanted no thanks—he just wanted me to be part of the joy."*

* Facebook comment in reply to my post requesting giving stories.

accommodations and food service on the *Logos Hope* are more like a warship than a cruise ship, and they often worked long hours at menial chores. Instead, we envied them, because while it wasn't a perfect life, for most it was clearly an authentic, rewarding, happy-making life.

Nanci and I met Audrey, a young woman from the Philippines who had been serving for a year in the ship's laundry. She told us a story about people trusting Christ after she spoke to them. Even though she didn't know their language and they didn't know hers, they had somehow understood her words. She'd witnessed a miracle. Her face beaming with joy, she said, "Every time I remember this story, I'm constantly amazed how limitless and how powerful our God is. It is such a privilege to be bringing this hope to all the people!"[4]

So who lives the good life: Owen Wilson or Audrey on the *Logos Hope*?

What Jesus Said about Wealth

Google "the good life," and you'll find advice from both secular and religious sources on how to achieve a life worth living. Some of these attempt to temper the money-centered worldview. An article on MarketWatch.com entitled "The Good Life Is Not Only about Money" says, "Being healthy and wealthy have always been two well-known ingredients of happiness," but it goes on to point out the importance of "being spiritually, emotionally, mentally, and physically healthy."[5]

Still, when I searched for "he's living the good life," the first two videos that popped up were people in plush surroundings, the first one flipping through a huge stack of cash and singing about partying, and the second one lounging in a luxury resort. A third was about a famous nightclub. One article was titled "The Keys to Building Wealth and Living the Good Life."

Neither the videos nor the article clearly defines the good life. Why? Because the creators assume the viewers and the readers agree it's about accumulating and spending lots of money to purchase happiness.

Yet despite both personal experiences and studies indicating money alone doesn't bring the good life, countless people think and live and make choices as if it does.

Every truth seeker must grasp how fundamentally flawed this worldview really is. To correct this fatal perspective, Jesus said, "Watch out! Be on your guard against all kinds of greed; life does not consist in an abundance of possessions" (Luke 12:15, NIV).

The last portion of this verse is rendered this way in different translations:

- Your true life is not made up of the things you own. (GNT)
- Life is not measured by how much you own. (NLT)
- Even if a man has much more than he needs, it cannot give him life. (WE)

Jesus immediately followed this statement with the parable of the rich fool, turning our idea of the good life upside down:

There was a rich man who had some land, which grew a good crop. He thought to himself, "What will I do? I have no place to keep all my crops." Then he said, "This is what I will do: I will tear down my barns and build bigger ones, and there I will store all my grain and other goods. Then I can say to myself, 'I have enough good things stored to last for many years. Rest, eat, drink, and enjoy life!'"

LUKE 12:16-19, NCV

So far, doesn't this story sound great? Store up lots of money for yourself, retire early, and live large!

These different translations of verse 19 capture the rich man's philosophy, which sounds remarkably like the American dream:

- Live it up! Eat, drink, and enjoy yourself. (CEV)
- Take your ease, eat, drink, be merry. (RSV)
- Relax! Eat, drink and have a good time! (PHILLIPS)
- You've got it made and can now retire. Take it easy and have the time of your life! (MSG)

Jesus didn't accuse the man of dishonesty, theft, or injustice. For all we know, he might have faithfully attended synagogue. He was living the life others dreamed of. What's wrong with that?

Then comes the big surprise: "But God said to him, 'You fool! Tonight you will die. Then who will get what you have stored up?'" (Luke 12:20, CEV).

What derailed the rich man's attempts to live what he believed was the good life? First, death. Second, God's judgment on his now irreversible life. In the predigital age, a high school photography teacher taught me how to develop photos by immersing photo paper in solutions. As long as the photograph remains in the developing solution, it can change. But once it's dropped into the stop bath, it's permanently fixed. Likewise, when we die and enter eternity, our lives on Earth will be permanently fixed, never again to be altered or revised. "People are destined to die once, and after that to face judgment" (Hebrews 9:27, NIV).

The rich man wasn't merely a fool like the kind described in the book of Proverbs, who still had an opportunity to repent and choose wisdom (see, for example, Proverbs 26). God's appraisal of us after we die is final. There's no reset button, no do-overs. If at the end of your life God calls you a fool, you'll be a fool forever.

This parable serves as a warning to all of us. Jesus applies the rich fool's experience to that of others: "So is the one who lays up treasure for himself and is not rich toward God" (Luke 12:21). To lay up treasures for ourselves and not be rich toward God means clinging to our riches instead of honoring God by helping those who are physically and spiritually needy.

God takes our stinginess or generosity personally. To give lavishly is to be rich toward him; to hoard or spend on ourselves without regard for others is to be impoverished toward God. He accepts our gifts to the needy as if they were given directly to him: "Whoever is generous to the poor lends to the LORD, and he will repay him for his deed" (Proverbs 19:17). Jesus reiterated the same principle: "The King will reply, 'Truly I tell you, whatever you did for one of the least of these brothers and sisters of mine, you did for me. . . . Whatever you did not do for one of the least of these, you did not do for me'" (Matthew 25:40, 45, NIV).

Any lifestyle that doesn't align with God's priorities and won't hold up after death is not a good one—no matter how glamorous or appealing or sensible it seems at the time.

What Makes Someone a Fool?

In Christ's story of the rich fool, the word translated "fool" literally means "unthinking one." Mindless. Senseless. The rich fool was out of touch with eternal realities. Despite death's inevitability, he failed to prepare for it—and failed to remember that he would give an account to God (Romans 14:12).

The rich fool stored up treasures for himself on Earth as if he were the center of the universe and as if this world was where he'd live forever. The man was a fool to imagine his silver, gold, crops, land, and barns were actually his. He was a fool to ignore God's claims on him and his possessions:

- The earth is the LORD's, and everything in it, the world, and all who live in it. (Psalm 24:1, NIV)
- "The silver is mine and the gold is mine," declares the LORD Almighty. (Haggai 2:8, NIV)

A wise person will regularly ask, "Lord, what do you want me to do with all you have put in my hands?" God reveals himself to us in the living Word—Jesus—and the written Word—Scripture. That means we don't have to wait until we die to discover how we should have lived. God's Word tells us exactly how to prepare now for the afterlife. Though our culture and even some of our Christian friends may encourage us to do so, we don't have to live like fools!

In the world's eyes, the rich fool was a great success. Today he would be admired, and he might even be placed on a church or ministry board. But in the end, all his success counted for nothing. D. L. Moody said, "Our greatest fear should not be of failure, but of succeeding at something that doesn't really matter."[6]

Had the rich fool acknowledged God as his Creator and Redeemer, and as the ultimate owner of everything he possessed, he would have been rich toward God and stored up treasures in Heaven. Instead, he stored up for himself treasures on Earth and was suddenly and eternally parted from them by death.

The most troubling aspect of this parable is that if we met this man, most of us would commend him for his foresight. *Yet foresight is exactly what he lacked.* He may have planned twenty years ahead, but he failed to plan twenty million years ahead. And as it turned out, he didn't even have twenty years before facing God in judgment. He had closer to twenty minutes.

When it comes to how we view money and possessions and what we do with them, what's right is also smart, and what's wrong is also stupid. In the end, this man's "good life" turned out to be an illusion. Notice he isn't called the rich *sinner*, but the rich *fool*.

Christian Smith and Hilary Davidson observed this about those who fail to live generous lives:

By clinging to what we have, we lose out on higher goods we might gain. By holding onto what we possess, we diminish its long-term value to us. In protecting only ourselves against future uncertainties and misfortunes, we become more anxious about uncertainties and vulnerable to future misfortunes. In short, by failing to care well for others, we actually do not properly take care of ourselves.[7]

Materialists are self-destructive keepers. Christ-followers are self-enriching givers. Why? Because giving inevitably enlarges our hearts, lives, and capacity for joy.

Don't misunderstand. The true good life doesn't say no to wealth or pleasures. Rather, it says yes to *greater and lasting* wealth and pleasures that are found when we cheerfully part with God's money and possessions for others' good and God's glory.

God graciously gives us money and possessions to meet real needs, both our own needs and the needs of others. He wants us to enjoy life, but he doesn't entrust excess to us so we can indulge excessive wants. Money and possessions are not life giving. They are utterly incapable of imparting to us the identity, purpose, significance, and security we crave.

I recently heard someone talk about the rampant unhappiness, disease, and disillusionment he and his friends experienced while, he said, they were "living the good life." Though I put that phrase in quotation marks, this person didn't use air quotes or note the irony that what he called the "good life" was in fact devastatingly bad. In his case, the "good life" included drugs and sexual immorality, led to the loss of his wife and children, and ultimately left him utterly empty.

Even when this so-called good life brought times of enjoyment, it was only "the fleeting pleasures of sin" (Hebrews 11:25). Such pleasures don't even last in this world, and they certainly won't outlive this life. The rich man in Christ's story learned the hard way that his prosperity was short lived. It came to a dramatic and eternal end at his death, when God proclaimed, "You fool!"

Our Source of Life

To understand what constitutes the good life, we need to understand what life really is, where it comes from, and where it's going.

ETERNAL LIFE INSURANCE

As a teenager, Art DeMoss loved gambling, and he eventually ended up in Las Vegas with the goal of getting rich. He opened a couple of betting rooms, handling upwards of $10,000 daily. "I was searching for something," he said, "and I never realized at the time what I was really searching for." Though he was remarkably successful, he had no peace or happiness.

One night Art attended an evangelistic meeting, where he heard the gospel. Jesus saved him, and he surrendered his life to the Lord. An amazing transformation took place in his heart: money was dethroned.

Knowing he needed a new profession, Art and his wife Nancy moved to Philadelphia and founded National Liberty insurance company. Their business grew quickly, but Art kept his eyes on his main purpose: to glorify God and advance God's Kingdom.

Art said to his pastor, "I'm going to give my life to full-time Christian service."

The pastor responded, "Are you going to become a missionary?"

"Oh, no," Art said. "We have enough missionaries. . . . We need people who will make a huge amount of money to support missionaries."

God is the eternal source of life. He gave human beings "the breath of life" (Genesis 2:7), and he designed the first people to experience communion with himself, the living God. In the presence of Eden's tree of life (Genesis 2:9), he walked with Adam and Eve as they enjoyed a life-giving and delightful relationship (Genesis 3:8). God warned them, though, that if they ate of the fruit of one particular tree, this beautiful life would tragically end in death (Genesis 2:17).

They disobeyed, and as promised, sin brought death. While

Over the years, Art and Nancy used their successful business to share their love for Jesus with other professionals. Art told his story to nearly everyone who met with him in his office. He challenged others, "Don't spend your life; invest it!"

Art joined the board of directors for Campus Crusade for Christ (Cru), where his significant financial investments enabled millions around the world to hear the good news of Jesus Christ. In 1979, Art died suddenly at the age of fifty-three. A plaque underneath his portrait at Cru's headquarters says, "His life was dedicated to Christ and his service."[*]

Without exception, those who knew Art DeMoss, including his daughter Nancy Leigh, testify that he was a man whose passion for Jesus and the gospel was matched only by his passion for giving. We can learn much from the fact that these passions were ultimately indistinguishable from each other.

After Art's death, the Arthur S. DeMoss foundation was created, which quietly funds evangelistic work, including publishing the widely distributed *Power for Living* evangelistic booklet.

[*] John Rinehart, "The Gospel Patron behind Cru," Gospel Patrons, December 7, 2017, https://www.gospelpatrons.org/articles/the-gospel-patron-behind-cru.

Adam and Eve's physical death came gradually, the end of their life-giving spiritual relationship with God was immediate.

Ever since, people have lived in a state of spiritual death, with dying bodies, decaying relationships, and failed dreams. Death is the new normal. But that's not the end of the story. The good news of the gospel is that Jesus' sacrifice conquers sin and death on our behalf.

John's Gospel tells us that God created the world through Jesus, bringing life and light to his creation (John 1:1-5). He raised Lazarus from the dead to display his power to make dead people alive again (John 11:42-44). Then he, too, rose from the grave, ensuring the ultimate death of sin and the defeat of death itself. His resurrection justifies us and gives us life (Romans 4:25). His coming back to life is the basis of God's moving us from death to life (1 Corinthians 15:17).

Jesus calls himself *life* in these four passages:

- the bread of life (John 6:48)
- the light of life (John 8:12)
- the resurrection and the life (John 11:25)
- the way, and the truth, and the life (John 14:6)

There's no way to overestimate the importance of life in John's Gospel. Consider these passages:

- For God so loved the world, that he gave his only Son, that whoever believes in him should not perish but have eternal life. (John 3:16)
- As the Father raises the dead and gives them life, so also the Son gives life to whom he will. (John 5:21)

- Truly, truly, I say to you, whoever hears my word and believes him who sent me has eternal life. He does not come into judgment, but has passed from death to life. (John 5:24)
- As the living Father sent me, and I live because of the Father, so whoever feeds on me, he also will live because of me. (John 6:57)

Further, John tells readers his Gospel was written "that you may believe that Jesus is the Messiah, the Son of God, and that by believing you may have life in his name" (John 20:31, NIV). Jesus said to the Father, "Now this is eternal life: that they know you, the only true God, and Jesus Christ, whom you have sent" (John 17:3, NIV).

Jesus is not just a signpost or a compass to life; he *is* life. He's not merely a map leading to water or an X that marks the spot where treasure is buried. Rather, he *is* the wellspring. He *is* the treasure.

We Can Choose Joy despite Our Afflictions

When Hudson Taylor opened a bank account for the China Inland Mission, the application form asked for an asset list. Taylor is said to have stated the following as the sum total of his assets: "Ten pounds and all the promises of God."[8]

Our greatest resources are spiritual, not material. They come from another world, not this one. And that's where the good life begins.

Author Alice Gray had lunch with a friend, Marlene, and over the course of the meal they spoke about difficulties they were facing. At a nearby table, Alice noticed a young woman with a radiant, joyful face. The woman smiled and said she'd overheard their conversation. She encouraged Alice and Marlene, telling them that God understood and cared about their heartaches and that nothing could separate them from the love of Christ.

When the smiling woman got up to leave, Alice saw that she used a walking stick, wore bulky shoes, and moved with a severe limp.

The waitress explained this woman had been in a near-fatal car accident the year before. She'd been in the hospital many times. Her husband divorced her, and she had to give up her home for an apartment. Unable to drive, she relied on public transportation. She hadn't been able to find a job.

Alice was stunned. She later reflected on that encounter: "This young woman's conversation had been filled with delights of the Lord. There had been no weariness about her. She had encouraged us with words of praise and promise. Meeting her that day, we never would have suspected that storms were raging in her life. Even as she stepped outside into the cold winter wind, she seemed to carry God's warm shelter of hope with her."[9]

Circumstantially, this young woman was immeasurably worse off than someone like Owen Wilson. But despite her adverse circumstances, or perhaps even through them, she knew God and was fully alive in Christ. She knew, not just in her head but at the core of her being, that wealth and fame are not the source of the good life—only Jesus is.

The living God says, "I have set before you life and death, blessing and curse. Therefore choose life, that you and your offspring may live" (Deuteronomy 30:19). He offers us true life and, with it, blessing. But he warns us against sin and the curse that always comes with it. Just as he did in the Garden, God offers us the quality of life that comes from obeying him. God says, "Let your heart hold fast my words; keep my commandments, and live" (Proverbs 4:4).

Our problem is the great problem of the ages: we have neither the righteousness nor the power to perfectly keep God's life-giving commandments. But God solved this apparently insurmountable problem by sending his Son, Jesus, as our Savior. The difference between life and death is actually quite simple: "Whoever has the Son has life; whoever does not have the Son of God does not have life" (1 John 5:12).

Aligning our identity with Christ's death and resurrection gives us power to live authentic, righteous, and beautiful lives so that "just as Christ was raised from the dead by the glory of the Father, we too might walk in newness of life" (Romans 6:4). This beautiful life is what the young woman in the restaurant experienced. It's a vibrant life overflowing with God's grace—what 1 Timothy 6:19 calls "the life that is truly life" (NIV). In other words, it's *the good life*.

And it's available to everyone who knows Jesus.

After establishing a restaurant chain, two banks, a ranch, a farm, and real estate ventures, Jerry Caven says the real fun started when his career was coming to an end:

At age 59 I was headed into retirement, looking for a nice lake home. Then God changed our plans and led Muriel and me to put our money and time overseas. It's been exciting. Before we gave token amounts, now we put substantial money into missions. Our hearts are in another country now. We visit and minister there often.[10]

The Cavens say, "After seeing the way poor Christians in other countries trust him, we've asked God if he wants us to give away all of 'our' money. He hasn't led us to do that yet. But we've meant it when we asked."[11]

When we live the good life, people quickly notice. The Cavens added this story: "A non-Christian couple saw us giving, and saw how much it excited and changed us. Then they started giving too, even before knowing Christ. They saw the joy and they wanted in on it!"[12]

The simplest statement made in Scripture about the life that Jesus brings his people is perhaps also the most profound: "I came that they may have life and have it abundantly" (John 10:10).

The giving life is not about obligation or guilt or drudgery or merely surviving. It's about life in abundance.

CHAPTER 3

A BETTER KIND OF ABUNDANCE

....

So now, take a man that hath all the fulness of the earth . . .
the man is an empty man, because his heart is not full of that
for which he was made, and that is Christ.

WILLIAM BRIDGE

I came that they may have life and have it abundantly.

JOHN 10:10

God took physician Renee Lockey completely by surprise one day while she was out running. At the height of her career, she sensed that he was planting an idea in her head: "Work like a doctor and live like a nurse."

Renee now lives on a nurse's salary and gives away the rest of her income. Renee believes God is worthy to be worshiped with all we have because we have nothing besides what he's already given us. "When we take this idea literally—that we are His—it results in a drastically different way of thinking and living," she says. "A different way of giving, as well. . . . When we are grounded more firmly in the Word than we are in the world, God moves us to countercultural ways of living and giving. Instead of living in fear, we live by faith. Instead of living for ourselves, we live generously for Him."[1]

While Renee's colleagues might assume she has denied herself the good life by living below her means, in reality, she has discovered the secret to the abundant life.

Treasure No One Can Steal

John 10 shows us that the false shepherds of Israel, the Pharisees, sought to keep people from Jesus, the one true Shepherd. Jesus promises abundant life, and in contrast, he speaks of false religious teachers as thieves and murderers who rob people of life. He said of himself:

> Truly, truly, I say to you, I am the door of the sheep. All who came before me are thieves and robbers, but the sheep did not listen to them. I am the door. If anyone enters by me, he will be saved and will go in and out and find pasture. The thief comes only to steal and kill and destroy. I came that they may have life and have it abundantly. I am the good shepherd. The good shepherd lays down his life for the sheep.
>
> JOHN 10:7-11

The religious shepherds were supposed to give God-centered hope and encouragement to downcast people in desperate need of the Messiah. Instead, they imposed bondage and duty-driven drudgery. Jesus, by contrast, is the Good Shepherd, who came to free us and bring abundant life.

Jesus said of the religious leaders, "You belong to your father, the devil. . . . He was a murderer from the beginning, not holding to the truth, for there is no truth in him. When he lies, he speaks his native language, for he is a liar and the father of lies" (John 8:44, NIV). Why would Jesus describe respected, Bible-believing religious leaders with such strong language? Because they used people for their own ends of financial gain, popularity, status, and power.

When Jesus said, "The thief comes only to steal and kill and destroy," he was alerting us to how much the devil hates life. But Satan isn't only a liar and a killer; he is also a thief. We get our word *kleptomaniac* from the Greek word *klepto*, translated "steal" in verse 10. Kleptomania speaks of an obsessive impulse to steal, independent of financial need. The devil is the original kleptomaniac.

A robber typically isn't subtle. He might put a gun in your face while demanding your cash. Conversely, a pickpocket uses crowds or staged distractions. With your focus on his partner blocking your way, you might be saying, "Excuse me," at the very moment the thief behind you lifts your wallet.

Were the devil more obvious in his temptations, we could see through them far more easily. When he tempts us to dethrone Jesus by making money our idol, he doesn't do so conspicuously or all at once. Rather, he works subtly and gradually until one day we wake up and realize we are spiritually bankrupt—or, like the rich fool, we don't wake up until we die and it's too late.

Ignorant people are easy targets for trickery, while those who know the tricks of con men and pickpockets clutch tightly to what's most precious. Paul's concern was "that Satan should not outwit us. For we are not unaware of his schemes" (2 Corinthians 2:11, BSB). An essential part of claiming victory is knowing our enemy. If we value the good life Jesus came to give us, we'll clasp it closely when Satan and his minions try to lay their hands on it. As 1 Timothy 6:19 commands us, we'll "take hold of that which is truly life."

Satan despises us and seeks to destroy us by robbing us of the good life God originally gave Adam and Eve—the life Christ came to restore to humanity. A key way Satan tries to destroy us is by convincing us that money and possessions are the source of an abundant life.

If you assume you'll never be burglarized, you'll leave your windows open and your cash lying on the dresser. Jesus knew our tendency to live in denial about the dangers of money-love, which is why he sounded this alarm: "Watch out! Be on your guard against all kinds of greed" (Luke 12:15, NIV).

The devil might not be able to deceive us into believing outright that nothing's more important than money and possessions. Instead, he might draw us to a catalog that shows us, as we flip through its pages, all those possessions we "really need." We might say no to Internet sites offering sexual temptation, only to succumb to websites where we indulge an unfiltered lust for things. We might buy dozens of utterly unnecessary things during Black Friday sales, which ironically mark the beginning of a holiday season that culminates in the birth of the one who told us that we need to be on our watch against greed and that life isn't about the things we possess (Luke 12:15).

People who are alert to the dangers of drugs, alcoholism, and sexual addictions often think that compulsive acquisition is normal. No one will suggest that we need an intervention for it or that we should attend a recovery group. We seem to have a silent agreement that keeps materialism mainstream and off limits from accountability.

Satan has numerous allies in his campaign to make us believe the lies of materialism. Advertising exists to sell us the "goods" that supposedly give us the good life. Fortunately for advertisers, no products exist that actually deliver on that promise, so we keep right on buying more things, hoping *this time* they will deliver.

They never will.

Let's Not Buy Ourselves to Death

Attempting to experience the abundant life Jesus spoke of while burying ourselves in material abundance isn't just difficult; it's impossible. That's not because material things are inherently bad. It's because accumulated stuff suffocates us, crushes us, and blocks us from Jesus.

In moderate quantities, certain possessions might draw our attention to him as our provider. For instance, when I buy a good book or my wife gives me a thermal mug or my daughters give me photos of my grandchildren, I am truly grateful to God. Other possessions, such as clothes I will never wear or the third version of a gadget I already own and don't use, do nothing for me or God's Kingdom. If it's something that will sap hours of my time, it may even draw my attention away from God and his Word.

Many things may be neutral or even fun, but it's too easy to end up trusting our stuff instead of our Savior.

In some circles, the abundant life has been confused with material wealth. Prosperity theology says that God's plan is always for us to be wealthy—and to spend our money primarily on ourselves. Jesus, who didn't even have a place to lay his head and who owned nothing but a robe and sandals (Matthew 8:20), clearly didn't live a money- and possessions-centered life. Surely that's not what he wants for us either.

Jesus told the church in Laodicea, "You say, 'I am rich; I have acquired wealth and do not need a thing.' But you do not realize that you are wretched, pitiful, poor, blind and naked" (Revelation 3:17, NIV). These were church people. What had buried their sense of spiritual poverty? Their material abundance. It tricked them into believing they were living the abundant life when in reality they were sabotaging it.

If abundant stuff equaled the abundant life, wealthy unbelievers wouldn't need Jesus—nor would the rest of us. Materialism dresses the corpse and puts makeup on it, but it's still dead. Jesus redirects us from death disguised as life to true abundant life. He says the very reason he came into the world is to give us "a rich and satisfying life" (John 10:10, NLT) or "life to the full, till it overflows" (AMP).

Jesus promises, "Whoever drinks the water I give them will never thirst. Indeed, the water I give them will become in them a spring of water welling up to eternal life" (John 4:14, NIV). The abundant life isn't measured in gold dust or material goods. It's rooted in the precious fact that our Creator and Redeemer himself indwells us, lovingly imparting his delight-giving presence to us. The same life Jesus speaks of will culminate in our resurrection and will ultimately mean total and final deliverance from sin, death, and suffering (Revelation 21:4). Meanwhile, we can experience victory over the destructive powers of evil while still living in a cursed world (Romans 6:13-14; 1 Corinthians 15:57). We're told we'll not merely be conquerors *after* we die but "in all these things we are [presently] more than conquerors through him who loved us" (Romans 8:37, NIV).

THE BOOMERANG EFFECT OF GIVING

The Wilsons wanted to show their kids opportunities to help people in other countries. Since several of their children loved to play soccer, their Christian financial adviser recommended giving to a soccer program for at-risk kids in Guatemala.

The family learned that Global Soccer Ministries (GSM) had a $40,000 yearly budget, but the Wilsons wanted to give much more. They committed to funding a complex that could facilitate all special GSM events and earn rental income from outside use.

With the help of donated land and discounted turf, the Wilsons' gift of $600,000 built a $1.2 million soccer complex, which in turn created more than $200,000 in revenue each year, sufficient to fund and expand GSM's entire operation. Now many people enjoy this wonderful gift—but perhaps no one enjoys it more than the Wilsons.*

* This story was sent to me by Al Mueller, president of Excellence in Giving, based in Colorado Springs (http://excellenceingiving.com).

Abundant Life Begins Today

When we trust in Christ—not just when we are first converted, but every day—we can lay hold of powerful realities. Jesus doesn't make us wait until things get better or until we die to start living the abundant life. The abundant life begins *now*! So if you're a Christian and you're searching for the good life, you don't have to go far to find it. Look no further than Jesus. Know him, delight in him, serve him, learn from his people, and do what he says. (Of course, you must study his Word to know what he says.) There's no life better than that.

Jesus himself is the entrance to an Eden of the heart—the ultimate refuge for refugees, and the home for every homeless and heartsick person in this world, whether they live in poverty or wealth.

Buddha isn't the door. Krishna isn't the door. Muhammad isn't the door. Joseph Smith isn't the door. Even Moses and Elijah and David and John the Baptist, who were true prophets of God, are not the door. Mary, mother of Jesus, though she was godly and faithful, is not the door (she affirmed her need of a Savior in Luke 1:47).

God didn't send a spokesperson, a prophet, or an angel to give us life, protection, provision, safety, and guidance. He sent his Son—his very best. He's the only Savior, and he freely offers all of himself to us.

When I was a young Christian, some sincere believers tried to convince me that I should seek a life in which miraculous events were the norm. After a year spent searching for more, I recall reading the promise that God has "blessed us in Christ with every spiritual blessing in the heavenly places" (Ephesians 1:3). I also read, "[God's] divine power has granted to us all things that pertain to life and godliness" (2 Peter 1:3).

That's when I asked myself, *What more do I need than what God has already given me?* I realized that Jesus, along with the power of God's indwelling Spirit (Romans 8:11), was enough for me to enjoy abundant life.

The same is true for all of us who know Christ. We simply need to enter into and enjoy the abundant life Jesus promises. It's a life that's tied to the happiness of God—a life that finds present joy in anticipating Heaven's infinite gladness. It's a life in which future eternal realities are front-loaded into our current experience.

The Good Life Begins and Ends with Christ

Before the Israelites entered the Promised Land, God promised them a land with "houses filled with all kinds of good things" (Deuteronomy 6:11, NIV). Then he stipulated a condition for enjoying the good life: "Do what is right and *good* in the LORD's sight, so that it may go well with you and you may go in and take over the *good* land the LORD promised on oath to your ancestors" (Deuteronomy 6:18, NIV, emphasis added). There is a direct connection here between doing good in God's sight and enjoying his good provisions.

Similarly, Peter said, "Live such good lives among the pagans that, though they accuse you of doing wrong, they may see your good deeds and glorify God on the day he visits us" (1 Peter 2:12, NIV). So a major part of the good life is living a moral, ethical, and God-centered life that shows itself outwardly in good deeds.

However, don't miss this: while it is necessary to live a good life to enjoy the abundant life, it's not sufficient. We all know unbelievers who are kind and warmhearted people, and from all appearances live very good lives. All people are created in God's image and, by his common grace, can reflect aspects of his character. But God says that without Christ, our righteous deeds are ultimately filthy rags (Isaiah 64:6). Only embracing Christ as our Savior can cleanse us from unrighteousness. His indwelling Spirit then empowers us to live a life that is pleasing to him.

Even once we know Christ, we need to understand that the good life isn't always the "fun life." Sometimes it demands that we step up and tell the truth when it's unpopular. Sometimes it means people will dislike us or malign us. It might even mean putting our lives at risk. But it's not our job to be safe or popular. We exist solely to please an audience of one—the God who alone defines the true good life. Knowing that we are pleasing him, even when for the moment it costs us to do so, can bring great joy and peace: "Rejoice insofar as you share Christ's sufferings, that you may also rejoice and be glad when his glory is revealed" (1 Peter 4:13).

What does this look like? Consider what happened to Paul and Silas in Philippi: "The crowd joined in attacking them, and the magistrates tore the garments off them and gave orders to beat them with rods. And when they had inflicted many blows upon them, they threw them into prison. . . . [The jailer] put them into the inner prison and fastened their feet in the stocks" (Acts 16:22-24).

God's people have been treated this way throughout history, but Paul and Silas's response in the next verse is astonishing: "About midnight Paul and Silas were praying and singing hymns to God, and the prisoners were listening to them" (Acts 16:25). Why were the prisoners listening? Because singing hymns was an expression of joy in circumstances that didn't call for joy. Why did the Philippian jailer believe in Jesus (verses 31-33)? Partly because he saw Paul and Silas living a life so abundant that happiness and praise overflowed from them in their darkest hour.

Richard Wurmbrand, who was tortured for decades in Romanian prisons and later founded Voice of the Martyrs, wrote, "It was strictly forbidden to preach to other prisoners. . . . It was understood that whoever was caught doing this received a severe beating. A number of us decided to pay the price for the privilege of preaching, so we accepted [the Communists'] terms. It was a deal: we preached and they beat us. We were happy preaching; they were happy beating us—so everyone was happy."[2]

After decades of imprisonment, Christ-follower Aleksandr

Solzhenitsyn said, "I turn back to the years of my imprisonment and say, sometimes to the astonishment of those about me: 'Bless you, prison!'"[3]

Even in the worst of circumstances, it's possible to experience

MORE THAN A HOBBY

David Green, the founder of retail giant Hobby Lobby, grew up financially poor but spiritually rich. His father was a pastor and his two brothers became pastors. Two of his sisters married pastors, and the third became an evangelist.

David, meanwhile, became a store manager for a variety store chain, working his way up through the company. But he wanted to find a way to provide for his family's needs while also spending more time with them. So he and a business partner purchased a wood-cutting machine for $600 to make picture frames, never expecting that their small business would one day produce significant wealth.

As his business grew, David began to realize that God had a sovereign plan for his career. He says, "My longstanding uneasiness about not going in the ministry like all my brothers and sisters went away. . . . Maybe God has a purpose for a merchant after all."[*]

Today Hobby Lobby has more than eight hundred stores in forty-seven states, with more than $4 billion in annual sales.[**] The company ministers to its 32,000-plus employees by closing at eight o'clock nightly and remaining closed on Sundays so they can be with their families and attend church. Hobby Lobby consistently pays the high-est starting wage of any comparable company.

The Green family gives 50 percent of the company's profits to Kingdom work. David's son Mart says, "Generosity is a gateway to intimacy with God. . . . That's why our family mission statement is 'Love God Intimately, Live Extravagant Generosity.'"[***]

[*] William F. High with Ashley B. McCauley, *The Generosity Bet: Secrets of Risk, Reward, and Real Joy* (Shippensburg, PA: Destiny Image, 2014), 144.
[**] "Our Story," Hobby Lobby, accessed January 27, 2019, https://www.hobbylobby.com/about-us/our-story.
[***] "Treasuring Jesus," Gospel Patrons, April 14, 2017, https://www.gospelpatrons.org/journal_authors/mart-green/entries/5.

a full, deep life in this world that's under the Curse, and that's what sets the Christian life apart. This soul-level abundance means that believers who are living in oppressive circumstances can be far more joyful than unbelievers who are living in luxury and popularity.

In short, even on their worst days Paul, Silas, Wurmbrand, and Solzhenitsyn were all living the abundant life. When we deny ourselves, God rewards us. When we lose ourselves, we find ourselves. When we accept that the good life isn't always the fun life and we make hard choices, God infuses our lives with far more enduring pleasures and greater happiness than anything we gave up for the moment.

Abundance Naturally Overflows

Jesus said, "The one who believes in me, as the Scripture has said, will have streams of living water flow from deep within him" (John 7:38, csb). There's an unmistakable sign of an overflowing, abundant life that comes from knowing Jesus, the author of life: generosity to others.

An old but helpful illustration applies to the abundant, generous life. In northern Israel lies the beautiful Sea of Galilee, where Jesus often sailed with his disciples. Water freely flows into the Sea of Galilee from the Jordan River, and its water is fresh and life giving.

Eighty-eight miles to the south is a larger and radically different body of water. One of the lowest places on the planet, the Dead Sea collects large volumes of water but disperses none. Its salt concentration is so high—ten times greater than ocean water—that no fish or vegetation can survive there.

While the Jordan River flows into the Sea of Galilee, it also flows out. The water simply passes through, allowing it to support fish life and plants. Trapped, with no outlet, the Dead Sea keeps taking water in, but no water leaves it except by evaporation. No outlet means no life.

This is a good parable of the Christian life in general—and an even better parable of the generous life in particular. In order to be faithful stewards and to love others, we must be not only recipients of God's provision but also outlets of it. Only then will we experience the true and abundant life he intends for us.

Such a dramatic overflow can have an amazing effect even on those who are hostile to the Christian faith. My friend pastors a church that rents a public school auditorium on Sundays. When a new principal arrived, he showed hostility toward Christians. His lifestyle was the kind he figured the church wouldn't approve of, and he was probably right.

One day the principal saw a Bible on the desk of one of his teachers—someone who was also a member of the church. He was told that teachers have the legal right to have their Bibles in plain sight, but he wasn't impressed. He urged the pastor to find another place to meet.

But over the next few years, something happened. The principal discovered that church members cheerfully give time and money for the sake of the school—a practice that was in place before he came. They schedule cleanup days. They serve teachers meals during parent-teacher conferences. They give teachers gift cards each year. They do this not simply to win favor but because Christ's love and kindness overflow from their lives.

The pastor of the church told me, "Three years later, this principal is no longer an antagonist; he's our advocate. Our works of service have softened his heart toward the Lord. He's confiding in me, and he invites me to speak to his school staff.'"

The pastor calls it an astonishing turnaround. And what was the cause? It was simply Christians living the good life, which always entails good deeds of generosity. Jesus put it this way: "Let your light shine before others, that they may see your good deeds and glorify your Father in heaven" (Matthew 5:16, NIV).

Generosity Is Contagious

The more we give in Christ's name, the more life he will put into us. And the more life we have flowing into us, the more that life will flow out of us to others. "Give, and it will be given to you," Jesus said. "A good measure, pressed down, shaken together and running over, will be poured into your lap" (Luke 6:38, NIV).

By giving generously of our money and possessions, we're able to open our hands to receive the abundant life God has for us. God is the greatest giver in the universe, and it's impossible to outgive him. This is not prosperity theology. It is simply the way our generous God delights to work in the lives of his children.

Out of a deep love for Jesus, Pete and Debbie Ochs decided to acquire a business constructing industrial products in prisons. They employ inmates, some of whom have committed violent crimes. They invest in these prisoners' lives by offering life lessons on topics like parenting, finances, and relationships. Pete says, "In one of our life lessons, we presented this whole concept of generosity and challenged [the prisoners] that we would match dollar for dollar any dollar that they gave to one of a number of charities and we gave them a list. It was amazing the

A BRIGHTER FUTURE

Biswanath, who lives in Bangladesh, had a terrible accident as a young adult that resulted in a loss of mobility. He couldn't find a job, and he was losing hope. After he married Sumi, they had a child, Sumonto. As a result of his disability, Biswanath struggled to provide for his family and began selling marijuana.

When a Compassion child development center opened at a local church, Biswanath jumped at the chance to send his son to school in the hope of giving him a brighter future. Sumonto has received tutoring as well as educational supplies, lunch, and care for his medical needs. When Sumonto's sponsors provided a monetary gift for the family to purchase six cows, Biswanath was able to leave the marijuana business. After selling three cows, his family bought a small piece of land and opened a shop that sells herbal products and spices. Biswanath's previously unemployed older brother now helps run the shop.*

Through sponsorship, these two families have been given new lives. And thousands of miles away, a third family has been changed as well. The sponsors have experienced the joy of being part of this life transformation—and they are richer for it.

* David Adhikary, "What Impact Does Giving a Family Gift Have in a Child's Life?" Compassion, August 9, 2016, https://blog.compassion.com/child-sponsorship-the-impact-of-family-gifts/.

amount of money that these prisoners gave to charity. . . . Most of the charities . . . existed to help the victims of the crimes that they committed."[4]

Pete's ministry to prisoners reflects the heartbeat of Scripture. Ephesians 4:28 says, "Anyone who has been stealing must steal no longer, but must work, doing something useful with their own hands, that they may—"

That they may what? Have only enough to live on so they no longer have to steal? No. "That they may *have something to share with those in need"* (NIV, emphasis added). Giving isn't just for those with squeaky-clean records; it's for all of us.

Pete and Debbie's overflowing good life has not only brought these men the gospel but has also introduced them to the overflow of joyful giving so they, too, can experience abundant life.

The good life in Christ is not only wonderful for those who live it; it is also a joy for those who behold it. Generosity is just as contagious as materialism. However, it brings life instead of death.

CHAPTER 4

WHAT LOVE LOOKS LIKE

....

You can give without loving, but you cannot love without giving.
AMY CARMICHAEL

My command is this: Love each other as I have loved you.
JOHN 15:12, NIV

My wife, Nanci, met an elderly man at the supermarket who asked her where to find flour. "I don't know my way around here," he explained. "My wife did all the shopping, and she died last month."

Nanci felt God's prompting to give him one of my books on Heaven, but they were in the car. So she prayed she would see him later in the very large parking lot. No sooner did she get to our car than she saw an elderly man wheeling his cart in her direction. She reached for one of my books, handed it to him, and said, "Are you the one whose wife recently passed away?"

He said, "Well, yes, my wife died three months ago. We were married forty-nine years." Suddenly Nanci realized it wasn't the same man. But he was clearly grateful to receive the book, and

Nanci felt certain he would read it. (Perhaps all the more because a total stranger seemed to know his wife had recently died!)

Since God is sovereign and is the orchestrator of divine appointments, Nanci knew her act of love was intended for this man after all. When we allow ourselves to be vessels of God's generosity and love, those on the receiving end experience joy, and we experience the pleasure of seeing God at work through us.

Nothing's Better than Loving God and People

When a religious leader asked which command was the greatest, Jesus responded, "Love the Lord your God with all your heart, with all your soul, and with all your mind. This is the greatest and most important command. The second is like it: Love your neighbor as yourself. All the Law and the Prophets depend on these two commands" (Matthew 22:37-40, CSB).

When we love God most, we will love others best. Love isn't just something we display on a wall hanging; it's something we do: "Little children, let us love not in word and speech, but in action and truth" (1 John 3:18, BSB). Jesus said, "Anyone who loves me will obey my teaching" (John 14:23, NIV). Jesus' teaching often centered on loving people, as in the story of the Good Samaritan who freely gave of his time and money to care for a stranger who'd been beaten and robbed (Luke 10:25-37). Jesus told us to love the poor, even to put on a feast for them (Luke 14:12-14). He said we should tend to the disadvantaged just as we would if he himself were the one in need (Matthew 25:31-46).

Jesus also said to love the spiritually poor by bringing them the gospel (Matthew 28:19-20) and by praying that God would send out workers to reach them (Matthew 9:37-38). He modeled evangelistic outreach that took into consideration the unique needs of the individual (for example, John 4:1-42).

Each of these passages, and many others, demonstrate that loving the physically poor and the spiritually poor both involve generously giving of ourselves and our resources. When humble service comes from the heart, it is gratifying and helps us to live the good life. Loving others is *really* living large, because it breaks us out of our own minuscule orbits. It puts us in orbit around God, who graciously meets the needs of those who meet the needs of the needy.

Jesus commands us to love our enemies, and he asked, "If you

THE GIFT OF LOVE

The video "I Like Adoption" tells the story of the Dennehys. With three biological children and nine specially chosen from around the world (including two from the American foster care system and some who have special needs), their home is, in their words, "an intriguing tapestry of hues, cultures, laughter, and love."*

On the video, Sharon, the mom, says, "People discouraged us. They thought we were going to ruin our lives by taking all of these special kids, and they said, 'You don't know what to do.' And it's true that we had no experience, and we didn't really know how to raise them. But you see what happens with unconditional love. You give a person unconditional love, and they blossom."** Of course, there are difficult days. But the generous life of investing in these children has paid off. And every family that has stepped in to help has become part of this joy-giving eternal investment.

* Ryan Scott Bomberger, "New Short Film Will Change Hearts: I Like Adoption," Radiance Foundation, December 14, 2012, http://www.theradiancefoundation.org/new-short-film-will-change-hearts-i-like-adoption/.
** Bomberger, "New Short Film," see "I Like Adoption," Vimeo video, 6:31, http://www.theradiancefoundation.org /new-short-film-will-change-hearts-i-like-adoption/.

love those who love you, what credit is that to you? Even sinners love those who love them" (Luke 6:32, NIV). Sinners typically don't love those who hate them, because there's nothing in it for them. Why go to the trouble when your love won't be returned or rewarded? But Jesus promises that even if our love isn't reciprocated, God will greatly reward us: "Love your enemies, do good to them, and lend to them without expecting to get anything back. Then *your reward will be great*, and you will be children of the Most High, because he is kind to the ungrateful and wicked" (Luke 6:35, NIV, emphasis added).

Part of the reward that awaits believers is in the afterlife. But part of the reward is here and now, with the peace, contentment, and joy we receive as we learn to be like him in our giving.

Love Can't Help but Give

In the King James Version, the Greek word *agape* is often translated "love." But twenty-nine times, this same word is translated "charity." Translators believed that when the word was used of vertical action, whether God toward us or us toward God, "love" was the proper translation. But when used of horizontal actions (toward a neighbor or an enemy), "charity" served the meaning best.[1] Why? Because loving someone is inseparable from giving to them. If you love, you give. If you don't give, you don't love.

In India, people rely on a family member or a paid assistant to care for them in hospitals. When a team of Christ-followers met a man with no one attending him, the first thing they did was wash him. He made it clear they could help him as long as they didn't try to convert him from his strong Hindu faith.

Days later the hospital discharged the man, as there was nothing more they could do—he was dying.

The team placed the old man in a home for the elderly, where they visited and cared for him regularly. The day the man died, a Christ-following staff member asked him where he thought he would go when he died. The believer held the man's hand while sharing the good news of God's love with him.

The Christian asked the old man if he'd like to repent of his sins and live forever with Jesus in Heaven. Unable to speak, but clearly responsive, the man squeezed his hand to indicate agreement. The old man squeezed his hand again when the staff member asked to pray for him. The faint smile on this man's face was a great encouragement to the team that loved him right up to the moment he moved from this life to the next.[2] By showing love through meeting his physical needs, the team was able to prepare this man to hear the gospel and ultimately meet his spiritual needs.

One of the best-known Bible verses is "For God so loved the world that he gave his one and only Son, that whoever believes in him shall not perish but have eternal life" (John 3:16, NIV). In short, love gives. Love gives up time. Love gives up money. Love gives up privileges. Love gives up what others might consider ours but what we know to be God's. And when we do give in these ways, we feel privileged to share with others.

The life God's Son offers us cost him his life. That's the essence of love, defined by example in the greatest act of love in the history of the universe: "This is love: not that we loved God, but that he loved us and sent his Son as an atoning sacrifice for our sins" (1 John 4:10, NIV).

Generosity Is Love in Action

Our love for God and others is not merely sentiment or words; it is something we actively give—both to God and to people.

Imagine if God had stayed in Heaven and, instead of sending his Son, sent us a message through an angel: "Too bad you're going to Hell. Remember, though, I love you!" Instead, he loved us as Immanuel, God with us.

If our love is genuine, when we see the picture of a hungry child, we don't just feel bad for the moment or merely think, *I wish that child weren't hungry.* Love finds a way to help feed that child or children like him. Love means giving.

If you still doubt that love is about generous giving, consider these words: "By this we know what love is: Jesus laid down His life for us, and we ought to lay down our lives for our brothers. If anyone with earthly possessions sees his brother in need, but withholds his compassion from him, how can the love of God abide in him?" (1 John 3:16-17, BSB).

This passage portrays love as inseparable from giving. In fact, it's impossible to truly love without giving. No, we can't give everything to everybody. Yet to withhold our money and possessions from the needy is to withhold from them God's love and compassion. God doesn't need our help—he could do everything without us. But he chooses to entrust us with his mission of love. We are the body of Christ, his hands and feet to the needy.

We can ignore people without hating them. But in the end, if we don't help them, it will be no consolation that we didn't hate them. As Holocaust survivor Elie Wiesel famously said, "The opposite of love is not hate, it's indifference."[3]

HEAVENLY JOY

Eun Young Park of Seoul, South Korea, is a partner at Kim & Chang. He has served as both an attorney and a judge in multiple jurisdictions, and has taught in Korean law schools. As he was commuting to work one day, he started thinking not about international arbitration but about a boy his family had recently stepped out in faith to help. Thinking of how the boy's life had changed, he was struck with so much happiness that he started trembling. He had to pull over until he could calm down.

Park says, "It was almost a heavenly joy. The kind that we might experience when we see Jesus face to face. . . . God gave me a special gift in that joy."*

It's probably safe to say Eun Young Park never pulled off the road due to overflowing gladness about court proceedings or the classes he taught in law school. This was something far greater. His work as an attorney and a judge and a professor—though good in itself—transformed into something far greater by producing an income that allowed him to invest in eternity.

* "Three Lessons from Eun Young Park, South Korea," JoyGiving.org, accessed January 27, 2019, https://joygiving .org/eun-young/.

The abundant life, which is itself a gift to us from the God of love, pours forth abundant love to others. That is the essence of giving.

What Story Do Your Financial Records Tell?

Evangelist John Wesley didn't just preach the gospel; he lived it.

Wesley had just bought pictures for his Oxford room when he noticed that the chambermaid at his door was cold. She needed a winter coat, but he had very little money left to give her. He asked himself, *Will thy Master say . . . "Thou hast adorned thy walls with the money which might have screened this poor creature from the cold!*"[4]

Wesley started limiting his expenses so he would have more to help the poor. At one time his book royalties gave him what today would be an annual income of $160,000. Yet he lived like someone today might at an income of $20,000.

Wesley's financial records tell a powerful story. One year his living expenses were £28. The next year his income doubled, but he still lived on £28 and gave away £32. In the third year, his income jumped to £90; again, he lived on just £28, giving the rest away. The fourth year he made £120, lived again on £28, and gave £92 to the poor.

Even when his income rose to £1,400, he kept living simply and gave away all but £30. His lifestyle increased only a marginal amount while his giving increased dramatically. Wesley feared laying up treasures on Earth, and he eagerly gave away money to help the needy as quickly as it came in. Wesley preached that Christians shouldn't merely tithe but should give away all extra income once their other obligations were met. He believed that whenever income increased, the Christian's *giving* should increase.

Perhaps you aren't as radical as Wesley—I'm certainly not—but his example of love and generosity inspires me to reevaluate my lifestyle and giving as well as the way I view the people I encounter daily.[5]

You Don't Have to Be Rich to Give

I know miserly people with enormous incomes and generous people who live far below their earnings in order to give. Likewise,

I know people making midlevel incomes who give sacrificially and others who live above their means, going deeper into debt every month. Regardless of their income, those who overspend never think they can afford to give.

I've also met generous poor people and stingy poor people. Generosity isn't dependent on how much we make but on what's happening inside our hearts. It's the overflow of our love for Jesus and for others.

The most striking model of generosity in the Bible is the poor widow. Jesus made an example of her to his disciples:

> Jesus sat down opposite the place where the offerings
> were put and watched the crowd putting their money
> into the temple treasury. Many rich people threw in large
> amounts. But a poor widow came and put in two very
> small copper coins, worth only a few cents.
>
> Calling his disciples to him, Jesus said, "Truly I tell
> you, this poor widow has put more into the treasury than
> all the others. They all gave out of their wealth; but she,
> out of her poverty, put in everything—all she had to
> live on."
>
> MARK 12:41-44, NIV

The greatest scriptural example of a group of people giving generously is the Macedonian churches of 2 Corinthians 8, whom Paul commended for insisting on taking an offering to help the needy saints in Jerusalem. The apostle said of these believers, "In the midst of a very severe trial, their overflowing joy and their extreme poverty welled up in rich generosity" (verse 2, NIV). Notice that their giving was the opposite of dutiful drudgery—it came out of "overflowing joy." Giving was their way of living the good life.

I've seen this every time I've traveled in poor countries where believers are eager to feed us. On a trip to Kenya, our group gathered for a feast. Missionaries there told us the people, who owned so little compared to those of us from the United States, had spent a large part of their weekly wages to put on the meal they were delighted to share with us.

On another trip, this one to Ukraine, my pastor friend and I spent the evening with a large family, feasting and singing hymns and laughing and exalting Jesus together. We felt bad when we learned our hosts had served an entire month's ration of butter at the meal, but we were assured there was nothing they would rather have done than open their hearts and home to brothers in Christ. It was humbling to be served when we had envisioned ourselves going to serve them. Giving is a great equalizer among God's people.

To the selfish person, the giver's behavior appears foolish and against his best interests. (Why part with a month's ration of butter to serve rich visitors who have unlimited amounts of butter at home?) Scripture says the opposite: "One person gives freely, yet gains even more; another withholds unduly, but comes to poverty" (Proverbs 11:24, NIV). *The Message* puts it this way: "The world of the generous gets larger and larger; the world of the stingy gets smaller and smaller."

I've certainly known generous people who were facing serious problems, but I've never known a generous soul—of any income level—who was chronically unhappy. Sure, we all struggle with life's tough circumstances. But I've found in life what studies confirm: even in hard times, loving, generous people always default not only toward gratitude but happiness.[6] That wonderful Ukrainian family might have missed their butter, but the payoff of loving Jesus and us by showing hospitality was, to them, a far greater treasure.

Giving from the Heart Really Matters

God commanded his people, "Give generously to the poor, not grudgingly, for the LORD your God will bless you in everything you do. There will always be some in the land who are poor. That is why I am commanding you to share freely with the poor and with other Israelites in need" (Deuteronomy 15:10-11, NLT). This was a command, yet God said they should "share freely." He cares about the state of our hearts as we give.

Paul made it clear that it's possible to give sacrificially without being motivated by love: "If I give away all my possessions, and if I give over my body in order to boast but do not have love, I gain nothing" (1 Corinthians 13:3, CSB). That means it's not just generosity that's the good life; it's generosity that flows out of love.

Paul also said that "God loves a cheerful giver" (2 Corinthians 9:7, ESV). What keeps us from giving cheerfully? We instinctively imagine that spending on ourselves will make us happiest. But Jesus said our greatest joy comes when we give to others: "There is more happiness in giving than in receiving" (Acts 20:35, GNT). You might have heard that verse translated "It is more blessed to give than receive," but the well-documented fact is that the Greek word *makarios* here, translated "blessed," really means "happy" or "happy-making."[7]

Notice what Jesus did *not* say: "Naturally, we're happier when we receive than when we give, but giving is a duty, so grit your teeth, make the sacrifice, and force yourself to give."

Money won't make us happy, but giving away money can make us profoundly happy! When we give out of love for Christ and others, we experience dramatic and lasting returns for the investments we've made—far more than if we'd kept or spent it. Therefore, it's not only receivers who come out ahead—it's givers, too.

Sociologist Christian Smith's study on generosity yielded this observation: "People rightly say that money cannot buy happiness. But money and happiness are still related in a curious way. Happiness can be the result, not of spending more money on oneself, but rather of giving money away to others. . . . The data examined here show this to be not simply a nice idea, but a social-scientific fact."[8]

The thought that giving makes us happier than receiving seems counterintuitive. What could be better than receiving a gift? Don't we love Christmas and our own birthdays? Isn't it fun to get a package in the mail?

Sure, receiving a gift is great, and our hearts should be full of praise to God for what he has given us—first and foremost his Son, but also thousands of other smaller gifts we seldom think about. We should be profoundly grateful for what others have given us too. But have you ever worked hard to find the perfect gift for someone you love? Or thrown a surprise party for someone or given them tickets to a concert or game? Or given a bag of groceries to a person in need? Don't you get great happiness in the planning and giving of that gift? And isn't your joy multiplied by the receiver's joy?

As I write, two days ago I received a totally unexpected gift of a framed black-and-white photograph of me sitting at a desk in

1985, in front of my first book and my first computer (a Kaypro, for those over fifty who remember or care). My friend tracked down and bought the photo, taken by a photographer from the local paper more than thirty years ago.

Looking at the photo was like time traveling, and it brought back a flood of memories. Did my joy in receiving negate what Jesus said? No, because when I contacted the woman who had given it to me, she told of her utter delight in finding, framing, and sending it to me. As much as I enjoyed receiving it, she seemed to enjoy giving it even more. And though I've received a lot of great gifts over the years, many of those that make me smile the most are those I've given to my wife, daughters, friends, people I met in a store or on a plane, and even people I haven't met who have received food, clothes, clean water, and the gospel through organizations my family and I have supported.

If we understand what Scripture says about how giving touches lives for eternity, stores treasures for us in Heaven, and brings us

A GIFT THAT KEPT ON GIVING

Marjorie Yates says, "I received $1,000 in insurance money after the death of my grandfather. I had decided to give some of it away, and an opportunity arose to send a girl from the juvenile parole program to Young Life's Malibu Club summer camp, where I was volunteering. As a camp counselor, I was assigned a cabin of girls from juvenile parole, all of whom had been sent there by gifts from others. I watched their hearts open to the gospel, and all six made a profession of faith. What a joy it was to see what God did with my gift!"*

* Facebook comment in reply to my post requesting giving stories.

great happiness here and now, we'll realize there's no greater privilege than to live lives of overflowing love and joyful generosity. It's a no-brainer.

God Has Wired Us to Give

Arthur Brooks writes, "Our brains are actually wired to serve others. When we give charitable money and service to others, our brain releases several stress hormones which elevate our mood and cause us to feel happy. Serving and giving help to others makes us happier, healthier, more prosperous, and therefore greatly blessed and more successful than non-givers."[9]

To voluntarily serve someone—to give of ourselves—is to show love to them.

It's God who has wired us to love and serve others, and to find happiness in doing so. We should give because it's right, but also because it's smart. When we give, God is happy, those who receive our gifts are happy, and we're happy. Everyone but Satan wins.

I spoke at a Jesus Film Project missions conference and invited a farmer from my church to join me. People from all over the world told powerful stories about how God had changed their lives through this ministry.

After the conference, this normally reserved man told me with bold passion, "I want to give as much as I possibly can to this ministry!" Someone might have thought he'd won the lottery. Yet what excited him wasn't winning money; *it was giving it away*.

This man had made money for years, and it hadn't filled his heart with delight. What he was gaining now was purpose, direction, a deeper love for God's work, and joy (as well as eternal reward, though that wasn't foremost in his mind). All it cost him was money he didn't need—money that, had he kept it, might have harmed him and his family.

A banker who had read my books *The Treasure Principle* and *Why ProLife?* called me and said, "I want to save the lives of unborn children and help out their mothers. Tell me the best places I can give a million dollars." I didn't hear obligation in his voice. All I heard was excitement and joy.

We don't have to wait until we're nearing the end of our lives to experience the joy of giving! This is something that can be instilled in the hearts of our children and grandchildren from a young age. I learned yesterday of a family sponsoring a child whose son asked them, "Can you help me sell my game system on eBay?" The parents were surprised, since this was one of their son's most prized possessions. They asked him why. "So I can send our [sponsored] child a Christmas present," he replied.

I'm sure the boy was happy when he originally received his game system. I'm also sure that when he gave a Christmas present to a truly needy child across the globe, his happiness was both greater and more enduring.

The way of loving generosity may sound like dutiful obedience to the uninitiated. But generous givers know the truth: the habit of generosity ultimately explodes into enduring happiness.

CHAPTER 5

THE BEST INVESTMENT WE CAN MAKE

···

We make a living by what we get; we make a life by what we give.
ATTRIBUTED TO WINSTON CHURCHILL

*Let your light shine before people, so that they can see your good deeds
and give honor to your Father in heaven.*
MATTHEW 5:16, NET

In 1893, Rowland Bingham, a penniless twenty-one-year-old Canadian, believed God was calling him to Sudan, in distant Africa. When he announced his plan to his community, one farmer gave five dollars. Another said, "I will give you all I have in the bank, and then I shall borrow more, if need be."

Bingham and his fellow missionaries made the journey. Though they had no organization and no regular supporters backing them, they committed to share the gospel with the 60 million people of sub-Saharan Africa, who were among the least-reached people groups.

Once the men arrived in Africa, other missionaries urged them not to go to Sudan, in the interior. They said that given the obstacles and dangers, it couldn't be done. But each man vowed, "I will open up Central Africa to the Gospel, or I will die in the attempt."

Bingham and his partners prayed for a week. During that time, a letter arrived from a housekeeper named Mary Jones. She sent the full $300 of her inheritance (the equivalent of $12,000 today) and rallied others to give.[1]

Was Mary's inheritance wasted when two of those missionaries died of illness the very next year and only Bingham survived?[2] It likely seemed so at the time. Surely someone said to her, "Think of what you could have done for yourself or needy people nearby with that money!"

Fifty years after Bingham left for Africa, he wrote this about Mary Jones, "The gift of this servant girl came just at the moment of our greatest need and made possible that first journey up into the Sudan. Out of that gift . . . has come the great harvest of hundreds of converts every year, which we are seeing today."[3]

Seen in retrospect, Mary's gift was an eternal investment. What began as the vision of three young missionaries, aided by the sacrificial gifts of two poor farmers and a housekeeper, became Sudan Interior Mission, or SIM. Today this organization's four thousand missionaries work on six continents and in over seventy nations.

Mary's gift launched a work that would eventually bring the gospel to what may now exceed a hundred million people. Thousands of years after the Resurrection, I expect to still be meeting people on the New Earth who were touched by the giving of housemaid Mary Jones.

When it comes to high-risk corporate investments, some people go "all in," banking their life savings on a stock that may tank or earn incomparable dividends. But there are also risky Kingdom investments. While it's important to be wise stewards, we are sometimes called to follow God's promptings to give when we're uncertain of the results. God surely would have said "Well done" to Mary if Rowland Bingham had also died before SIM was begun. But it's beautiful to see the return he brought on her eternal investment!

GOD REDEEMS THE FORMER THINGS

I asked my friend Francine Rivers to share about her book *Redeeming Love*, which she wrote more than twenty-five years ago. From the very beginning, she devoted this book to Jesus, with all the royalties going to God's work: "After a successful career in the general market writing steamy historical romances, . . . my relationship with Jesus became the most important thing in my life. I sensed God telling me, 'This is the love story I want you to write—*my* story.' *Redeeming Love* was the result. It was and is *his* story, not mine. *Redeeming Love* was my firstfruits as a Christian writer. Hence, whatever royalties came from the book belong to the Lord, not to me. It was an act of obedience in the beginning but very quickly became a joyful offering."

More than one million copies of her book have been sold, and it is used by numerous ministries, including outreaches to prostitutes and organizations that help survivors of sex trafficking. Not only have many people benefited from reading *Redeeming Love*, but untold numbers have also been helped through its royalties.

Let's Deposit into Our Eternal Account

Paul rejoiced over the Philippians "because of your partnership in the gospel from the first day until now" (Philippians 1:5). This was a financial partnership in support of his ministry (Philippians 4:10-20). The "good work" he said God had begun in them was specifically the good work of Kingdom-centered generosity (Philippians 1:6).

He told the Philippians, "I have received everything in full, and I have an abundance. I am fully supplied, having received from Epaphroditus what you provided—a fragrant offering, an acceptable sacrifice, pleasing to God" (Philippians 4:18, csb). Their financial gifts were gifts to God. Since they gave so generously to provide for him and his work, Paul was confident

God would provide the same for them: "My God will supply all your needs according to his riches in glory in Christ Jesus" (Philippians 4:19, CSB). This is a familiar promise, but most people don't realize that in context, it is specifically for givers who have stretched themselves to become sacrificial partners in Kingdom ministry.

Notice Paul's invitation to the church in Philippians 4:17: "Not that I desire your gifts; what I desire is that more be credited to your account" (NIV). Or, "I want to see profit added to your account"

GOD NEEDS BUSINESSMEN TOO

R. G. LeTourneau's life didn't start out looking like it would be a success according to the world's definition. With only a seventh-grade education, he moved across the country, working as a welder, a woodcutter, a bricklayer, a farmhand, a miner, an electrical machinist, and a carpenter. He became a contractor and a self-taught engineer, and eventually a business owner.

Nearly 70 percent of the earthmoving equipment and engineering vehicles used by the Allied forces during World War II were built from his designs and machinery. LeTourneau invented and manufactured machines that laid most of the original highway infrastructure in the United States.

Arguably the greatest mechanical engineer of the twentieth century, LeTourneau had God-given creativity and vision that were decades ahead of his time. By the end of his life, he held more than three hundred patents.

LeTourneau's sister, a missionary, felt that R. G. should not pursue business but should instead prove his commitment to Christ by becoming an evangelist, a pastor, or a missionary. R. G. was willing to serve God in any way, and he went to his pastor, seeking

(GNT). He was giving people an opportunity to support his ministry not because he needed them to—he knew if they didn't give, God would provide for his work through other means. Rather, he was doing this *for their sake,* that God might credit it to their account in Heaven.

It's amazing but true: the eternal beneficiaries of our giving are not only God and other people. *We* benefit too. We need to ask ourselves if we've been making regular deposits into our accounts in Heaven.

advice. After they prayed together, his pastor told him, "God needs businessmen as well as preachers and missionaries."*

LeTourneau determined to be the best businessman he could for the cause of Christ.

He didn't find instant success. In his thirties, deeply in debt, he made God his senior business partner. This led him to live on 10 percent and give 90 percent of his income and business profits to God's Kingdom.

LeTourneau eventually established a school, which became LeTourneau University. He understood that missionary technicians were every bit as important as traditional Bible-teaching missionaries. One of LeTourneau's numerous projects included agricultural development in Liberia, which involved both growing crops and spreading the gospel. Ultimately, through his testimony and his giving, R. G. ended up reaching far more people than he could have as a pastor or missionary.

LeTourneau's tombstone cites Matthew 6:33: "Seek ye first the kingdom of God, and his righteousness; and all these things shall be added unto you" (KJV). He did, and they were.

* R. G. LeTourneau, *Mover of Men and Mountains: The Autobiography of R. G. LeTourneau* (Chicago: Moody, 1972).

Giving Is a High-Yield Investment

When she was in her seventies, Dottie Tillstrom started volunteering at Adorned in Grace, a bridal shop in my hometown of Gresham, Oregon. The store sells donated wedding and formal gowns. All proceeds are used to promote awareness and prevention of sex trafficking, as well as provide restoration for victims.

As Dottie became more involved in reaching out to victims, she recognized the need for a prevention program for young girls who come from difficult family situations. So she started a beginning sewing class for young refugees. She and her friends went door-to-door inviting girls to join their after-school program. Most had never used a sewing machine. "They caught on quickly and were eager to learn," Dottie says. "The girls were so happy, and I always went home feeling I'd received such a blessing for sharing my skills."

Dottie may have decreased her net worth by giving generously of her money and time, but she certainly increased her "Kingdom worth." God calls us to do good works (Ephesians 2:10; Romans 12:6-8). All good works involve service and generosity, whether it's spending time in prayer, providing hands-on help, sharing our gifts or talents, or giving our money and possessions. Most people think of giving as losing, since time and money are valuable, and we think, *I can't get it back*. But generous giving doesn't result in loss. It produces gain—both here and now, and in the life to come.

For thirty years, Nanci and I have had the privilege of giving away all our book royalties to God's Kingdom work. On occasion, people ask if I realize what we could have done with all the money from the sale of more than eleven million books. The answer is easy: "Nothing that would bring us nearly as much joy!"

When investors get excited about real estate and business deals, they call their friends and share the opportunity. Shouldn't we get even more excited about investments in Christ-centered ministries that help the poor, reach the lost, plant churches, and get God's Word into people's hands for the first time? Think of it—in God's new universe, our investments via giving will still be yielding dividends a billion years from now!

Giving Is Pure Gain

Musician Kyle Hutton went on a trip to Haiti with his wife and three teenage children, and they were touched by the many orphans there. It struck Kyle that these children weren't much different from the kids in the United States who needed homes, especially the ones in foster care who often spend their lives in insecurity, never knowing where they'll live next.

Kyle took this personally since he, too, had been in foster care the first six weeks of his life. So the Huttons became certified as foster parents and started taking in kids.

Kyle says, "If we love the kids right that come through our house, it's going to hurt when they leave. But when I look back, the only other option is that I never met the children who came through our home. The joy that these kids bring in—there's nothing like that in the world." Kyle laughingly adds, "I do miss sleeping, but I just drink more coffee now."[4]

Missionary martyr Jim Elliot wrote, "He is no fool who gives what he cannot keep to gain what he cannot lose."[5] Some interpret this quote to mean we are not to care about personal gain but only about great sacrifice. But read the statement again. Jim Elliot was saying that the fool clings to what he can't hold on to anyway. In contrast, giving away our lives and our time and our money will gain something far better that we can never lose. Hence, his statement about giving was *all about gain, not loss.*

Though Jim Elliot and his four missionary friends were speared to death in an Ecuadorian jungle, they gave up lives they would have eventually lost anyway to gain eternal reward. In addition, he and his friends and their wives inspired thousands to take the gospel to desperate souls around the globe.

Peter speaks of an inheritance God has awaiting us after death that includes both our salvation and the eternal treasures we store up through generous giving: "He keeps them for you in heaven, where they cannot decay or spoil or fade away" (1 Peter 1:4, GNT).

Jesus said, "The kingdom of heaven is like treasure, buried in a field, that a man found and reburied. Then in his joy he goes and sells everything he has and buys that field" (Matthew 13:44, CSB). Do you feel sorry for the man because of his huge sacrifice? Don't. That expression "in his joy" is the key. Someone might lament, "But it cost him everything he owned." Yes—*but it gained him everything he wanted!* He happily parted with a large amount of money to obtain what was worth far more. That's what happens when we give.

When a rich young man pressed Jesus about attaining eternal life, Jesus told him something that seems (even to many Christians) negative, not to mention unrealistic: "Sell your possessions and give to the poor, and you will have treasure in heaven. Then come, follow me" (Matthew 19:21, NIV).

But Jesus knew possessions were the man's god. Unless he dethroned his money idol, the rich man would never be free to serve the true God. Sadly, instead of embracing gain he'd never lose, the man foolishly held on to what he couldn't keep. He lost out on the good life. (Maybe he later changed his mind; I hope so.)

Both the investor of Matthew 13 and the rich man of

Matthew 19 valued treasure. The difference is, the investor happily took a short-term loss for the superior joy of long-term gain.

Giving Is an Adventure

Sometimes I meet Christians who seem utterly bored with their lives. There is a great cure for boredom, although it's one people don't typically consider: giving more time, money, and energy to God's Kingdom work, and inviting God to open our eyes to the needs surrounding us.

One hot summer day I stopped at a store for a Diet Mountain Dew, but when I saw the price, I changed my mind. However, as I often do, I prayed that God would connect me with someone in the store. The few people inside didn't look like they needed anything, so I thought, *Next time,* and walked out the door.

Outside, six feet from me, stood a young man who was probably in his early thirties. With long, stringy hair and worn sandals, he looked like he'd been living on the streets. He hadn't been there three minutes earlier when I walked in. I knew he was my answer to prayer.

"Hey, it's a hot day," I said. "Can I get you a bottle of water? Something to eat?"

He looked at me.

Reaching out my hand, I said, "I'm Randy."

He shook my hand. "I'm John."

I was unprepared for what happened next. He looked at me intently and said, "Are you a servant of Yeshua Adonai?"

Recognizing the Hebrew words for Jesus and Lord, or Master, I responded with a stunned, "Yes, I am."

He immediately put his hand on my shoulder and prayed for me—as if I were the needy one, which in fact I was that day. He asked God to use me to do great things for his Kingdom. His prayer was insightful, biblically resonant, and articulate—in fact, one of the most powerful prayers I've ever heard.

Then I prayed for John. When I finished, I asked him again if I could get him something in the store. He chose a small water bottle, but I pulled out a large instead (next to the Mountain Dew I was too cheap to buy). "Why don't you pick out something to eat?" I said. He chose some chips, and the total came to $4.50.

When we walked out the door, I tried to engage John further. But it seemed he had some place to go, so we said good-bye. I went to my car and wept, overcome with the deep sense that I'd met an angel. Hebrews 13:2 says, "Do not forget to show hospitality to strangers, for by so doing some people have shown hospitality to angels without knowing it" (NIV).

If John wasn't an angel, I knew he had been sent by God to pray for me. Who knows—maybe he was Jesus himself, given his age and general appearance—and anyway, Jesus said whatever we do to the needy we do for him (Matthew 25:37-40).

After thanking God and regaining my composure, I headed home, deeply touched. At a stoplight, I looked to my right and saw John thirty feet away, leaning against a building, drinking from his large water bottle. With a big smile, he waved at me in a way that seemed to say, "See you later."

No matter who John really was, I knew without a doubt that I would, in fact, see him later. I suspect we'll sit together at a banquet on the New Earth, and I'll find out who he really is and hear his story. The thought of it thrills me even now.

And I suspect that $4.50 will turn out to be one of the best investments I've ever made.

CHAPTER 6

THE DANGERS OF BEING RICH

....

Christ says, "Give me All. I don't want so much of your time and so much of your money and so much of your work: I want You."

C. S. LEWIS

It is easier for a camel to go through the eye of a needle than for someone who is rich to enter the kingdom of God.

MATTHEW 19:24, NIV

In the 1890s, Youssuf Ishmaelo, the "Terrible Turk," was an international wrestling phenomenon known for overwhelming his opponents with his immense strength. As his popularity grew, so did his wealth. Always suspicious, he demanded his winnings in gold and strapped them into his belt, which he never removed.

While he was sailing home from a victory in America, his ship sank. Survivors of the shipwreck reported that Ishmaelo became "like a wild beast." He bullied his way through frightened crowds and jumped into a fully loaded lifeboat. His weight, together with the force of his leap, overturned the boat, throwing its occupants into the sea. Ishmaelo, though a good swimmer, was dragged underwater by the weight of his $10,000 gold belt.[1]

We may not carry all our money with us like Youssuf Ishmaelo did (I certainly don't recommend it). But his story graphically portrays the way such an attitude toward material wealth weighs us down—and, in the end, sinks us.

There's Some Very Bad News about Wealth

While many (though far from all) Old Testament references to wealth are either positive or neutral, most New Testament references warn, rebuke, and outright condemn the attitude toward money prevalent in most cultures. This may be partly because Israel was a unique people of God, located in one place, and he blessed the country as a whole. Today, however, God's people are spread out among the nations and must more actively resist the beliefs and values that surround us. God withheld his full picture of the dangers of wealth until Christ came to teach and model biblical stewardship, and until the indwelling Holy Spirit could empower his people to live radically, going against the flow of pagan worldviews and lifestyles. We are citizens of a heavenly Kingdom (Philippians 3:20), and we are called to invest in *that* Kingdom, not our own earthly one.

Given their previous understanding of wealth, it would have been startling for Jesus' listeners to hear him promise that good things are in store for the godly poor: "Happy are you poor; the Kingdom of God is yours! Happy are you who are hungry now; you will be filled!" (Luke 6:20-21, GNT). But he also singled out the rich: "Woe to you who are rich, for you have received your consolation" (Luke 6:24).

The greatest danger of wealth is the illusion that we don't need God. Who prays, "Give us this day our daily bread" if they own the bakery or could easily afford to buy every loaf in the store?

James warned, "Come now, you rich, weep and howl for the miseries that are coming upon you. Your riches have rotted and your garments are moth-eaten. Your gold and silver have corroded, and their corrosion will be evidence against you and will eat your flesh like fire. You have laid up treasure in the last days" (James 5:1-3).

The word *treasure* in James 5 has the same root as the word used by Jesus when he talked about treasures stored on Earth and treasures in Heaven (Matthew 6:19-21). The only escape from judgment for those who hoard earthly treasures is to find real life in Christ, who calls us to surrender material goods to help the needy.

The Poor Are Close to God's Heart

Scripture clearly teaches that helping the poor and needy is right at the top of God's priority list for us. This includes the physically deprived as well as the spiritually impoverished—those hungry for the gospel and the Word of God.

God said, "I command you to be openhanded toward your fellow Israelites who are poor and needy in your land" (Deuteronomy 15:11, NIV).

He promises to reward those who obey his command to give:

- Whoever has a bountiful eye will be blessed, for he shares his bread with the poor. (Proverbs 22:9)
- When you give to the poor, it is like lending to the LORD, and the LORD will pay you back. (Proverbs 19:17, GNT)
- Share your food with the hungry, and give shelter to the homeless. Give clothes to those who need them, and do not hide from relatives who need your help. Then your salvation will come like the dawn, and your wounds will quickly heal. Your godliness will lead you forward, and the glory of the LORD will protect you from behind. (Isaiah 58:7-8, NLT)

The New Testament is full of similar themes about rewards for those who give to the poor (see, for example, Matthew 6:3-4; Matthew 6:19-21; Matthew 10:42; 2 Corinthians 9:6-8). When people asked what they should do to demonstrate true repentance, John the Baptist said, "Anyone who has two shirts should share with the one who has none, and anyone who has food should do the same" (Luke 3:11, NIV).

Jesus said, "The Spirit of the LORD is upon me, for he has anointed me to bring Good News to the poor" (Luke 4:18, NLT). James wrote, "If one of you says to [the poor], 'Go in peace; keep warm and well fed,' but does nothing about their physical needs, what good is it? . . . Faith by itself, if it is not accompanied by action, is dead" (James 2:16-17, NIV).

Paul's words powerfully reflect the giving priorities of the early church leaders who had been with Jesus: "James, Cephas and John . . . agreed that we should go to the Gentiles, and they to the circumcised. All they asked was that we should continue to remember the poor, the very thing I had been eager to do all along" (Galatians 2:9-10, NIV). Both tithing and freewill giving have prominent places in the Old Testament, but Jesus and the apostles raised the bar to a whole new level.

We Are the Rich

Wealth is gauged by comparison; people are considered rich or poor in relation to the people around them. As much as our incomes and assets may vary, the great majority of people reading this book—and the person writing it—are wealthy compared to the rest of the world.

AN NFL PLAYER WHO DRIVES A REALLY OLD CAR

While most professional athletes drive top-of-the-line cars, running back Alfred Morris still drives his trusty old 1991 Mazda, which he has affectionately dubbed "Bentley." A genuine follower of Jesus, Alfred bought the car from his pastor when he was in college—for two dollars. He has come a long way since then; with his NFL contract, he certainly would be able to afford any car he wants. But he says he keeps the car as a reminder to stay humble.*

* Alysha Tsuji, "Cowboys' Alfred Morris Refuses to Stop Driving 25-Year-Old Car He Bought for $2," *USA Today Sports*, July 19, 2016, https://ftw.usatoday.com/2016/07/cowboys-alfred-morris-old-car-bentley.

In 2017 a family of four in the United States with an annual income of $24,600 was at the US federal poverty level.[2] Yet when I entered that amount at globalrichlist.com, it indicated this income level is in the top 2.09 percent of people worldwide. In 2018 the median household income in the United States was $62,175.[3] That amount lands not just in the top one percent of the world's wealthy but *inside the top one-fifth of one percent.*[4]

Some readers will be far more or less rich than others, of course, and many may not *feel* rich. Still, on a relative global scale, the great majority of us clearly are.

It's critical for us to recognize when the Bible is talking to and about us. Later in this book, we will look closely at 1 Timothy 6:17-19, which says, in part, "Command those who are rich in this present world . . . to be rich in good deeds, and to be generous and willing to share" (NIV). If we fail to realize that we really *are* rich, we will imagine that this command (along with other principles and parables) applies to other people, but not us.

Why Is the Bible So Hard on Us Rich People?

Now that we know God's commands to the rich apply to us, the question isn't just "Why is the Bible so hard on rich people?" but "Why is the Bible so hard on *us*?"

As I've studied Scripture, I've come to the conclusion that the Bible is hard on those with wealth because *certain undesirable attitudes and actions tend to characterize rich people*. These include pride, arrogance, presumption, entitlement, and indifference to the needy. While poor people can have all these characteristics, the danger tends to increase if they become rich.

Paul Piff gives an interesting TED talk called "Does Money Make You Mean?" It describes a study in which participants play a particular game and begin to demonstrate unfavorable qualities when they "get richer" as the game goes on.[5]

The admonitions to the rich in James 5:1-5 likewise list some of these unfavorable qualities. James began with these words: "Listen, you rich people," and then he went on to warn them, "The wages you failed to pay the workers who mowed your fields are crying out against you. The cries of the harvesters have reached the ears of the Lord Almighty. You have lived on earth in luxury and self-indulgence. You have fattened yourselves in the day of slaughter" (NIV).

Many people limit their concept of entitlement to poor people wanting the rich to take care of them. Sometimes that's true, but studies indicate that the *rich* easily become narcissistic and often feel entitled.[6] They expect preferential treatment because of their special status. This might include the corner office, the best table at the restaurant, or a prominent position at church.

Paul told Timothy, "As for the rich in this present age, charge them not to be haughty" (1 Timothy 6:17). The final word is also rendered "arrogant" (NIV), "egotistical" (CEB), and "proud" (NLT, GNT). The fact that this warning is specifically intended for the rich suggests that pride, arrogance, egomania, and narcissism are common temptations for them. The rich will fall prey to these sins unless something bold and significant is done to ward them off. (As we'll later see in 1 Timothy 6, generous giving is precisely the prescription to avoid the downsides of wealth.)

God emphatically warns us, "Pride goes before destruction, and haughtiness before a fall" (Proverbs 16:18, NLT). But how are we to view all these warnings to the rich, as well as the severe condemnation of pride, arrogance, and entitlement? How can we reconcile them with God's love for his people? The answer is that God warns his children *precisely because he loves us!*

If you see someone about to cross a street in front of an oncoming car, do you whisper a prayer or ask, "May I make a suggestion?" No, you warn them! If necessary, you scream at them. It doesn't matter if they are startled, embarrassed, or annoyed.

If the one in danger of being hit by a car is your child or grandchild, would you lower your voice so as not to alarm them? No, you'd raise your voice! They *need* to be alarmed. You'd rather have them alive and momentarily frightened than dead.

In our grandson's football game, one of his teammates intercepted a pass. When he ran the wrong way, his coaches and teammates started yelling at him. No one in the stands thought that was mean. He heard their shouts, turned around, and ran the right direction. Out of love (and a desire to win), they spared him the embarrassment of scoring points for the other team!

That's why God raises his voice to warn the rich—because he loves us. A judge may condemn the guilty and impose punishment.

A father, in contrast, warns his child of the dire consequences of wrong behaviors. The judge is concerned with law and justice; the father is concerned for his child's welfare. And if the child understands that, he listens carefully to the father's warnings, no matter how countercultural they may be.

Can Rich People Go to Heaven?

In the story of the rich young man, we're told that he "ran up to [Jesus] and fell on his knees before him" (Mark 10:17, NIV). The man's eagerness and sincerity are evident.

"Good teacher," he asked, "what must I do to inherit eternal life?" So far, so good. This man wants to live with God in Heaven forever.

After the rich young man spoke to Jesus, we read something remarkable that's often overlooked: "Jesus looked at him and loved him" (Mark 10:21, NIV).

When you love people, you act in their best interests. What Jesus said next should be seen in light of the immediately preceding statement that Jesus loved him: "One thing you lack. . . . Go, sell everything you have and give to the poor, and you will have treasure in heaven. Then come, follow me" (Mark 10:21, NIV).

Unlike many of us, Jesus clearly grasps eternal realities, and that knowledge informs his love for rich people. He knew what stood between this young man and the good life God offers: his wealth. He wouldn't have been seeking something more from Jesus if he already had the abundant life. His question suggests unease, dissatisfaction, and discontentment with the life he'd been living.

Because of his loving grace, God desires to remove any obstacle between us and eternal, abundant life. Sure, Jesus showed love for the poor by commanding the rich man to donate his wealth to them. But he simultaneously showed love for the man by offering him liberation from the false god of wealth.

Tragically, we're told, "At this the man's face fell. He went away sad, because he had great wealth" (Mark 10:22, NIV). What the rich man thought he owned actually owned him. Money was his god. "No one can serve two masters. . . . You cannot serve both God and money" (Matthew 6:24, NIV).

The man thought he was acting in his own best interests by clinging to his wealth. He couldn't have been more wrong. He didn't understand that Jesus, by telling him to give it away, was actually offering him freedom, joy, and the life that's truly life.

Seeing the rich man's unwillingness to be freed from the bondage of wealth, Jesus turned to his disciples and said with sadness, "How hard it is for the rich to enter the kingdom of God! . . . It is easier for a camel to go through the eye of a needle than for someone who is rich to enter the kingdom of God" (Mark 10:23, 25, NIV).

Many books and sermons, and even some commentaries, claim that there was a narrow passage or gate in Jerusalem called "the eye of a needle." Supposedly camels had to be unloaded of everything they were carrying before they could fit through it. Some say the camels could enter on their knees. Therefore, rich people can enter God's Kingdom, but only if they dump all their baggage and enter Heaven in humility.

This all sounds very spiritual, and indeed endless articles online suggest that such a gate existed. Commentator William Barclay is sometimes cited as a source for this idea, but Barclay doesn't document this claim; he simply indicates, "It is said that . . ." which of course is no help.[7] In fact, despite my extensive search for a credible historical reference to back this up, I have never seen any evidence there was actually a gate called by ancients the "eye of the needle."

Jesus used the normal word for a sewing needle, and what's translated "eye" means "hole." We don't have to come up with a creative way to negate the possibility of a camel going through a needle's eye. Obviously a camel *can't* go through a needle's eye—and that's the whole point, humorously pictured by Jesus. Apart from a miracle, rich people can't stop trusting in their riches and instead turn to Christ. That's what the disciples understood Jesus to be saying, which explains their shocked response: "They who heard it said, 'Then who can be saved?'" (Luke 18:26, NASB).

Why their astonishment? Because in Jesus' day, wealth was seen as a sign of God's approval. The logic went like this: if the wealthy, whom God obviously approves of, have a hard time going to Heaven, how could the poor, whom God apparently disdains, ever make it?

But Jesus qualified his shocking statement by saying, "The things that are impossible with people are possible with God" (Luke 18:27, AMP). Just as it's impossible for a camel to go through the eye of a needle, it's impossible with people—but *not* with God—for a rich man to enter Heaven. Jesus can and ultimately did provide a way for rich people—and all who believe in him—to enter God's Kingdom.

Peter seemed stunned by Jesus' statement that it's humanly impossible for the rich to inherit God's Kingdom. He said, "We have left everything to follow you!" (Mark 10:28, NIV).

Instead of rebuking him, Jesus said to Peter, "Truly I tell you, . . . no one who has left home or brothers or sisters or mother or father or children or fields for me and the gospel will fail to receive a hundred times as much in this present age: homes, brothers, sisters, mothers, children and fields—along with persecutions—and in the age to come eternal life" (Mark 10:29-30, NIV).

Jesus indicated here that not just some but all of his followers must turn away from various forms of wealth that get in the way of following him, whether that wealth comes in the form of money, property, security, family, prestige, or popularity. Short-term rewards and eternal ones await anyone who follows Christ. The life we obtain far surpasses anything we leave behind.

After saying we should take up our crosses to follow him, Jesus taught, "If you try to hang on to your life, you will lose it. But if you give up your life for my sake, you will save it" (Matthew 16:25, NLT).

At first glance, we might imagine Jesus calls us to utter disregard for our self-interests. In fact, his call is the opposite. Jesus

STANDARD OF LIVING . . . OR STANDARD OF GIVING?

Brothers Alex and Edward Foster in the United Kingdom are radical young givers. As a new physician, Edward has seen his friends spend lavishly since they started making higher salaries. But Edward says, "I don't want to increase my [standard of] living as I earn more. I'm committed to increasing my standard of giving."

Alex, a former investment banker who's now an entrepreneur, says, "I try to live as simply as I can. I cap my budget at 15,000 pounds. That's really hard, but really good."

Edward and Alex have experienced some awkward conversations—even with their family and friends. "What's alienating isn't just that you have slightly different logic. It's that the logic is upsetting to people," Edward says. Still, Alex says, "Being free of materialism makes you incredibly happy. There's so much more joy in my life than when I was owned by the things I wanted."*

* Cameron Doolittle, "Three Lessons on Giving from the Foster Brothers," Generosity Path, January 27, 2017, http://www.generositypath.org/morestories/foster-brothers.

supplies the reason we should give up our lives: *to save them*. We give up empty lives and grab hold of the good life. We give up an impoverished spiritual life to enjoy the abundant life in Christ. This is like being offered ownership of Coca-Cola in exchange for a sack of pop bottles. Only a fool would pass up the offer.

Wealth Has Mortal Dangers

Henry Kaestner's company, Bandwidth, received a lucrative contract they really needed to stay afloat. When they discovered that business's affiliation with the adult entertainment industry, Bandwidth could have looked the other way. But they knew that would put them at odds with God's principles. Heeding the warnings in his Word, they canceled the deal. Soon their financial position looked bad.

Sometimes making ethical business decisions reduces profits. Refusing to compromise morally can even result in a failed business.

In Henry Kaestner's case, Bandwidth turned around dramatically after that decision, becoming the fourth-fastest-growing privately held company in the country.[8] For a while, Henry and his wife, Kimberley, gave away 20 percent of their income, thinking double tithing was impressive. But Henry said, "[God] wants our hearts. Now we can give much more radically. We intend to give away half, and the lion's share of the rest is invested in Christian-led private companies in Asia."

Henry added, "There's an incredible joy when you participate in the work of God. It's remarkably fulfilling, because it fills up the hole that would otherwise contain idols that take the place of God."[9]

Only after comprehending our imminent risk of drowning will we reach out to take hold of the life preserver God has thrown us in Christ. Grabbing that life preserver will require us to do what Youssuf Ishmaelo wouldn't—free ourselves from the weight of our possessions.

There's implicit good news in the bad news about wealth: since we can still hear God's warning, it's not too late for us. Heeding it can still save our lives.

We know a woman who appeared physically fit but had a routine annual medical exam and received bad news. Her test results were abnormal. This led to another test and more bad news. The doctor said she had cancer and needed surgery. This led to further bad news. The cancer might have spread, so more procedures were recommended. She heeded the recommendations, and the cancer hasn't recurred. She is alive today because she subjected herself to medical tests, took the results seriously, and followed the professional diagnosis. Accepting the bad news resulted in the good news that she is alive and healthy.

It is necessary for us to hear the explicitly bad news about materialism, which is indeed cancer-like. Learning about it prepares us to eagerly and gratefully embrace the wonderfully good news that follows—about a lifesaving cure to an otherwise terminal disease.

God doesn't call all Christ-followers to give away everything. In fact, he doesn't instruct the rich to become poor. Rather, he instructs them to counterbalance their wealth with generosity. We are to be rich in good deeds and ready to share (1 Timothy 6:17-19). This good news of life-altering generosity serves as a life preserver. It results in treasures awaiting us in Heaven, and meanwhile it gives us the life that is truly life.

At some point for all of us, the ship of our lives will sink. When that happens, and it's time to die, will we cling to our money belts like the Terrible Turk, or will we cling to Jesus and the eternal life he offers?

CHAPTER 7

PUT YOUR TREASURE WHERE IT WILL LAST

....

Little kingdom living is an endless search for earthly treasure and unending focus on personal need; grace calls you to a bigger kingdom.
PAUL DAVID TRIPP

The Kingdom of heaven is like this. A man happens to find a treasure hidden in a field. He . . . sells everything he has, and then goes back and buys that field.
MATTHEW 13:44, GNT

There were some people of times past I wished I could have interviewed for this book. One of them was Stanley Tam, whom I'd read about years earlier. I couldn't find Stanley's date of death online, but considering he was born in 1915, it seemed safe to assume he had already died. I contacted a friend who'd known Stanley to find out more about his life. I was shocked by his response: "Want to talk to Stanley on the phone this Saturday?"

So to my delight, I spoke with 102-year-old Stanley Tam (since then he's turned 103). Here's his story, with parts of our conversation woven in.

In 1934, as a young door-to-door salesman, Stanley Tam met a farmer's wife who told him about Jesus. Six weeks later, while in a church, he placed his faith in Christ.

With twenty-five dollars of his own in his pocket, plus

twelve dollars from his father, he launched United States Plastic Corporation, in Lima, Ohio.

Stanley told me, "I started the business in 1936, and I soon went broke. I was so discouraged. Then the Lord spoke to me: 'Turn it over to me; I'll make it succeed.'"

So Stanley legally made God the company's majority owner—51 percent of company stock was given to a nonprofit, which in turn gave all the earnings to God's Kingdom. Stanley believed that God wanted to run the business with Stanley as his employee.

God Was Just Getting Started

It turned out 51 percent wasn't enough!

Stanley became familiar with an effective international ministry that he heard was closing due to lack of funds. He contacted them and said, "If I could trust God to provide $50,000 more per year to give you, would you open the ministry back up?"

They said yes.

In our conversation over the phone, Stanley's voice grew animated, and he sounded half of his 102 years. He told me, "That ministry is still going. We're now in forty-two countries, and we have thousands of people going door-to-door bringing people God's Word and the plan of salvation."

I loved that he said "we." Where your treasure is, there your heart will also be (Matthew 6:21), and when you give to God's work, you invest in his Kingdom. You are thinking and acting like someone with vested interests. When we spoke in 2017, more than 140,000 people had professed Christ the previous year through the ministry Stanley supported, and many churches had been planted.

BETTER THAN FINANCIAL SECURITY

Sophie, founder of a training center in the Netherlands, says, "In our culture, our money is our security, and when this security vanishes, people start to panic." Sophie built a successful business, but after her radical conversion, she realized she'd been building it because "I wanted to prove I was worthy. Then I found my identity in Christ and didn't need to prove to anyone how worthy I was."

Now that she is involved in Generosity Path, Sophie decided to give away a substantial portion of her savings. "We're giving away our company, and we're looking at ways to offer our house to the church."

Through Generosity Path, she connects with a group of other radical givers who share testimonies and encourage one another. This sense of community is important to Sophie: "Let's walk together where similar people are thinking about similar things."*

* This story was sent to me by Cameron Doolittle, senior director of Generosity Path (www.generositypath.org).

Stanley told me about a meeting in South America in 1955 where he spoke and saw God work powerfully in people's lives. He explained, "God spoke to me and said, 'Stanley, if a soul is the most precious thing in the world, would you go back to the United States and turn your entire business over to me? And would you use the profits to spread the gospel around the world?'"

"Lord, you already have 51 percent of it," Stanley replied. "Isn't that enough?"

Then Stanley sensed God saying to him, "Stanley, on the cross, I paid it all for you. Now you're my disciple. And I want you to do what I ask."

You might be thinking that since Stanley is an extraordinary man of faith, this all came easily for him. It didn't.

Stanley said, "You'll never know the struggle I went through that night. Finally I said, 'All right Lord, you can have it.'" He added, "I just wanted to be obedient."

Stanley's wife, Juanita, agreed to follow the Lord in this too, and the Tams gave 100 percent of the company to God, meaning all the profits went to gospel ministry. It was only then that Stanley found the joy in giving over to God what he knew belonged to him. Stanley had a new plant built, four times bigger and facing an interstate, with huge letters installed on the side of the building: "Christ Is the Answer."

Though Stanley's salary was a mere fraction of that of a typical CEO, he gave substantially out of his income. In fact, he told me, "When my salary was $78,000, our personal giving was about $30,000."

The company now produces more than 30,000 products and serves more than 85,000 customers. Stanley Tam had a wonderful business career in which he brought the world high-quality plastics. But more important, he brought the world what will last forever.

So what did Stanley do when he retired? He opened a small woodworking shop a mile up the street. His sign outside said, "Are you seeking peace in your heart? The answer is in the Bible." Underneath was this offer: "Come inside for a free Bible."

Wes Lytle, Stanley's successor as president of U.S. Plastic Corp., said, "We're different than most companies. We're similar in that we want to make as much money as we possibly can, but the purpose is totally different. . . . What is that purpose? To give away as much money as we possibly can, for the glory of Jesus and the good of others!"[1] U.S. Plastic Corp. has cumulatively contributed more than $150 million to God's Kingdom.

Is Stanley Tam "coasting" now that he's nearing the end of his life? Not even close. Over a century old, living in a retirement home, he prays a few hours in the morning and again in the evening. He told me, "I've talked to more than one hundred people about Jesus in this retirement home. And I've led twelve to the Lord."

If we truly believe that God owns everything and that we owe him everything for giving us all the goodness we've ever known or will ever know, then Stanley Tam's actions make perfect sense. While the details of our circumstances may vary, the heart behind generosity can be the same. Stanley's life, and the lives of others like him, should stir us to say, "What can I do that would express the same faith in God's ownership and lordship of all I am and all I own?"

At the end of our conversation, Tam said, "People used to tell me, 'Stanley, you're giving it all away! Why aren't you keeping it?' I told them, 'I am putting it in the bank account in Heaven.'"

As I heard Stanley speak, I could imagine another voice— a louder and stronger voice—saying to him, "Well done, my good and faithful servant."

Being Rich Comes with Responsibility

If you are working a "secular" job like Stanley Tam did, you are not second class in God's Kingdom. You are no less called or gifted than a pastor or a missionary. Your ministry is to represent Jesus in your own sphere of influence and to provide financial support that enables others to do the work God equips them to do. You may not have the wealth of someone who started a successful corporation, but if you are living on more than $5.50 a day, you are richer than 3.4 billion people.[2] That kind of blessing isn't something to take lightly; it comes with responsibility.

John Rinehart tells many compelling stories in his excellent book *Gospel Patrons: People Whose Generosity Changed the World*.[3] These include how God raised up William Tyndale five hundred years ago to be an English preacher. But he also raised up Humphrey Monmouth, a wealthy cloth merchant who joined forces with Tyndale to steer their nation back to faith in Jesus. God used Tyndale to provide six million English speakers with their first English translation of the Bible. God used Monmouth to fund Tyndale, strategize with him, and smuggle Bibles into hostile England. Tyndale was later martyred for his work, but the fruit of his partnership with Monmouth birthed a reformation that shook England—and later, the world.[4]

Similarly, 250 years ago, God used Lady Huntingdon and her connections in high society to bring the Good News to England's aristocracy in conjunction with preacher George Whitefield. Their partnership gave Whitefield a powerful preaching platform to reach not only Britain's elite but thereafter to bring the gospel to 80 percent of the American colonies. God used the two of them to spearhead the Great Awakening.[5]

Two and a half centuries ago, as John Rinehart notes, God brought together an English sailor-turned-minister, John Newton, and one of the wealthiest businessmen in England, John Thornton. Newton was a patriarch to the next generation of England's church leaders, missionaries, and leading laymen, including William Wilberforce, who almost single-handedly brought an end to the slave trade in England. Thornton financed the first thousand-book print run of Newton's hymns. Their partnership helped raise up two generations of gospel preachers and shaped the spiritual and political future of England.

Meanwhile, Newton's hymnbook spread to American congregations in the Deep South, where the words of one of his hymns were paired with a new tune, which they renamed "Amazing Grace." This song went on to become what is probably the world's most beloved hymn. And behind the success of this song was not just John Newton but also businessman John Thornton, who gave generously so more people could hear and sing God's Word. And now, 240 years later, God's people around the globe still sing this song![6]

So why did God give business success and wealth to Humphrey Monmouth, Lady Huntingdon, and John Thornton? For exactly the reason he gave skills in preaching and translation to William Tyndale, George Whitefield, and John Newton—to further the cause of Christ and expand his Kingdom all over the world.

Why has God entrusted you with more money than you need, whether that's a little more, a lot more, or a whole lot more? I would venture to say it's for that very same reason. (Doesn't that excite you?)

WHAT IF PEOPLE TAKE ADVANTAGE OF YOUR GENEROSITY?

Martin Luther was generous to the point that he and his wife, Katherine, were sometimes taken advantage of. At one point, a woman traveling through showed up at their home needing help. Martin and Katherine provided food and housing for her. They later discovered that she had lied and stolen. Yet Luther "believed that no one would become poor by practicing charity, [saying] 'God divided the hand into fingers so that money would slip through.'"*

* Mark Galli, "Martin Luther's Later Years: Did You Know?" *Christian History*, no. 39 (1993), https://christianhistory institute.org/magazine/article/martin-luthers-later-years-did-you-know.

God Has Reasons for Entrusting Us with His Resources

Most of us don't start companies that enable us to give $150 million, like Stanley Tam did. But we can follow his example of serving God not only by generating funds to give to God's servants around the world but also by *being* God's servants—ambassadors for Christ, his representatives in our places of influence.

Jesus told his disciples a parable in which he described a "faithful and wise manager" as one who gave his servants food and other resources "at the proper time." When the master returned and saw one servant faithfully managing his resources, he "put him in charge of all his possessions" (Luke 12:42-44, NIV). Jesus continued the parable by describing an unfaithful servant who forgot about his master and failed to manage his assets according to his principles. This servant got drunk and beat the other servants. Jesus promised the master would return when the servant didn't expect it and bring harsh judgment on him (Luke 12:45-47).

In contrast to the faithful servant, the unfaithful servant mismanaged the master's resources. Instead of carefully managing the owner's possessions, he greedily squandered them on himself.

Jesus then summarized the point of the parable with these words: "Everyone to whom much was given, of him much will be required, and from him to whom they entrusted much, they will demand the more" (Luke 12:48).

Make no mistake about it, you and I have been entrusted with much. So in light of Jesus' words, we need to ask ourselves, *Am I a faithful servant or an unfaithful servant when it comes to what I do with my Lord's resources?*

WOULD YOU GIVE IT ALL AWAY?
David Tjokrorahardjo's company in Jakarta, Indonesia, was earning a couple of million dollars annually. That's when God prompted him and his wife, Julia, to "close it down and give it away." So they did. David says, "It was a time of testing for us, but something inside told us that this was from God and we wanted to be available." The couple has invested both time and money in the JPCC Foundation, a humanitarian organization that responds to victims of natural disasters and proactively works with forgotten people in remote areas.*

* "Three Lessons from David Tjokrorahardjo, Indonesia," JoyGiving.org, accessed January 23, 2019, https://joygiving.org/david/.

God Has Given You a Unique Platform

If God has wired you to be good at what you do—whether business or art, manufacturing or farming, music or medicine, or anything that allows you to freely help the needy and further the cause of Christ—rejoice! This is a great use of your life.

Leaving your job for "full-time ministry" may not be a step up for the Kingdom of God but a step down. God may have given you the ability, right where you are, to help churches and missionaries reach those God has called them to, as well as the ability to reach others in your own unique sphere of ministry.

So whether you are a grocery clerk, an assembly line worker, a salesperson, a flight attendant, a stay-at-home mom, or a professional athlete, or whether you have a primary ministry of prayer or encouraging people, God has given you a unique platform. In all likelihood, no pastor or missionary will reach your neighbors, teachers, coworkers, coaches, or teammates. We each have our own God-given mission fields to serve every day. So use your platform for the glory of God, and then give generously to the causes of evangelism, justice, and mercy that are close to his heart.

God doesn't just call his people to the far reaches of the Earth for his Kingdom. He also equips many servants to support and supply workers and to meanwhile represent him in their own territory right where they live and work. Whatever he has called you to do, do it with your whole heart, giving generously out of the overflow he's entrusted to you.

May each of us live daily in such a way as to look forward to hearing the Lord say to us, when we meet him face to face, "Well done, you good and faithful servant! . . . You have been faithful in managing small amounts, so I will put you in charge of large amounts. Come on in and share my happiness!" (Matthew 25:21, GNT).

PART 2

THE BAD NEWS AND GOOD NEWS ABOUT MONEY

There is great gain in godliness with contentment; for we brought nothing into the world, and we cannot take anything out of the world; but if we have food and clothing, with these we shall be content. But those who desire to be rich fall into temptation, into a snare, into many senseless and hurtful desires that plunge men into ruin and destruction. For the love of money is the root of all evils; it is through this craving that some have wandered away from the faith and pierced their hearts with many pangs.

1 TIMOTHY 6:6-10, RSV

CHAPTER 8

CONTENTMENT: WHEN ENOUGH IS ENOUGH

....

You say, "If I had a little more, I should be very satisfied."
You make a mistake. If you are not content with what you have,
you would not be satisfied if it were doubled.
CHARLES SPURGEON

Godliness with contentment is great gain.
1 TIMOTHY 6:6

In 1996, Life.Church began in Oklahoma with a handful of people. By 2005, church growth brought floods of requests to purchase Pastor Craig Groeschel's sermons. A staff member asked, "What would happen if we just gave them away?"

"That moment changed us," Craig says. "Generosity became one of my top values."

Craig and his church decided to give away something of value without expecting a return. From the moment they made that decision, giving became contagious at Life.Church. He says, "Generosity is not something we do—it is something we are."[1]

Their giving went far beyond not charging a fee for sermons. Life.Church has contributed more than 9 million resources to more than 355,600 church leaders around the world.[2] They also created YouVersion, which has been downloaded 355 million times, making it the most popular Bible app in the world.[3] To date, Life.Church has given more than $30 million to fund this project alone.[4]

Life.Church's emphasis on giving has had a significant effect on its leaders. They've found deep-rooted contentment in knowing that their church honors God by freely giving away what otherwise could have been sold for a great deal of money. Because of their commitment to trust God instead of money, they model what Scripture teaches about both generosity and contentment.

Contentment Is the True Measure of Godliness

We are living in an era when we have more material possessions than any generation before us. Compared to Americans living in the 1950s, we have countless more conveniences, including big-screen TVs, microwaves, online shopping, smartphones, and twice as many cars.[5] It's easy to assume our purchases will automatically lead to greater contentment.

But will they? Dr. David G. Myers claims that this generation is actually less content than generations before it. "Compared with their grandparents, today's young adults have grown up with much more affluence, slightly less happiness and much greater risk of depression and assorted social pathology."[6]

The false idea that prosperity brings contentment is nothing new. Paul warned Timothy and the church at Ephesus about false teachers—first-century equivalents to modern prosperity theology proponents—who were "depraved in mind and deprived of the truth, imagining that godliness is a means of gain" (1 Timothy 6:5).

Like the Pharisees, these false teachers were religious braggarts, and most of what Scripture says about the one group applies to the other. Jesus put it this way: "Everything they do is just to show off in front of others" (Matthew 23:5, CEV). They impressed people with their clever interpretations and personality-driven communication. Instead of faithfully teaching God's Word, they misused their platform to perform and make money. We know from historical documents that some prominent religious teachers in that time charged exorbitant speaker fees.[7] Like their counterparts today, they embraced the secular culture's materialistic values while baptizing them with verses taken out of context.

A CHILD'S ACT OF GENEROSITY

Four-year-old Sidney made national news when she asked a police officer to check for monsters in her new home. Out of gratitude, she donated the contents of her piggy bank (nine dollars and change) to the police department's efforts to raise funds for the medical treatment of another officer, an Army vet and father of three who had been diagnosed with cancer.

"It's the nice thing to do," she said.

Now Sidney frequently visits the police station and brings the officers candy and cookies.

Her mother said, "It all started about two years ago when she saw an officer directing traffic. It was hot outside and she said, 'He looks thirsty; he needs water,' and she brought him a bottle of water. . . . It feels good that she's so giving. She wanted to save the money for a toy but decided someone needed it more than her."

The police department stated, "Words are not available for what this means to us."*

* Aliyah Frumin, "4-Year-Old Girl Donates Piggy Bank Money to Police Officer with Cancer," Today, October 31, 2017, https://www.today.com/news/girl-donates-piggy-bank-money-police-officer-cancer-t118140.

Many people believed such preachers were wealthy because God approved of them. But he didn't then, and he doesn't today.

After describing the false teachers as "imagining that godliness is a means of gain," Paul immediately followed with "but godliness with contentment is great gain" (1 Timothy 6:6).

Like the Pharisees, the false teachers used superficial, outward godliness as a means to the ends of popularity, power, and wealth. Paul, however, wasn't talking about a *show* of godliness. He was referring to genuine, inward godliness centered on the person and work of Jesus Christ. This is a humble godliness that manifests itself as a natural outflow, never as a calculated performance.

The New Living Translation renders 1 Timothy 6:5-6 this way: "To them, a show of godliness is just a way to become wealthy. Yet true godliness with contentment is *itself great wealth*" (emphasis added). When it comes to lasting gain, true godliness definitely pays off! But the measure of such godliness is our *contentment*, not our bank balance. And *that* is the great gain.

What Is Contentment?

Contentment is being satisfied in whose you are, who you are, and what you have. Those who love and serve Jesus can be truly content. Those who love and serve money can never be. Contentment isn't dependent on favorable life circumstances, nor is it the product of material abundance. That's why there are people who struggle with poverty or other difficult life circumstances and yet are content, and rich and healthy celebrities who aren't.

Puritan Jeremiah Burroughs defined Christian contentment as "that sweet, inward, quiet, gracious frame of spirit, which freely submits to and delights in God's wise and fatherly disposal in every condition."[8]

Money-love robs us of contentment, while God-love fills us with it. God, our Creator and Redeemer, has transformed us and opened the doors of Heaven to us. No matter what happens, no matter how much or how little money we have, "nothing in all creation will ever be able to separate us from the love of God that is revealed in Christ Jesus our Lord" (Romans 8:39, NLT).

Hebrews 13:5 gives us the formula for finding contentment, as well as the ultimate reason for it: "Make sure that your character is free from the love of money, being content with what you have; for He Himself has said, 'I WILL NEVER DESERT YOU, NOR WILL I EVER FORSAKE YOU'" (NASB).

While most translations of this verse have two negatives—*never* and *nor*, the original has three. Young's Literal Translation renders the verse in keeping with this: "For He hath said, 'No, I will not leave, no, nor forsake thee.'" Here we have the strongest possible assurance that God will never abandon his children. That alone is the best reason to be content with whatever we have—and don't have.

Jesus said of those who know him, "I give them eternal life, and they shall never perish; no one will snatch them out of my hand" (John 10:28, NIV). We have God, and even in life's most difficult circumstances, he holds us securely in his hands.

Jerry Bridges wrote, "Contentment is one of the most distinguishing traits of the godly person, because a godly person has his heart focused on God rather than on possessions or position or power."[9]

If our trust is in money, possessions, power, or fame, we'll never be content. All of these are cruel false gods. They always break their promises and send us the bill. Proverbs 23:5 puts it this way: "Your money can be gone in a flash, as if it had grown wings and flown away like an eagle" (GNT). Money is a false god that, when we love it, will disconnect us from loving God and living the good life.

God, on the other hand, has promised and proven that he loves us unswervingly, that he will never abandon us, and that he is sufficient for all our needs. He is our true God, and when we love him, our hearts can always be at rest. Then we will be free to live the abundant life.

Contentment Must Be Learned

An airline pilot, while flying over the Tennessee mountains, asked his copilot, "See that little lake? When I was a kid, I used to sit in a rowboat down there, fishing. Every time a plane would fly overhead, I'd look up and wish I was flying it. Now I look down and wish I was in a rowboat, fishing."[10]

Many of us can relate to that pilot's sentiment. We desperately wish we had something we once had, or perhaps something we never had, so we're discontent. We imagine we won't be happy until we have that thing. But if we do attain it, we're surprised to find that it doesn't satisfy us the way we thought it would. And instead of learning from our mistake, we continue to want more, imagining that if only we had *that* instead of *this*, we could be content.

There's a secret to being content, and Paul discovered what it was:

> I know you have always been concerned for me, but you didn't have the chance to help me. Not that I was ever in need, for I have learned how to be content with whatever I have. I know how to live on almost nothing or with

BETTER THAN A DRIVEWAY FULL OF HUMMERS

Alan and Katherine Barnhart (whose story is told in chapter 12) have given away more than a hundred million dollars from their company, which now belongs to God and his Kingdom. At a Celebration of Generosity event,* I enjoyed hearing what their adult son Nathan, then in his twenties, had to say about growing up in their home.

"We were raised in a culture of generosity and contentment," he explained. Then he told an unforgettable story.

"When I was probably eleven or twelve . . . I went to my dad and said, 'Hey, Dad, I think we should get a Hummer.'"

"Nathan, that's a great idea," his father said. Then he surprised Nathan by saying, "What if we got *two* Hummers?"

After letting that sink in, Alan said, "I can do that for you. . . . In fact, I could buy you enough Hummers to fill up our driveway."

Nathan said, "We had a really long driveway . . . so I'm thinking, *This is too good to be true. Where's he going with this?*"

He said his dad then asked him, "What if we took that money and instead blessed . . . people who don't know where they're going to get their next meal or don't know where they're going to sleep at night? Nathan, there are thousands, millions of people around the world . . . who don't have access to the gospel. What if we used that money to bless them?"

Nathan's genuine response, from his heart, was, "That is a great idea!"**

* For more information about Celebration of Generosity events, see https://generousgiving.org/celebrations.
** "Alan and Nathan Barnhart," Vimeo video, 19:33, posted by Generous Giving, April 25, 2015, https://generous giving.org/media/videos/alan-nathan-barnhart.

everything. I have learned the secret of living in every situation, whether it is with a full stomach or empty, with plenty or little. For I can do everything through Christ, who gives me strength.

PHILIPPIANS 4:10-13, NLT

Paul said the key to contentment is living for Jesus and doing everything through Christ, relying on his power.

The phrase "I have learned how to be content" tells us something. Contentment doesn't come naturally. So if you struggle, be encouraged! We shouldn't give up on seeking contentment, because Paul tells us that we *can* learn it. However, to learn anything, we must invest the time and effort to develop our skills. We must ready ourselves to have our contentment tested and deepened, as Paul did.

For years I coached high school tennis—first girls, then boys. Every player wanted to win, but many were unwilling to make the effort to practice hard and learn the necessary skills. The successful players did whatever was necessary, and their games improved dramatically. Even when it didn't feel natural at first, they learned to keep their eyes on the ball, bend their knees, and step into their shots, as well as to get enough sleep, eat the right food before the match, and drink water even when they didn't think they needed to. Eventually, these practices became second nature, and their games steadily improved.

Contentment requires learning new habits and new ways of viewing God, money, and life itself. Since even the apostle Paul had to learn to be content, we shouldn't be discouraged that it takes us time to learn it too.

Is God Enough?

A primary Greek root word for *contentment* is often translated "sufficiency." It's used in 2 Corinthians 9:8: "God is able to make all grace abound to you, so that having all *sufficiency* in all things at all times, you may abound in every good work" (emphasis added).

This sufficiency—"in all things at all times"—is not because all things and all times are sufficient, but because *God* and his abounding grace are.

In 2 Corinthians 12:9, God told Paul, "My grace is sufficient for you." We often admire the quality of self-sufficiency in ourselves and others, but the key to contentment is recognizing that Christ is our sufficiency. *We are not enough.* We should admit that we lack the power, knowledge, moral strength, and stability necessary to be self-dependent. Self-reliance never leads to contentment.

Our satisfaction with Jesus—and our happiness in him—exists independently of large bank accounts and retirement funds. (In fact, it can often be impaired by them.)

Job said, "Naked I came from my mother's womb, and naked shall I return" (Job 1:21). Paul, clearly alluding to teachings such as this in the biblical books of wisdom, said, "We brought absolutely nothing with us when we entered the world and we can be sure we shall take absolutely nothing with us when we leave it" (1 Timothy 6:7, PHILLIPS). *The Message* paraphrases the verse this way: "We entered the world penniless and will leave it penniless."

The Egyptians weren't alone in their belief that being buried with precious metals and money would transfer treasures from this life to the next. At least five tombs unearthed in Ephesus, where Timothy lived, contained substantial treasure, fine clothing, and even slain servants.[11]

As moderns, we may smirk at this seemingly primitive belief that the dead could take their assets into the afterlife. The saying "You can't take it with you" may seem self-evident. But in practice, many of us cling to our possessions with a similar mind-set, desperately and nonsensically clutching them as if we really could take them with us.

"Here today and gone tomorrow" is true of money, possessions, and even our loved ones. In contrast, God says, "I the LORD do not change" (Malachi 3:6), and "Jesus Christ is the same yesterday and today and forever" (Hebrews 13:8). God is permanent and he will always be there, never vacillating in his love, sovereignty, power, and sufficiency. He is an unwavering source of security and contentment.

We can't keep our money and possessions, and even while we have them, they are pitifully insufficient to satisfy our souls. Only God can do that. Once we understand this, we'll never again be surprised to find that material things can't bring us contentment and that money can't buy us happiness. The knowledge that money and things won't satisfy us frees us to look to Jesus instead.

In the Old Testament, priests and Levites received no land when the tribes divided Israel. That's because their portion wasn't property; God himself was their portion as they served him daily (Numbers 18:20). Under the new covenant, believers are called God's priests (1 Peter 2:5). This suggests that God—not real estate or wealth—is our true inheritance.

Trying to find contentment in anything less than God is a waste of time. Scripture asks, "Who is God, but the Lord? And who is a rock, except our God?" (Psalm 18:31). God is the Rock of Gibraltar; we are tiny pebbles with the structural soundness of dirt clods. God is our stronghold and refuge; we are too weak and vulnerable to find contentment on our own.

C. S. Lewis said, "He who has God and everything else has no more than he who has God only."[12] God himself is the primary goodness, out of which all secondary goodness flows. If we are stripped of the secondary, we still have God. And we always will. His promises are not as good as gold—they are far better.

How Much Is Enough?

Paul followed his statement about contented godliness by saying, "But if we have food and clothing, with these we will be content" (1 Timothy 6:8). The word translated "clothing" literally means covering. If we have the basics in life—food, clothing, and shelter—we have everything we need.

Sure, we could have all that and also wish for a bicycle or a car. But what we *want* isn't the same as what we need. The contented person recognizes the difference. The "wants" God often generously provides are not the foundation of our contentment.

Paul's words "with these we *will* be content" (emphasis added) convey a determined resolution. We can, with God's help, decide to embrace contentment and gratitude. Even if our circumstances suddenly improve, we won't magically become content. But our *eternal* circumstances are secure, and God is fully available to us right now. Therefore, it is possible to be content and live the good life no matter what's happening. Even when our current circumstances, in and of themselves, are not good, God is. And God's sovereignty, justice, goodness, love, and grace trump even the greatest adversity.

I learned this time and again over a period of several years when I was researching a book on having faith in the midst of evil and suffering.[13] I interviewed person after person who had lost their health, jobs, homes, and even loved ones, yet displayed an authentic contentment far greater than most whose lives have been much easier.

In terms of money and standard of living, how much is enough? Always a little more or a lot more than we'll ever have—unless we learn contentment. Once we experience contentment and gain an eternal perspective, we'll realize God has given us more than we need—often far more.

The excess is given to us partly for our enjoyment. That's made clear in 1 Timothy 6:17 (we'll explore that more in chapter 13). But the "above and beyond" God graciously entrusts to us is principally intended to help those who truly don't have enough: "so that in all things at all times, having all that you need, you will abound in every good work" (2 Corinthians 9:8, NIV). Notice the perspective that frees God's people to give generously: seeing that we have all that we need and that others have greater needs God has called us to help meet.

If we say we believe all of God's Word, then why waste our lives chasing more stuff, which only robs us of contentment? Instead, let's pursue more of God. As Paul put it, thirty years after his conversion, "I want to know Christ and experience the mighty power that raised him from the dead" (Philippians 3:10, NLT). We don't just come to know Jesus at our conversion. The adventure of the Christian life comes as we get to know him better daily. In the process, we become more like him, which means being more full of grace and generosity. When we do, we'll experience many magnificent side effects, including one of the most precious: contentment.

Less Really Can Be More

For twenty-five years, Mark and Jennifer Higinbotham owned a successful medical equipment dealership. It was good work that paid well, but eventually their hearts were no longer in it. They thought, *There must be more to life than this.*

Mark and Jennifer felt God's prompting to sell their business, along with their custom-built house. They sold their expensive cars and ski boat, and liquidated or gave away most of their possessions. They traveled for two years in a motor home, took mission trips to Russia and Africa, served at homeless shelters, and volunteered at their church.

They then sold the motor home and bought a fixer-upper. When they were trying to determine what God had in mind for them next, they heard that Family Life Ministries was looking for someone in their area to work with financial donors. They were longtime supporters of the ministry, and with their hearts for marriage ministry and their background in business, they could relate to donors. They've found the calling God prepared and wired them for. And in the process, they've found contentment.

Mark says, "None of those material possessions were inherently bad, we had no debt, and we used those things for ministry. But they were no longer important to us. We've never regretted or looked back for one moment, and we're thrilled to be serving the Lord."[14]

Of course, professional ministry isn't the key to contentment either. (Many are content outside of professional ministry; many inside are discontent.) The point of Mark and Jennifer's story is their willingness to ask God what *he* wanted them to do and how they could serve him best. That led to them living the life that is truly life.

Are you ready to ask God if he wants you to downsize your house, career, hobbies, or lifestyle in order to upsize to the good life—to live in greater service and Christ-centered contentment?

CHAPTER 9

MONEY: A BLESSING OR A CURSE?

....

Remember this—you can't serve God and Money,
but you can serve God with money.

SELWYN HUGHES

No one can serve two masters. Either you will hate the one and
love the other, or you will be devoted to the one and despise the other.
You cannot serve both God and money.

MATTHEW 6:24, NIV

Before attending a Journey of Generosity event,[1] business owners Caspar and Esther Jiang believed all their money belonged to
them. "We worked, we worried, we spent energy. . . . But money
was like a burden. We were slaves to money. . . . Money is very
important in Shanghai, but we don't want to live like slaves."[2]

They've come to look at money differently: "The real boss is
our Lord. We know the richest man in the whole universe is our
Lord and we belong to Him."[3]

Anxiety used to accompany the Jiangs' giving, as they would
carefully scrutinize each decision. But then they realized they
needed confidence in the Lord. "We started to offer giving help
and giving what we have to other people. We feel touched by the
Holy Spirit. The joy is different. We can really feel it."[4]

The Jiangs realized that God, not money, is their proper master. This realization is what ultimately freed them.

In his Lord of the Rings trilogy, J. R. R. Tolkien portrayed the pathetic creature Gollum as obsessed with the ring of power. By calling it "my precious," Gollum essentially affirms that the ring is his god. Ultimately his greed for and worship of it leads to his doom.

Gollum's greed destroys him. We see that clearly from outside the story, but we fail to grasp how our own obsession with wealth threatens our life stories. Twice God tells us that greed is idolatry (Ephesians 5:5; Colossians 3:5). How seriously should we take this powerful claim? As the first two commandments emphatically reveal, nothing is more repulsive to God than idolatry (Exodus 20:3-5). In ancient Israel, idolaters were put to death (Deuteronomy 13:6-9). That's pretty serious!

Twice Scripture condemns greed in the same breath as sexual immorality, suggesting the two should be regarded as equally scandalous (Ephesians 5:5; Colossians 3:5). But why is greed more acceptable to most Western Christians than sexual immorality? Why are we far more shocked by sex scandals than we are by our own greed? Is it because we've bought the lie of Satan and our culture that greed is good or necessary or normative, even for God's people? Do we fail to see how much God hates greed and the spiritual ruin it brings to us and our families?

In two powerfully descriptive verses, Paul concisely reveals the perils of craving wealth:

> Those who desire to be rich fall into temptation, into a snare, into many senseless and harmful desires that plunge people into ruin and destruction. For the love of money

is a root of all kinds of evils. It is through this craving
that some have wandered away from the faith and pierced
themselves with many pangs.

1 TIMOTHY 6:9-10

Various translations of "those who desire to be rich" can help
us understand its meaning:

- those whose goal is to be rich (CJB)
- those who long to be rich (NET)
- [those] who set their hearts on being wealthy (PHILLIPS)

This God-breathed truth hits close to home. After all, who
among us doesn't want to get rich?

Sometimes when we read Scripture, we may doubt we have
much in common with the original readers, making us think,
These words may be inspired, but they don't really apply to me. But
the first-century citizens of Ephesus held cultural values surprisingly similar to ours.

Timothy was responsible for churches and their leaders in
Ephesus, a crossroads of great commercial importance strategically
located on the Aegean Sea, in what is now Turkey. Archaeological
digs have uncovered a large marketplace, gymnasiums, theaters,
a library, and numbers of baths. The city also boasted the "hall of
Tyrannus," a prominent building where Paul taught God's Word
(Acts 19:9), and a great Ephesian amphitheater (Acts 19:23-41),
which seated 25,000 people.

The most impressive building in Ephesus was the Temple of
Artemis, at the time one of the largest structures in the world. The
temple also functioned as a bank, financing much of the city's

commerce. Ephesus was so wealthy, the city declined Alexander the Great's offer to help fund temple renovation.[5]

Despite their comparatively low-tech culture, the Ephesians were far more like us than unlike us. Material prosperity was the goal, and materialism the norm. They had the same longings and temptations we do. The desire—and the opportunity—to be rich was as normative in Ephesus as it is anywhere in our world today.

God's Focus Isn't on How Much We Make

Paul's first-century readers in Ephesus, many of them wealthy, no doubt found Paul's warnings not to pursue wealth very unsettling. But we need to understand that Paul condemned their motives and values, not their income.

Paul's concern isn't about how much money we make or even whether we're richer than others (everyone except perhaps two people in the entire world is always richer than some and poorer than others). Rather, he focuses on what we treasure most and how much we keep in relation to what we give. Jesus commanded us not to seek first material wealth, but God's Kingdom and his righteousness (Matthew 6:24, 33).

Certainly Paul wasn't condemning desire in and of itself. Scripture says plenty about righteous desires (Psalm 20:4; 37:4; Proverbs 11:23; 13:12). When he spoke about desiring to be rich, Paul was criticizing the underlying selfish intent—the desire to spend on oneself or keep riches rather than share them.

Proverbs 30:8-9 says, "Give me neither poverty nor riches, but give me only my daily bread. Otherwise, I may have too much and disown you and say, 'Who is the LORD?' Or I may become poor and steal, and so dishonor the name of my God" (NIV). Too little isn't good, but too much isn't helpful either. It's okay for riches to *come to us*, but it is dangerous when they *stay with us*. When we're quick to give to needy people and worthy causes, riches effectively *go through us* to honor God and help others. Then and only then can wealth be defanged.

There's room for only one on the throne of our lives. That's why Paul warned us against the enslaving power of desiring riches. It is fatal to our spiritual lives.

The Wealth Trap Will Destroy Us

The list of warnings against money-love given in 1 Timothy 6:9-10 is sobering. Here's what desiring to get rich entails (these key words are from the New International Version):

- Falling into temptation
- Becoming ensnared in a trap
- Succumbing to many foolish desires
- Giving in to many harmful desires
- Plunging us into ruin
- Resulting in our destruction
- Leading us into all kinds of evil
- Causing us to wander from the faith
- Piercing ourselves with many griefs

The desire for riches is inseparable from "many senseless and harmful desires" (1 Timothy 6:9). These desires "plunge" us into ruin and destruction, because fools inevitably make choices that harm themselves and those around them. The Greek word rendered "plunge" in twenty-nine English versions is translated "drown" in seventeen others. It's hard to imagine more graphic words than *plunge* or *drown*, and more fear-inducing words than *ruin* and *destruction*.

The life described here should be utterly repulsive to any thinking person. It is the polar opposite of Jesus' promise of a "life in all its fullness" (John 10:10, NCV). Following the drive to get rich for the usual purposes, and thereby loving money, is not the good life. It's a deeply troubled and spiritually impoverished life—one that both studies and observation confirm leads to moral decay, sexual sin, family breakdown, loss of faith in God, and ultimately death.

If we were to write out the pros and cons of the money-centered life, what would we list as the pros? If we allow this passage to guide our thinking, we have to ask what the payoffs are of stepping into a bear trap. What is the profit of drowning? What is the upside of ruin? What are the benefits of destruction?

In 2002, a sixty-two-year-old French man went to the emergency room, suffering from severe stomach pains. X-rays showed a twelve-pound mass. Incredibly, the man had swallowed 350 coins, valuing $650, in addition to necklaces! Surgeons removed his stomach and its contents, but the man died from complications a few days later.[6]

The existence of psychiatric illness aside, this story graphically symbolizes how money obsession kills us spiritually. Materialism is not simply wrong; it is immensely foolish, horribly destructive, and in the end, fatal. God warns us that desiring to be rich will ultimately ruin us—and often our families as well.

Money opens up a world of possibilities, some good and some not. A friend told me that when he and his wife were first married and made little money, they never went to the mall or flipped through catalogs or shopped online. They spent their time on simple pleasures, including taking walks, playing games, and reading together. They were content.

Later, as their income rose, they bought a few luxuries and acquired a mortgage. They gradually found themselves trapped by shifting priorities and habits. Little by little, money and possessions took precedence over God, church, and meaningful time together. The last I knew, sadly, my friend hadn't done much to change the trajectory he had come to regret.

It has been said, "Money can buy medicine, but not health. Money can buy a house, but not a home. Money can buy companionship, but not friends. Money can buy entertainment, but not happiness. Money can buy food, but not an appetite. Money can buy a bed, but not sleep. Money can buy a crucifix, but not a Savior. Money can buy the good life, but not eternal life."[7]

In short, money's power is extremely limited, and often deceitful.

WHY HAS GOD GIVEN US ALL THIS PROSPERITY?

Tricia Mayer, a Microsoft executive, believes that stewardship is vital to the Christian life. She says, "Sharing the money God has given us has given us more pleasure than any of the stuff we've bought with it. We still don't know why God put us in the situation we're in, with all this prosperity, but we're always on guard to do His will in it. . . . Being a faithful steward of money also takes more energy than one would ever imagine. . . . We need God's help to manage the temptations that come along with money. . . . Every time we give, we acknowledge that everything we have has been given to us by God."*

* Randy Alcorn, "Twelve Giving Stories," Eternal Perspective Ministries, February 16, 2010, https://www.epm.org /resources/2010/Feb/16/twelve-giving-stories/.

"Better a little with the fear of the LORD than great wealth with turmoil" (Proverbs 15:16, NIV). While the poor can have plenty of turmoil, great wealth is nearly inseparable from its own kind of turmoil. The fact that money-induced trouble takes us by surprise shows that we expect wealth to satisfy us when it has no power to do so.

That's why we should regularly ask ourselves, *What will be the consequence of this purchase? What would be the result if I gave or saved that money instead?* Sure, God intends for us to find pleasure in some wants along with our needs. But if we aren't careful, money-love will trap us in a lifestyle that is dishonoring to God and harmful to us and those we love.

"If Only I Won the Lottery . . ."

In 2016, Americans bought over $80 billion in lottery tickets. That's more than they spent on books, movies, music, sporting event tickets, and video games combined.[8] This amounts to an average of $300 per adult. Half of all lottery tickets are bought by the poorest one-third of the population.[9]

The saddest stories tell of what happens to winners, not what happens to losers. According to *Forbes*, 70 percent of those who suddenly gain large amounts of money lose it all within a few years.[10] This isn't just the huge jackpots. Winnings of $50,000 to $150,000 make it 50 percent more likely that a person will be bankrupt in three to five years than winnings of less than $10,000.[11]

Why the bankruptcy? Suddenly gaining lots of money doesn't change the underlying heart issues and wisdom issues related to greed and money-love. The more we have, the more we qualify for bigger loans. Acquiring more allows people to overspend in larger quantities. Those who don't handle a small amount of money well will never handle a massive amount well.

A Texas man won $31 million, and less than two years later, with his spending out of control, he committed suicide.[12] One "winner" said, "My life was brilliant. But the lottery has ruined everything. What's the point of having money when it sends you to bed crying? I thought the lotto win was going to be the answer to my dreams. Now those dreams have turned to dust."[13]

After Willie Seeley and some coworkers won $450 million in a 2013 lottery, he took the microphone at a press conference. Beaming, Willie said that they were "very happy, happy, happy."

After only two months, Willie and his wife were full of regrets. He said, "There are days I wish we were back to just getting paid every two weeks. . . . You have to change your whole way of life, but we didn't want to change the way we lived."

His wife, Donna, dubbed their winnings "the curse." Seeley said, "The drama is nonstop," and offered this advice for the new winner of a $400 million lottery: "Just disappear. . . . Get lost while you still can."[14]

There are many similar stories of lottery winners who end up taking their lives, becoming drug dealers or alcoholics, losing their families, and even being murdered by relatives. If you want proof that the Bible's warnings against desiring to be rich have merit, the biographies of lottery winners should be sufficient.[15]

I've looked for stories of lottery winners whose lives didn't fall apart. They're not easy to find. In each of the three cases I came across, the winners gave away most or all of their winnings. (Think of the blessings that might replace the curses if instead of buying lottery tickets, people gave that money away in the first place.)

People dream of winning the lottery because they're certain it will bring them lasting happiness. As long as they don't win, hope remains. But once they do, both happiness and hope gradually disappear. When money is exposed as the idol it is, those who have worshiped it are left devastated.

Money Is Not Evil; People Are

Though it's commonly misquoted this way, 1 Timothy 6:10 does *not* say "money is the root of all evil."

This point is vital: money itself is not inherently evil. What we do with money can be either good or bad. Money can be used to purchase sex, bribe a judge, buy cocaine, and fund terrorist acts. But in each case, the way one uses money—not money itself—is evil.

Money can also be used for good. It can purchase life-giving aid, feed a family, further the cause of justice, and fight oppression. Money can also help build wells, finance housing, save children's lives, support churches, and fund Bible translations for unreached people groups. In so doing, money can help store up for us treasures in Heaven.

If money were evil in and of itself, it could not be used to do such good. Paul would not say in 1 Timothy 6:18, "Be generous and ready to share," since sharing money would impose evil on others.

Every time we do anything with money—for instance, spend it, save it, or give it—we get something in return or position ourselves to get a return in the future. The question is, what will we get in return for what we do with the money God has entrusted to us? If what we get with money is sex, we have used money for evil.

If what we get is food for our children and other people's children, we have used money for good.

John Wesley, like Paul, spoke of the good money can do:

> In the hands of [God's] children, it is food for the hungry, drink for the thirsty, raiment for the naked. It gives to the traveler and the stranger where to lay his head. By it we may supply the place of a husband to the widow, and of a father to the fatherless. We may be a defence for the oppressed, a means of health to the sick, of ease to them that are in pain. It may be as eyes to the blind, as feet to the lame: yea, a lifter up from the gates of death![16]

We love money when we always keep it, hold it close, or spend it on countless things we don't need. Radical giving can sanctify our desire for financial gain. It's possible to want more not so we can become rich ourselves but so that we'll have more to give away. In this way, our money can be used as a conduit of God's grace.

The Love of Money Is the Root of All Evils

Wait. Shouldn't that heading read, "The love of money is the root of all *kinds* of evils"? After all, that's how it appears both in the most literal translations (such as the New American Standard Bible and the English Standard Version) and the more dynamic translations (such as the New Living Translation, the Good News Translation, and the New Century Version).

Actually, prior to the more recent Bible versions, the nearly universal English translation of 1 Timothy 6:10 was this: "The love of money is the root of all evils." Not all *kinds of* evils, but simply *all evils*.[17]

John Piper comments,

> Paul is tracing the cause of these "many desires" back to the love of money as the root of "all evils." Why does the desire to be rich not just result in *one* desire for money but "many desires"? Because the love of money is the root of vastly more than we usually think it is. It is the root of all evils that men do. Paul is tracing the multiplicity of desires that flow from the desire to be rich.[18]

Adding the uninspired "all kinds of" tampers with Paul's original Greek words and dulls them. Translated correctly, this passage forces us to conclude, "Wow, money-love is way bigger and way more damaging than I realized!" The wrongful pursuit of wealth destroys morality, marriages, families, business relationships, church relationships, and everything else, while robbing us of contentment and happiness. It results in spiritual ruin because money-love always displaces God-love.

Jesus said, "No one can serve two masters. . . . You cannot serve both God and money" (Matthew 6:24, NIV). We can have money and use it to serve God. But we cannot serve both. It's not simply wrong; it's impossible.

Even when we recognize the threat of money-love, it's difficult to avoid its grasp. Materialism is behind advertising, spending, credit, and debt. It drives entertainment, music, and sports, and sometimes it even drives churches. Advertising is designed to convince us of needs we don't actually have. Materialism and the pursuit of wealth are so frequently hammered into our thinking that

EXPERIENCE THE JOY

A commodities trader from Chicago attended a conference on generosity and heard about the joy of giving. After the event, he called the leader. "What does this 'experience the joy' mean?" he asked. "Every year, I'm giving away between three and five million dollars, and I'm not experiencing the joy."

He'd been giving out of duty and habit, but the leader challenged him to read and meditate on certain Scriptures, asking the Lord to give him joy in giving.

God began to answer those prayers, and he started to get excited about giving. Soon his wife noticed his radical change of heart.

Eventually the couple sold their eight-million-dollar home so they could give more to ministries they loved. Now he and his family travel with some of these ministries, building connections with the poor and with those serving the poor.

He is no longer a spectator when it comes to giving; he is a joyful, active participant.

we would have to live in a cave to avoid their allure. This means we must appeal to something greater than our culture in order to resist these temptations.

My friend Tony Cimmarrusti offers this analogy for fighting the money-god:

Jesus changed my life thirty years ago when I finally surrendered to him on Wall Street. The Lord quickly showed me how dangerous materialism was. It's like kudzu, that creeping vine that grows in the South. That's what materialism is. And you ask people, How do you get rid of that vine? And they all give you the same answer: "You don't! You just keep whacking away at it." That's how materialism works. [Martha and I have] found that the only thing that breaks the hold of materialism on our lives is giving. Giving, giving, and giving. Giving wisely, giving smartly, giving spiritually, giving generously.[19]

Money is a curse whenever we allow it to become the center of our affections, get a stranglehold on us, and choke out the abundant life God intends for us. But it becomes a blessing when we use it wisely and generously to bless others. In the process, we, too, are blessed.

CHAPTER 10

WHAT MONEY CAN DO TO YOUR SOUL

....

Generosity is to materialism what kryptonite is to Superman.
LLOYD SHADRACH

Be on your guard against all kinds of greed; life does not consist in an abundance of possessions.
LUKE 12:15, NIV

As MBA students, friends Greg Baumer and John Cortines took a course called "God and Money" at Harvard Divinity School. One of the Scriptures they studied—Luke 12:13-21, about the rich fool—hit them hard. They paraphrased Jesus' words with a modern take, building a bridge to their world:

> [Jesus] told them a parable, saying, "The stock options belonging to a manager vested after a major run-up in share price, and he thought to himself, 'What shall I do, for I already have enough saved to send my kids to college, my house is paid off, and I already max out my 401k every year!' And he said, 'I will do this: I will open an investment account and create a passive income portfolio, and I'll exercise my options and put the money

there. And I will say to my soul, 'Soul, you have a big enough portfolio to be financially independent; retire early, plan some vacations, play golf.'

"But God said to him, 'Fool! This night your soul is required of you, and the portfolio you've built, what use will it be then?' So is the one who endlessly builds his net worth and is not rich toward God."[1]

John says, "Putting the parable in these words was just like an arrow through my heart. I realized that I was that fool, or at least headed that direction."

Greg, who cowrote the book *God and Money* with John, says, "We realized that we were actually asking the wrong question. We were asking, 'How much do we need to give?' . . . The right question is actually 'How much do I really need to keep?'"[2]

By recognizing their trajectory toward a life of materialism, John and Greg have sought to avoid falling into the trap of money-love that Scripture warns us about. In doing so, they are also protecting and enriching the spiritual lives of their families.

Money-love is a temptation for all of us, regardless of the size of our financial portfolios—or whether we have them. That's why it's important for us to recognize the fundamental connection between money and faith.

Wandering from the Faith Is a Dangerous Detour

In this chapter, we'll take a closer look at the second half of 1 Timothy 6:10: "Some people, eager for money, have wandered from the faith and pierced themselves with many griefs" (NIV).

When people who have been lost for days in a remote forest

are finally found, they never say, "We thought it would be fun to wander so far we wouldn't be able to find our way back." But many who love money never even realize they're lost.

In talking about people who have wandered from the faith, Paul may have included some who have outright denied Christ. But this description surely includes many who maintain a nominal faith but have been slowly lured away from Jesus through their love of money.

When Jesus spoke of "the deceitfulness of wealth" (Mark 4:19, NIV) making hearers of the word unfruitful, he wasn't suggesting that they consciously wanted to be deceived. More likely, without their even realizing it, the father of lies (John 8:44) had torn down the road signs indicating the right destination and replaced them with detours. Whether we are rebellious or just gullible, the result is the same—thinking we are headed to the good life, while in reality we are wandering from it. Those following the wrong road maps seldom know they're wandering.

In a culture so alienated from the gospel, we may spend a small percentage of our time thinking like Christians and a large percentage living out a worldview diametrically opposed to our faith. Even more dangerous is how Jesus-followers view money-love as normal. We're as accustomed to an environment of materialism as a fish is to water. Fish take water for granted. It's their world. Likewise, we don't think about materialism; it's the cultural air we breathe. We don't see it for what it is or realize how it's causing us to drift from Jesus.

The believers in Ephesus, who lived in a city of great commercialism and wealth, were also tempted to wander from their first love. Paul witnessed the birth of the church in Ephesus around AD 54, perhaps ten years before he wrote 1 Timothy. In Acts 19,

Luke portrays the dramatic way the first Ephesian Christians said no to the false gods of magic and money:

> Many who had become believers came confessing and disclosing their practices, while many of those who had practiced magic collected their books and burned them in front of everyone. So they calculated their value and found it to be fifty thousand pieces of silver. In this way the word of the Lord flourished and prevailed.
> ACTS 19:18-20, CSB

These occult books were worth the modern equivalent of over six million dollars! The converts could have rationalized selling the books instead of burning them. After all, they could have used this vast sum of money to help the poor and build a place for the believers to assemble and still had plenty left to increase their standard of living. But these books trained people to embrace witchcraft, which God detests (Deuteronomy 18:10-12; Galatians 5:19-21). The people could be redeemed, but the books could not. The only Christ-centered option was to destroy these possessions that dishonored God. The Ephesians' radical actions were a powerful testimony to their conversions.

Paul warned Timothy and these same believers, and those who had since joined the church, of the ever-present temptation to surrender to their culture's materialistic values. It wasn't enough that some of them had burned evil books ten years earlier. He urged them back to the radical faith that had birthed the church.

Around twenty-five years after Paul wrote 1 Timothy, the apostle John recorded Jesus' words to this same church in Ephesus: "I have this against you, that you have abandoned the love you had at first. Remember therefore from where you have fallen; repent, and do the works you did at first. If not, I will come to you and remove your lampstand from its place" (Revelation 2:4-5).

Surely among those first good works was the burning of their magic books. Such far-reaching action—including the toppling of their money idol—was what Jesus, and Paul in 1 Timothy 6, called them back to.

Your Money Can Own You

How many people who followed Christ when they made modest incomes later wander from the faith after acquiring more possessions, power, and prestige? There's a good chance you've seen it in yourself, your friends, or your church. Think of those you knew in youth group or campus ministries who seemed to be true followers of Christ. Over the years, how many of them have been distracted from the pursuit of Jesus by the pursuit of wealth?

Attending class reunions has been an eye-opener for me. I've rejoiced over those who have come to Christ since high school or college while mourning those who once served Jesus and are now instead serving the money god and showing signs of unhappiness despite the image they try to project. How many people start out with seemingly justifiable financial goals, only to lose sight of their priorities somewhere along the way? I know a man who sacrificed his time with his family to work seventy-hour weeks in order to buy the house of his dreams. He did this, so he told himself, for the sake of his wife and children. Now he lives in that huge house by himself. Pursuing the good life, he ended up living a bad one.

In the third century, Cyprian, bishop of Carthage, wrote this description of the affluent:

> Their property held them in chains . . . chains which shackled their courage and choked their faith and hampered their judgment and throttled their souls. . . . If they stored up their treasure in heaven, they would not now have an enemy and a thief within their household. They think of themselves as owners, whereas it is they rather who are owned: enslaved as they are to their own property, they are not the masters of their money but its slaves.[3]

The various translations of 1 Timothy 6:10 describe what those who love money have done to themselves:

- pierced themselves with many pangs (ESV)
- wounded themselves with many sorrows (NIRV)
- impaled themselves with a lot of pain (CEB)
- caused themselves untold agonies of mind (PHILLIPS)
- broken their hearts with many sorrows (GNT)

Reread this list aloud and let it sink in. These words were carefully chosen by five different teams of Greek scholars attempting to capture Paul's meaning. Ponder them and ask yourself, *Is this what I want to happen to my family and me?*

No one in their right mind would desire grief, sorrow, pain, and agony. Nobody wants to pierce, wound, or impale themselves. Yet God says that's *exactly* what we do when we choose to center our lives on money and things. (How would the social media posts of God's people change if we really believed this?)

Everything spelled out in 1 Timothy 6:9-10 is a promise to "those who want to get rich." These promises are just as trustworthy as the promises of blessing we post on refrigerators, dashboards, and bathroom mirrors. I wonder what would happen if we contemplated these inspired warnings just as much as we do the feel-good verses.

Wealth Never Keeps Its Promises

As the wealthiest man on Earth, King David's son Solomon had a lust for more and more wealth that led him to flagrantly disobey God's prohibitions against accumulating large amounts of horses, gold, and silver—and also many wives (Deuteronomy 17:16-17). Solomon knew from experience that

HEROIC GIVING

In World War II, Orville Rogers was a bomber pilot. An avid runner later in life, Orville was featured on the ABC evening news when, as a one-hundred-year-old, he broke five world track records, bringing his total to eighteen.[*]

But Orville's greatest life achievement is not widely known. Over his decades-long career as a commercial airline pilot, his total earnings were $1.5 million—an impressive figure then. God blessed Orville's savings and investments. Instead of spending or hanging on to his wealth, he and his wife gave away more than $30 million, mostly to missions.[**]

We won't know until eternity how many people came to faith in Jesus because Orville gave what he could have kept.

[*] Enjoli Francis and Eric Noll, "100-Year-Old Runner Sets 5 New US and World Track Records," ABC News, March 19, 2018, https://abcnews.go.com/US/100-year-runner-sets-us-world-track-records/story?id=53859293.

[**] Randy Alcorn, "Meet Orville Rogers, 100-Year-Old Jesus Follower, Generous Giver, and Athlete," Eternal Perspective Ministries, January 12, 2018, https://www.epm.org/blog/2018/Jan/12/orville-roberts-100.

affluence didn't satisfy. All it did was give him greater opportunity to chase more mirages.

People tend to run out of money before mirages, so they cling to the myth that things they can't afford will satisfy them. Solomon's money never ran out. He tried everything, saying, "I denied myself nothing my eyes desired; I refused my heart no pleasure" (Ecclesiastes 2:10, NIV).

His conclusion? "When I surveyed all that my hands had done and what I had toiled to achieve, everything was meaningless, a chasing after the wind; nothing was gained under the sun" (Ecclesiastes 2:11, NIV).

This chart captures a powerful sequence of statements about wealth in Ecclesiastes 5. If you're just going to read part of it, read what's on the left. It's God breathed. My comments on the right are a paraphrase to help us understand and apply the inspired text.

ECCLESIASTES 5 (NIV)	
Solomon's Words	**Meaning and Application**
"Whoever loves money never has enough" (verse 10).	The more we have, the more we want.
"Whoever loves wealth is never satisfied with their income" (verse 10).	The more we have, the less we're satisfied.
"As goods increase, so do those who consume them" (verse 11).	The more we have, the more people (including the government) will come after it.
"What benefit are [goods] to the owners except to feast their eyes on them?" (verse 11).	The more we have, the more we realize it does us no good.

Solomon's Words	Meaning and Application
"The sleep of a laborer is sweet, whether they eat little or much, but as for the rich, their abundance permits them no sleep" (verse 12).	The more we have, the more we have to worry about.
"I have seen a grievous evil under the sun: wealth hoarded to the harm of its owners" (verse 13).	The more we have, the more we can hurt ourselves by holding on to it.
"I have seen a grievous evil under the sun . . . wealth lost through some misfortune" (verses 13-14).	The more we have, the more we have to lose.
"Everyone comes naked from their mother's womb, and as everyone comes, so they depart. They take nothing from their toil that they can carry in their hands" (verse 15).	The more we have, the more we'll leave behind.

When read in concert with the warnings in 1 Timothy 6, these statements should stop us in our tracks. Not only does wealth fail to solve our problems, but it creates massive problems of its own.

There's Danger in Passing on a Legacy of Wealth

First Timothy 6:9-10 couldn't be clearer. If families and churches model a life centered on wealth accumulation, we sabotage our lives and cultivate in our children the many foolish and harmful desires that will plunge *them* into ruin and pierce *them* with griefs.

In light of all the biblical warnings about wealth, John Wesley challenged parents, using the language of 1 Timothy 6:10: "Why should you purchase for them more pride or lust, more vanity, or foolish and hurtful desires? . . . Why should you be at farther expense to increase their temptations and snares and to pierce them through with many sorrows?"[4]

Most Christian parents who unthinkingly raise their children to love money don't set out with that goal in mind. In fact, they would probably say that more than anything else they want their children to walk with God (not wander from the faith) and be happy (not pierce themselves with many griefs). But children raised in materialism are prime candidates to wander from the faith. Why do I say this? Partly because of what Scripture itself says. But based on my personal observation of many lives, I would come to exactly the same conclusion.

Children with access to larger amounts of money will face larger and more frequent temptations. Just as a greater mass exerts stronger gravity, the more money and possessions our children have, the more strongly they will be pulled toward those possessions, and the more tightly our children will be held in their orbit. Though this isn't their desire nor their parents', those with access to more money find it easier to trust money rather than God.

Children raised in a climate of materialism will in all probability pierce themselves with many griefs. In contrast, if parents live more simply, say no to their and their children's momentary wants, and say yes to giving more radically, it is more likely that they and their children will be drawn to God, the source of happiness. This is a strong claim to make, but I don't think it's overstating the case: raising children in a home that embraces materialism is a form of child abuse. Even if our motive is to give our children the good life, we are actually *robbing* them of the life that is truly life. By not purchasing expensive electronics or the latest video games, we may free our children up to read and play outside and interact face-to-face with others. Ultimately, they will be healthier and happier for it.

Parents whose children have much must work all the harder to keep money and things from ruining them. Sometimes the easiest solution is to reduce the inventory of toys and devices. The most influential lesson in living simply and giving generously will be the way we live. Like everything else in the home, stewardship and generosity are caught as much as taught. Children will do what we do more often than they will do what we say. Through example, we can teach our children to avoid greed, to control spending, and to give generously.

When I asked a group at a conference to share their giving stories, Daniel J. Arnold told me, "Giving to the glory of the Lord Jesus Christ and the expansion of his Kingdom on Earth has become the common purpose of our family, our co-mission. We test the will of God for us in prayer and come together in agreement on every gift. Giving enters us into a life of faith and trust in God."

Raising money-loving, possessions-centered children isn't inevitable. With deliberate and sustained effort, and through the power of God at work in us and our children, we can model a different path. While proverbs are not a guarantee as much as a description of the way life normally works, this proverb can encourage us as parents as we pray for and guide our children: "Train up a child in the way he should go, and when he is old he will not depart from it" (Proverbs 22:6, NKJV).

ACCOUNTABLE GENEROSITY

Adam Walach, founder of Walmark Pharmaceuticals in the Czech Republic, was aware of the dangers of wealth when he started his business. His countermeasure was a plan to give away 50 percent of the profit.

He did not keep his promise at first, and he drifted away from God for a few years, until he read *The Treasure Principle*. He rediscovered the joy of giving and wrote down reasons to be generous. He regularly consults that list to keep his commitment to generosity.

Adam also knew he needed to be surrounded by like-minded people who are determined to follow Christ and pursue generosity, so he helped assemble the European Great Commission Collaboration (EGCC). This group takes seriously the biblical warning against the desire to be rich, and its members help one another think strategically about generous giving.*

* "Three Lessons from Adam Walach, Czech Republic," JoyGiving.org, accessed January 24, 2019, https://joygiving.org/adam/.

How Will You Steward What God Has Entrusted to You?

The church father John Chrysostom said what we don't like to think about . . . but need to. He warned his fellow believers, "You have taken possession of the resources that belong to Christ and you consume them aimlessly. Don't you realize that you are going to be held accountable?"[5]

As of 2019, many states are considering raising minimum wage to $15 an hour. That amounts to a salary of $31,200 per year. If you started working at that wage at age twenty and continued without any raises until you were sixty-five, you would make $1.4 million dollars in your lifetime. Obviously, this income has to cover basic needs like food and shelter, but the point is that God entrusts a fortune even to many who spend their lives wishing they made more. We will answer to him for what we've done with what we have (Romans 14:12). Where did that money go? What needs did we meet with it, both inside and outside our families? What difference did it make for eternity? Did it pierce our lives with grief because we clung to it, or did it fill our lives with joy because we honored God with it?

In the novel *Fahrenheit 451*, Ray Bradbury said, "Everyone must leave something behind when he dies. . . . The difference between the man who just cuts lawns and a real gardener is in the touching. . . . The lawn-cutter might just as well not have been there at all; the gardener will be there a lifetime."[6] As believers in Christ, we have the opportunity not just to tend flowers but to tend to people and leave an eternal impact, all for God's glory. May we never settle for anything less.

CHAPTER 11

THE GOOD NEWS ABOUT MONEY

....

If a person gets his attitude toward money straight,
it will help straighten out almost every other area in his life.
BILLY GRAHAM

He who is the blessed and only Sovereign,
the King of kings and Lord of lords.
1 TIMOTHY 6:15

Hugh Maclellan Jr. has long been involved in leadership of a large Christian foundation that supports missions across the globe. With the help of four other men, he launched a high-impact organization called Generous Giving, which puts on conferences where givers share their stories and inspire others to discover the joy of giving.

Hugh says that God used several experiences in his life to change his priorities. One was learning that God owns it all; another was a vision trip to see firsthand what God was doing through mission work. He was hooked, and he knew that's where he wanted to invest money in what would never stop paying off.

Hugh decided to give away a minimum of 70 percent of his income, starting with a tithe to his local church and then widening his giving from there. He and other foundation members choose ministries to invest in with just as much care as mutual fund investors choose their stocks. And why not? Kingdom-minded people seek to invest not just for a moment but for eternity.

One year the foundation increased its giving considerably. A merger soon followed that significantly reduced the value of the foundation's assets. Someone might have expected Hugh to say, "I wish we wouldn't have given away so much last year." But I've never forgotten what he told me: "I wish we'd given more of it away while we still had the chance!"

Hugh suggests we ask ourselves, *What are the barriers that keep me from being a generous giver?* If we ask God to deal with us in those areas, he will!

Hugh's story reminds us there really *is* good news about money. We can use it in a way that glorifies God and imparts life to others. In the process, the money we give draws our hearts toward Heaven. In doing so, it helps us instead of hurting us, as Scripture warns money can do.

We Should Run from Money-Love

As we saw in the previous chapter, in 1 Timothy 6:9-10 Paul affirmed the utter spiritual poverty of a life devoted to pursuing wealth. His emphasis on money just seven verses later, in 1 Timothy 6:17-19, suggests that what he said in the six verses in between is also intended to shed light, indirectly at least, on how we handle money:

> But you, man of God, flee from all this, and pursue
> righteousness, godliness, faith, love, endurance and

gentleness. Fight the good fight of the faith. Take
hold of the eternal life to which you were called when
you made your good confession in the presence of
many witnesses. In the sight of God, who gives life to
everything, and of Christ Jesus, who while testifying
before Pontius Pilate made the good confession, I charge
you to keep this command without spot or blame until
the appearing of our Lord Jesus Christ, which God will
bring about in his own time—God, the blessed and only
Ruler, the King of kings and Lord of lords, who alone is
immortal and who lives in unapproachable light, whom
no one has seen or can see. To him be honor and might
forever. Amen.

1 TIMOTHY 6:11-16, NIV

In chapter 3 of this same letter, a basic qualification for church
leadership is that a man not be "a lover of money" (1 Timothy 3:3).
So when Paul appealed to Timothy's identity as a "man of God," he
was saying he's not to be known as a "man of money." Likewise, a
qualified deacon is not to be "greedy for dishonest gain" (verse 8).
Paul told Timothy to avoid putting money, power, fame, sex, and
anything else before God.

Paul's command to "flee from all this"—namely, the catastro-
phes of money-love—implies vulnerability, danger, and urgency.

Flee is a dramatic word, the same one Paul used when he said,
"Flee from sexual immorality" (1 Corinthians 6:18). The command is not to amble or casually stroll away but to *run as if your
life depends on it*—because it does.

Fleeing money-love brings freedom from bondage, insecurity,
uncertainty, worry, emptiness, and confusion. In a culture like

Ephesus (and ours), money worship was normal, and seen even as commendable. Timothy, however, was told to turn his back and run, not walk, from pride and greed and materialism and all the false doctrines that flow out of them.

Will We Run toward Something Better?

When a child is chased by a bully, with his father in sight, he is not simply running *from* the bully; he is running *to* his dad. The fear of being caught is eclipsed by the anticipation of finding refuge in his father's arms. Likewise, we run from money-love not out of despair but out of hope. We are running toward God-love.

The word rendered "pursue" in verse 11 is a mirror image of "flee." Paul commanded Timothy to "pursue righteousness, godliness, faith, love, endurance and gentleness." These qualities don't come naturally to us, yet they are obtainable through the power of the Holy Spirit. In fact, some of them are among the ninefold fruit of the Spirit (Galatians 5:22-23). We are to pursue them with the same gusto with which we flee materialism.

Paul told Timothy to "fight the good fight of the faith" (1 Timothy 6:12). In Paul's writings, running and fighting connect to Greek athletic competitions, where notable events included foot racing, wrestling, and boxing.

Richard L. Pratt Jr. writes,

The Corinthians loved athletics. They sponsored the biannual Isthmian Games, which were second in importance only to the Olympic Games. They held these games only ten miles from Corinth, so most people in Corinth would have been familiar with the goals and practices of the games. They also would have had the opportunity to observe these games. Paul was in Corinth in AD 50–52, so he would have been present for the Isthmian Games held in the spring of AD 51.

The games included six events: wrestling, jumping, javelin and discus throwing, and, most importantly for Paul's analogy, racing and boxing. Competitors in

MOTORCYCLES FOR CHRIST

The chances of Rod Meyer winning a $20,000 Harley Davidson through a dice competition at a dealership were one in 375,000. On the way to the competition, Rod and wife, Diane, told God that he was in control of everything, even a dice roll, and that if they won, they would sell the bike and all the money would be given to worthy Christian ministries. As Rod rolled the first letter, he knew God was up to something. When the sixth die landed on the correct combination of letters to spell *Harley*, Rod became the first winner in the twenty years the competition had been running.

Rod shared with his motorcycle group about God's providence and his decision to sell the bike and give the money away. There was loud applause and delight. Since then, through the Black Sheep Harley Davidsons for Christ motorcycle ministry, Rod has had numerous ministry opportunities. He prays before group rides, and they've started up a small church service before Sunday rides, with the dealership advertising the service to customers.

Diane says, "The money has been a tool to make God known—not just for the various charities . . . , but also for those watching and being a part of the giveaway. . . . It was incredibly fun to see and be a part of."*

* Diane Meyer, "A Dice Game, a Harley Davidson Motorcycle, and a Delightful Story about Generosity and God's Providence," Eternal Perspective Ministries, September 19, 2018, https://www.epm.org/blog/2018/Sep/19/dice-harley-generosity.

the Olympic Games were required to train for at least ten months before the games in order to qualify for participation. It is possible that a similar requirement existed for the Isthmian Games, which may explain Paul's references to strict training and disqualification.[1]

Paul wrote, "Do you not know that in a race all the runners run, but only one receives the prize? So run that you may obtain it. Every athlete exercises self-control in all things. They do it to receive a perishable wreath, but we an imperishable. So I do not run aimlessly; I do not box as one beating the air. But I discipline my body and keep it under control, lest after preaching to others I myself should be disqualified" (1 Corinthians 9:24-27).

Pratt adds, "Winners received crowns either of pine or of celery, both perishable materials"[2]—hence Paul's contrast to serving God for eternal crowns, including rewards for giving. Fans often traveled to both Athens and Corinth for these competitions, and since evangelists are drawn to crowds, Paul probably was too. Significantly, Timothy also lived in Corinth when Paul did (Acts 18:1-5). They likely attended those games together. (In my graphic novel *The Apostle*, I portray Paul and Timothy playfully boxing with each other after watching champion athletes box.[3])

The fight Paul encouraged Timothy to engage in was the good fight of the faith. He wanted Timothy to defend the full body of precious truths God has revealed in his Word. This core value of fidelity to sound doctrine is why he also told Timothy, "Guard, through the Holy Spirit who dwells in us, the treasure which has been entrusted to you" (2 Timothy 1:14, NASB). This treasure isn't material and can't be bought with money. It's the gospel, the ultimate prize.

Grasping onto Eternal Life Starts Now

Paul says that we need to "take hold of the eternal life" to which we were called (1 Timothy 6:12). The Greek word translated "take hold" means "to grasp or seize."[4] Envision a wrestler, determined not to let go, or a father clutching his child in the midst of danger.

Because our concept of eternity is vague, ethereal, and unreal, this call to grasp it may seem meaningless. How can we possibly clutch smoke or vapor?

Eternal life isn't just some future experience but something we entered into at our conversion. Often we think of our present life on Earth as real and desirable, and eternal life as imaginary or unappealing. In many people's minds, the life we'll live forever is devoid of what we love about life now. That's why we make bucket lists, imagining this present life is the only chance we'll have to experience beautiful places and fascinating adventures.

When we use the term *eternal life*, often we put the emphasis on *eternal*, ignoring *life*. Eternal life isn't just about quantity of existence; it's about the highest possible quality of life, filled with vibrant energy and untold happiness.[5]

Peter says God's children are "looking forward to a new heaven and a new earth, where righteousness dwells" (2 Peter 3:13, NIV). If our concept of eternal life doesn't breed anticipation, then it's dead wrong. Believing Satan's lies about eternal life being unappealing will cause us to latch onto the present world and store up riches here, rather than invest them in the greater and eternal world that awaits us.

We will only expend the effort to take hold of an eternal life we consider worth thinking about and longing for. Once we believe God's promises about the magnificent everlasting life Jesus secured for us, which begins as an abundant life here and now, we'll grab it and cling to it for all we're worth. Since Jesus tells us to store up treasures in Heaven through giving and says that our hearts will follow our treasures (Matthew 6:19-21), we have a vested interest in the place we will live forever. Giving helps us take hold of our eternal life *now*.

Raja B. Singh, a chartered accountant in Mumbai, India, studied Scripture and discovered there were three tithes commanded in the Old Testament, one of which was to be given every three years. So the Jewish people were expected to give 23.34 percent of their income per year, plus freewill offerings. Though Raja and his wife, Shantha, knew they weren't bound by Old Testament laws, they wondered why they should give less now that we're living by grace.

That's when Raja and Shantha decided to increase their giving to 23.34 percent. Later they started giving more, not because God demands it, but because God is generous and because sharing with others is life giving. Raja says, "The joy of giving makes you increase your giving and not look at the figure!"[6] (By the way, there's no tax deduction for giving in India, so their total amounts are significantly larger than they'd be in the United States.)

Raja and Shantha believe that "financial generosity is the barometer of your spirituality."[7] They also have a passion for evangelism. Shantha leads Bible studies for housekeepers in their neighborhood, and she ministers to prisoners in Mumbai. Raja travels and speaks for the Gideons. In short, they have taken hold of eternal life, and as a result, they live a presently abundant life. Their children have experienced the same. The Singhs say, "Once you involve your children . . . they come on board with the idea of generosity. It's a great joy to us."[8]

The Good Life Begins and Ends with a Happy God

God "gives life to all things" (1 Timothy 6:13). The text now speaks of God, the Creator, who is life itself and is the source of all life. Three different Greek words in 1 Timothy are translated *life*. The English word occurs seven to ten times in the book, depending on the translation. It's worth seeing these instances together to get a sense of how important the word is (these are from the New International Version of 1 Timothy, emphasis added):

- [Paul is] an example for those who would believe in him and receive *eternal life*. (1:16)
- Physical training is of some value, but godliness has value for all things, holding promise for both *the present life* and *the life to come*. (4:8)
- Watch *your life* and doctrine closely. Persevere in them, because if you do, you will save both yourself and your hearers. (4:16)
- Fight the good fight of the faith. Take hold of the *eternal life* to which you were called. (6:12)
- In the sight of God, who gives *life* to everything, and of Christ Jesus . . . I charge you . . . (6:13)
- In this way they will lay up treasure for themselves as a firm foundation for the coming age, so that they may take hold of *the life* that is *truly life*. (6:19)

Embedded in the text is praise that flows from Paul's worship of God, whom he calls "the blessed and only Sovereign, the King of kings and Lord of lords, who alone has immortality, who dwells in unapproachable light, whom no one has ever seen or can see" (1 Timothy 6:15-16).

The word translated "blessed" here is better rendered "happy."[9] Paul was affirming not only God's control of the universe but also his happy nature. He did the same in 1 Timothy 1:11, when he said he'd been entrusted with "the gospel of the glory of the blessed [happy] God."

Charles Spurgeon said, "The Gospel . . . is the Gospel of happiness. It is called, 'the glorious Gospel of the blessed God.' A more correct translation would be, 'the happy God.' Well, then, adorn the Gospel by being happy!"[10]

Greek scholar A. T. Robertson translated 1 Timothy 6:15 this way: "The happy and alone Potentate."[11] Here's how other experts explain these verses: "The word translated 'blessed' here . . . means 'happy.' . . . We have a happy God, a happy Ruler . . . altogether happy and altogether powerful."[12] "The term 'blessed' indicates . . . *supreme happiness*."[13] A. W. Pink commented on the meaning of "the happy God" in 1 Timothy 6:15: "God himself, the triune God, is the source of all blessedness and joy. God is self-sufficient, infinitely blessed and happy in Himself."[14]

The statement that the happy and sovereign God "alone has immortality" means that unlike us, he has life in and of himself. All people live in this present world by his common grace. All who will live with him forever are granted eternal life through his special grace.

Any conversation about the good life is incomplete without an understanding of where the eternally good life comes from—the sovereign and happy God. Our vibrant and glad God is infinitely greater than money (and all other false gods). He is absolutely

A HUNDRED-DOLLAR BILL FROM HEAVEN

Jose is a Jesus-follower. As he and his coworker were talking outside one day, the man told Jose he didn't know where he would spend the night. As Jose listened to his friend, he noticed something floating in a puddle—a one-hundred-dollar bill!

Jose could have easily said, "Lord, this is great! There are so many things I could do with this money." But that's not what he did. Instead, he gave it to his amazed coworker and said, "God has provided for you." This temporarily homeless man said he only needed forty dollars to take a train to stay with friends. He insisted that Jose keep the other sixty dollars. But Jose's mind was on a roll with giving. He took the money to a struggling farmer instead, and yet another life was touched.*

* Facebook comment in reply to my post requesting giving stories.

holy, transcendent, and worthy of our worship. His dominion is complete and eternal. Unending life won't be long enough for his beloved children to explore the wonders of his attributes and the depths of his grace.

God Is Sovereign over Our Giving

I believe that God's sovereignty brings a special joy to giving. Recently I was driving with Luis, a thirteen-year-old boy I've been mentoring. I took a road I hadn't been on for a few years and found myself stuck at a long red light in a left-turn lane. A twenty-something woman called to me from the sidewalk, "Got change for a dollar?"

The lane between our car and the woman had no traffic, so I beckoned her over, gave her some money, and then handed her my little book *Everything You Always Wanted to Know about Heaven*, which includes the gospel message.

She said, "Cool," thanked me, and returned to the sidewalk.

Afterward I pointed out to Luis, "Had I driven a different street, or had that light turned yellow two seconds later, we wouldn't have been here. Had that woman come to the crosswalk thirty seconds earlier or later, she wouldn't have called to me."

I could have added that had I not felt moved the day before to replenish my supply of books in the car, I wouldn't have had any copies to give her. And to top it off, had it happened another time, Luis and I wouldn't have had the fun of together seeing God at work.

But Luis and I didn't sense only God's sovereignty in that moment; we also sensed his happiness. What a delight it was to have this unexpected encounter that I could never have orchestrated.

I don't know who that young woman was—whether she read the book or responded to the gospel, or whether the book ended up in the hands of someone else whose life might have been changed by it. But if it did, one day I'll see her again or meet the person God touched through it.

In his sovereignty, God orchestrates unique opportunities for us to be generous. He delights in those moments of divine connection, and so should we.

CHAPTER 12

THE SOURCE OF AUTHENTIC WEALTH

At its best, giving is an act of worship.
CORNELIUS J. DYCK

Remember the LORD your God, for it is he who gives you the ability to produce wealth.
DEUTERONOMY 8:18, NIV

Alan Barnhart is the CEO of Barnhart Crane and Rigging, one of the largest heavy-lift and heavy-transport companies in the United States. He and his wife, Katherine, and their children exemplify careful and generous management of God's money. "Everything that I have and everything that I am has come from God, and belongs to God, and I am a steward of it," Alan says. "My job is to figure out what God wants me to do with the things that he's given me."[1]

When he was finishing school, some friends encouraged him to go to seminary and then into full-time Christian work. Alan recalls, "I realized that all of us who are followers of Jesus are in full-time ministry. . . . And I felt that God had gifted me more in the area of business and engineering than he had in preaching or teaching."[2]

As a young believer, Alan took Jesus' warnings about wealth's downside seriously. So when he and his brother started a business, they put safeguards in place, including a lifestyle cap.

By God's grace, Barnhart Crane and Rigging has grown about 20 percent a year for the last thirty years, with more than one thousand employees. In their first year of business, they donated $50,000—more than Alan's salary. Since then, the Barnharts have contributed more than $100 million in profits to Christian ministries.

In 2007 Eric, Alan, and their families gave the company to the National Christian Foundation. Though they still run its daily operations and are paid by the company, the brothers do not own it, and their descendants won't either.

When asked why his family chooses to live so far beneath their means, Alan looks at it in relationship to their support of Kingdom work: "I don't think that the army cook should eat better than the troops."[3]

"Giving feeds our soul," Katherine Barnhart says. "Giving has us looking outward. . . . We are giving in order to serve the God we love."[4]

There's an Antidote to Materialism

The Barnharts' story proves it's possible to use material wealth in a way that avoids its temptations and builds God's Kingdom. Giving can topple the false god of materialism like nothing else.

After warning against the desire to be rich, 1 Timothy 6:17 includes instructions to readers who are rich, whether by diligence, ingenuity, or inheritance: "Command those who are rich in this present world not to be arrogant nor to put their hope in wealth, which is so uncertain, but to put their hope in God" (NIV).

These are not suggestions to consider but commands to obey. The word Paul used when talking about the rich is the same one Jesus used when he said, "It is hard for someone who is rich to enter the kingdom of heaven" (Matthew 19:23, NIV). So does this mean the rich must give away everything, as Jesus instructed the rich young ruler to do (Matthew 19:21)? No. Scripture demonstrates that this isn't his universal expectation. Lazarus, Mary, and Martha weren't required to give away their large estate, which they used to minister to Jesus and his disciples. Jesus himself was criticized for attending parties, including one at the home of an affluent tax collector (Matthew 9:10-11).

The passage from 1 Timothy neither condemns nor dismisses the rich, but recognizes that Christ-followers with extra resources can please God, serve his purposes, receive eternal rewards, and find true purpose and fulfillment in this life. While God doesn't call most of us to give everything away, as true disciples, we must put all our assets at God's disposal, holding back nothing.

Despite the many biblical warnings about being rich and wanting to be rich, it's good news that we can, in fact, honor God by recognizing that everything belongs to him, by asking what he wants us to do with it, and by giving generously.

Who Are the Rich?

When Paul addressed the rich in 1 Timothy 6:17-19, who was he talking about? If we don't consider ourselves rich, we'll conclude that this passage isn't intended for us.

You might think that giving is a good idea . . . someday, when you have more money. You may feel like you just don't have extra to give right now. True, compared to Bill Gates, you may not have much. But compared to 98–99 percent of the world, you have a great deal of money! That's our problem: when it comes to money and possessions, we tend to compare upward, not downward.

Millionaires make up about 4 percent of the US population.[5] It's easy to suppose that those are the people who qualify as rich. But consider that the quality, variety, and affordability of consumer goods available to lower- or middle-class Americans far exceeds those available to anyone, rich or poor, in the first century. In many respects, given our technology, electricity, plumbing, health care, education, travel opportunities, and variety of food and activities, our material advantages are far superior to those of kings throughout history!

The truth is, if you and your children are not malnourished or enslaved, and if you can access clean water and shelter, you are relatively rich—on that basis alone.

The next time you're tempted to think, *I don't have enough money to give*, don't compare yourself to the relatively small number of people who have more than you. Compare yourself to the seven billion others who have less—most of them far less.

As stated earlier, a family living at the poverty level in the United States is in roughly the top 2 percent of the world's income.[6] Of course, being rich is relative, but anyone in the top 2 percent of wealth in the world surely must be considered rich.

In other words, the instructions to the rich in 1 Timothy 6:17-19 certainly apply to us. Even if we're not accustomed to thinking of ourselves this way, by historical and global standards, we are, in fact, rich.

In saying this, I'm not minimizing the fact that some Americans struggle financially. In many cases, it's not their fault, and certainly we should help them.[7] Often, however, it's a matter of priorities. We may feel like we have nothing to give, but if we reduced our discretionary spending, lived in smaller homes or apartments, drove older cars, ate out less, or made fewer visits to the coffee shop, we would free up a significant amount to give. And once we experienced the joy of giving, we would find it more satisfying and of greater enduring value than the nonessentials we might otherwise purchase.

WHO ARE THE POOR?

- Although the world produces enough food for everyone to have well over the average number of calories needed, one in nine people in the world doesn't get enough food. That translates to more than 800 million hungry people worldwide.*
- Nearly one in four of the world's children are stunted in their growth due to malnutrition. Approximately 5.6 million children under the age of five die each year globally, and more than half of those deaths stem from malnutrition.**
- There are 20 to 30 million slaves in the world today. According to the US State Department, 600,000 to 800,000 people are trafficked across international borders every year. Of these, 80 percent are female and half are children. About 80 percent of human trafficking involves sexual exploitation, and the rest is labor exploitation.***
- In another form of poverty—that of being deprived of the most basic human right, the right to life—globally there are about 56 million induced abortions per year.****

* "Global Hunger Continues to Rise, New UN report says," World Health Organization, September 11, 2018, https://www.who.int/news-room/detail/11-09-2018-global-hunger-continues-to-rise---new-un-report-says.

** World Child Hunger Facts, World Hunger Education Service, accessed January 28, 2019, https://www.worldhunger.org/world-child-hunger-facts/.

*** "11 Facts about Human Trafficking," DoSomething.org, accessed January 24, 2019, https://www.dosomething.org/us/facts/11-facts-about-human-trafficking.

**** "Induced Abortion Worldwide," Guttmacher Institute, March 2018, https://www.guttmacher.org/fact-sheet/induced-abortion-worldwide.

God Owns It All

For those who are rich, the key to avoiding greed, pride, and possessiveness is recognizing God's ownership of everything. That's what God's Word emphasizes:

- To the LORD your God belong the heavens, even the highest heavens, the earth and everything in it. (Deuteronomy 10:14, NIV)
- The land belongs to me. You are only foreigners and tenant farmers working for me. (Leviticus 25:23, NLT)
- Yours, LORD, is the greatness and the power and the glory and the majesty and the splendor, for everything in heaven and earth is yours. (1 Chronicles 29:11, NIV)
- Everything under heaven belongs to me. (Job 41:11, NIV)
- Every animal of the forest is mine, and the cattle on a thousand hills. . . . The world is mine, and all that is in it. (Psalm 50:10-12, NIV)

And to those who think, *Well, at least I own myself,* God says, "You are not your own; you were bought at a price" (1 Corinthians 6:19-20, NIV). We are twice God's—first by creation, second by redemption. Recognizing God's total ownership is a pride killer. We aren't tempted to boast about what doesn't belong to us.

If we were the ultimate owners of our possessions and money, no one would have the right to tell us what to do with them. So until we truly grasp that God owns everything and that we're stewards, we won't be generous givers.

Simply put, a steward is someone an owner entrusts with the management of his assets. The steward's job is to handle the owner's assets with integrity, making sure to consult the owner about what he does with his owner's belongings. We are God's stewards, and we will give account to him for how we've done our job: "It is required of stewards that they be found faithful" (1 Corinthians 4:2). Another translation puts it this way: "It is a prime requisite in a trustee that he should prove worthy of his trust" (PHILLIPS).

Stewards or trustees who are unclear about who owns—and who does *not* own—what they're responsible for managing become embezzlers, stealing what belongs to God and doing with it whatever they please.

Someone told me recently, "There's no point in saying 'It all belongs to God.' Everybody already knows that."

I disagree. First, many people have never actually heard it. Second, of those who *have* heard it, many don't really believe it. Or they agree in theory without living as if it's true.

When someone asked my friend Ron Blue, a well-known Christian financial adviser, "How would you sum up your life's message in a single sentence?" he replied, "God owns it all." That may be the most biblically grounded four words of financial insight ever given.

Once we truly embrace God's ownership, it's a small step to regularly ask him what he wants us to do with *his* money and possessions. Until we get to that place of laying before him all he has entrusted to us, we cannot be true disciples of Jesus.

We Can't Take Credit for Our Bootstraps

We become arrogant when we forget that God is our primary provider. We give too much credit to our hard work and ingenuity.

We easily forget the advantages of our upbringing, heritage, and education, and we view ourselves, even if unconsciously, as better than others, particularly the poor.

Some of us talk about people needing to pull themselves up by their bootstraps. Yet had we not had stable parents or gone to a good school or had positive role models, we might have grown up without bootstraps—or even boots. As has been said in other contexts, many rich people who were born on third base routinely congratulate themselves for hitting a triple.

Scripture says, "Value others above yourselves" (Philippians 2:3, NIV). Our example is Jesus, who humbly gave up the place in Heaven he fully deserved (Philippians 2:3-11). We must fight our misplaced pride, remembering that the air we breathe, the lungs with which we breathe it, and our ability to make money are from God's generous hand (Deuteronomy 8:18).

Pride, by its very nature, is self-focused. If we live for the purpose of celebrating our own greatness, we'll endure small, pitiful lives. But if we focus on God's greatness and live to serve others, then we will, in the best sense, live large.

Ever since I was a child, I've loved stargazing. For many years, night after night, I went outside, needing something bigger than myself to be in awe of. While I gazed at the wonders of the universe, I was *not* thinking about myself (I could have stayed warm indoors and done that!). Similarly, as an adult, I love snorkeling. Sometimes for hours on end, I'm immersed in ocean waters, lost in the wonder and worship of God, and I'm therefore supremely happy. Giving is one of the ways we can take a step back and recognize there's something much bigger than ourselves—and then to stand in awe as we realize God is at work and that he invites us to play a part in it!

Wealth Is Fleeting

Paul reminds the rich that their wealth is temporary: they are "rich *in this present age*" (1 Timothy 6:17, emphasis added). When we understand that our wealth is God's gift to us meant to glorify him, we'll lose ourselves in him and in Christ-honoring causes, whether feeding the hungry, supporting Bible translation, fighting injustice, or reaching the unreached. Our hearts will have no room for arrogance. We'll be humble and profoundly grateful servants who feel privileged to be children of the King!

The Bible offers this humorous commentary on pursuing riches: "Cast but a glance at riches, and they are gone, for they will surely sprout wings and fly off to the sky like an eagle" (Proverbs 23:5, NIV).

It's tempting to put our hope in money, but in the long term, money always disappoints. There's only one sure way to escape this disappointment: give away so much that God becomes your all.

Hope as we use the word often has an element of wishful thinking to it, with little likelihood of success (for example, "I hope I become president someday" or "I hope I win the sweepstakes"). The Bible views hope differently. To put our hope in God is to *know* him as our source of life, significance, and security. He is all powerful, and he loves us too much to ever fail us. That means hope placed in him isn't merely a wish but a rock-solid certainty.

Money, in contrast, is fickle: "Whoever trusts in his riches will fall, but the righteous will flourish like a green leaf" (Proverbs 11:28). God alone is forever certain, dependable, and trustworthy.

Our hearts will always follow our money. That means when

we give, we will naturally put more hope in God and in Heaven, where we've laid up our treasures.

God Is Generous, Not Stingy

Paul commanded those who are rich in this present world to put their hope in a God who "generously gives us everything for our enjoyment" (1 Timothy 6:17, GNT). When we follow God's example, we give generously to the needy in a way that brings them joy. God portrays our call to give not as an act of self-deprivation but of overflowing abundance and joy.

In 1 Timothy 6:6-10, Paul warned against money-love and, by implication, condemned extravagant, self-centered lifestyles. Yet verse 17 is remarkable in that it gives God's children permission to enjoy the pleasures of his creation and his provisions. God usually doesn't intend for us to give everything away but affirms that we are also recipients, since he has given us all things to enjoy.

There is clearly a place for enjoying what money can buy, when accompanied by generous giving. Scripture doesn't exalt socialism, endorse asceticism, glorify poverty, or condemn the enjoyment of material possessions.

God is not stingy with his children—he models the same extravagant generosity he calls us to show others. He is immeasurably rich—and abundantly generous. God owns the universe itself and gives generously even to those who don't know him (Acts 14:17). But he takes special pleasure in giving gifts to his children. Jesus said, "If you sinful people know how to give good gifts to your children, how much more will your heavenly Father give good gifts to those who ask him" (Matthew 7:11, NLT).

HOW DOES MOST OF THE WORLD LIVE?

Sometimes it's hard for us to wrap our minds around what life is really like for others around the world. Economist Robert Heilbroner recommended visualizing step-by-step the daily reality for billions of people:

1. Take out all the furniture in your home except one table and a couple of chairs. Use blankets and pads for beds.
2. Take away all your clothing except your oldest dress, suit, or shirt. Leave only one pair of shoes.
3. Empty the pantry and the refrigerator except a small bag of flour, some sugar and salt, a few potatoes, some onions, and a dish of dried beans.
4. Dismantle the bathroom, shut off the running water, and remove all the electrical wiring in your house.
5. Take away the house itself and move the family into the toolshed.
6. Place your "house" in a shantytown.
7. Cancel all your subscriptions to newspapers, magazines, and book clubs—you can't read anyway.
8. Leave only one radio for the whole shantytown.
9. Move the nearest hospital or clinic ten miles away, and put a midwife in charge instead of a doctor.
10. Throw away your checkbooks, debit and credit cards, stock certificates, pension plans, and insurance policies. Leave the family a cash hoard of ten dollars.
11. Give the head of the family a few acres to cultivate, where he can raise a few hundred dollars' worth of cash crops, of which one-third will go to the landlord and one-tenth will go to the moneylenders.
12. Lop off twenty-five or more years in life expectancy.*

* Robert L. Heilbroner, *The Great Ascent: The Struggle for Economic Development in Our Time* (New York: Harper & Row, 1963), 33–36.

The Worldwide English Bible renders 1 Timothy 6:17 this way: "He gives us richly all things to make us happy." The key to our happiness is recognizing the source of our gifts and loving the God who gives them to us. Material gifts are secondary, but we enjoy them most when we see them as the loving provision of a kind and generous Father.

In the previous chapter, I pointed out that the description of God in 1 Timothy 6:15 is best translated "God, the happy and only Sovereign." After Paul described God as happy in 1 Timothy 6:15, he said just two verses later that God "richly provides us with everything for our enjoyment" (verse 17, NIV). If verse 15 were translated "the happy God," it would be obvious to us that verse 17 flows naturally from that reality. Who else but a happy God would richly provide for our enjoyment?

God gives more than a few sources of enjoyment; he has happily gifted us with a world of abundance to enjoy. Some of these gifts come to us for free—it costs us nothing to view a sunrise or to take a walk and smell the flowers. Trips to places like the Grand Canyon or the Smoky Mountains cost something, but I believe taking such trips to connect with God and our family or friends can fall within the generosity of our gracious God. First Timothy 6:17 also opens the door to buying good books that draw our hearts and minds closer to the Lord, eating a meal at a favorite restaurant with people we love, or enjoying the company of a beloved pet, all of which prompt us to thank God for his kindness.

God doesn't expect his followers to live like monks in a stark cell, never feasting or celebrating or enjoying life. He is like a parent who puts specially selected presents under the Christmas tree and delights in watching his children enjoy the gifts he chose just for them.

The God of Riches Richly Provides

There's a play on words in 1 Timothy 6:17: "Command those who are *rich* . . . [not] to set their hope on *riches* . . . but on God who *richly* provides" (NET, emphasis added).

Sometimes we take for granted God's many wonders, such as the beauty of the hummingbird, the glories of a rose, or the taste of grapes picked off the vine. For me, late-summer bike rides in Gresham, Oregon, are highlighted by the scent of ripe blackberries and the warm sun on my face. Are these small things? Sure. But how encouraging that God has intended "all things" for our good!

God's generosity abounds. His gifts surround us—everywhere we look, and everywhere we don't.

In the middle of instructing those who are rich, Paul took a moment to comment on the character of God. He described God not as demanding or restrictive or begrudging, but as a God full of joy who provides all things with our delight in mind.

Paul wasn't telling us "Stop enjoying life" but rather "Start enjoying the good life—the true and abundant life! Take pleasure in all God's gifts to you." He wasn't telling us "Don't care about treasures" but "Enjoy the superior treasures and joys of generosity." Our Father doesn't prize our misery or insist that we live a life of stoic sacrifice. Rather, the Creator delights in our joy. Who should enjoy God's world more than God's people, who know and love him as their loving Father? The things we love are not merely the best this life has to offer—they are previews of the greater life to come. So we simultaneously feel profound gratitude for what he gives us now and great anticipation for the treasures he promises us in the world to come.

God is the ultimate good parent. He does not cater to our

whims or submit to our demands. Yet he is a kind, gracious, and loving Father who cares for our needs and even has a place in his heart for our wants. He gives us surprising, delightful, frequent treats (if our eyes are open to see them), while not spoiling us with overindulgence or trouble-free ease.

After spending a week with the crew of the *Logos Hope* in Jamaica, Nanci and I were deeply touched by the hard work of the four hundred young people who serve people in the port, both on and off the ship. They sell great books at great prices to people who otherwise might not have access to Christian materials. While they're in port, they help provide eye exams, reading glasses, and dental work, and they often build playgrounds as a gift to locals.

Before leaving the ship, I asked the leaders, "In addition to supporting the ship in general and giving a few of my books to each of them, is there something more we could do to encourage the crew?"

They told us about their upcoming annual sabbatical week, the only time the crew gets anything close to a vacation. It's a week of special teaching and reflection, and mostly a lot of fun. They told me they wanted to take the crew to a nearby island for swimming and snorkeling, but even with special rates, renting the necessary small boats would be costly.

The moment they said *snorkeling*, my eyes lit up, because that's one of my greatest God-given passions.

With joy in our hearts, Nanci and I committed a portion of my book royalties to pay for a day of snorkeling and fun for the whole crew. A few weeks after we left, they went to the island for their sabbatical. Afterward we received letters and e-mails from some of the crew telling us what an amazing and unforgettable experience it was.

I've had many snorkeling adventures in my life. In doing so, I've enjoyed the pure pleasure of worshiping the God who made the undersea wonders—from multicolored fish, sometimes in schools of thousands, to eels, crabs, turtles, monk seals, octopuses, dolphins, sharks, and rays. But a snorkeling trip that brought me perhaps the greatest joy is one I wasn't there for!

And yet I *did* participate, because when I thought of those hardworking, Christ-serving young people from sixty countries snorkeling off a beautiful island and praising God, I entered into their joy. With tears in my eyes even now, I thank God for the incredible and undeserved privilege of helping make it happen. In countless small ways and sometimes big ones, our loving Father truly does richly provide for our enjoyment.

CHAPTER 13

RICH IN GOOD DEEDS

....

Small deeds done are better than great deeds planned.
PETER MARSHALL

While we have opportunity, let us do good to all people, and
especially to those who are of the household of the faith.
GALATIANS 6:10, NASB

Dave and Jessica Lindsey were invited to help build a house for a Mexican family, which dramatically changed their perspective on generosity and what it means to love the poor.[1] Later, they and their three children served for three months in Japan with a mission group. They shared their one-bedroom apartment with three single staff men, who slept in the living room. They had one bathroom and a tiny kitchenette. That challenging experience heightened their sense of world need and made them want to do more to make a difference.

The Lindseys decided they shouldn't keep these experiences to themselves. So their $450 million company, Defender Direct, now sends hundreds of employees and their families to Mexico every year to build homes, paying all expenses.

The giving only grew from there. Defender employees are also given days off to volunteer, and they are invited to participate in what the Lindseys call the Super Service Challenge. After employees volunteer with a ministry, they're asked, "What would this nonprofit do if they were given $5,000 or $10,000?"[2] The chosen teams win that amount of money for the charity they serve. Dave says, "We went from being a giving company to a company of givers. It is really fun to work at a company full of givers." He adds, "There is a greater purpose for our business than simply making money."[3] That purpose is not only to give away profits but also to create a climate in which people see giving consistently modeled. Generous giving becomes the conscious norm rather than the occasional exception.

Excited by the transformation he saw in his own company, Dave also founded Companies with a Mission to encourage other businesses and their employees to live generously. The affiliated national Super Service Challenge, with the motto "Transforming business through service," uses a strategy of friendly competition between companies in serving worthy causes. In its first four years, the Super Service Challenge spurred 800 companies from 42 states across the United States to engage more than 94,600 of their employees into service for 1,100 charities. More than $3 million was awarded to winning nonprofits.[4]

The Lindseys didn't stop at discovering the personal joy of giving. They became giving warriors, thoughtfully strategizing how to expose those around them to the contagious generous life, then taking the next step to spread the good news of giving to businesses around the country. The result has been transformation at every level—for both givers and receivers.

Goodness Can't Be Separated from Generosity

The Lindseys and the employees at their company are living out the command of 1 Timothy 6:18, which says to "do good, to be rich in good works, to be generous and ready to share." Everything in verses 1-17 has paved the way for this four-part command. Each component is interconnected, yet distinct, and together they create a cumulative effect. In this chapter, we'll focus on the first three.

First, we are to "do good." The Greek word Paul used here appears in only one other New Testament passage. In a message to unbelievers at Lystra, Paul presented God as a doer of good things: "He has always given evidence of his existence by *the good things* he does: he gives you rain from heaven and crops at the right times; he gives you food and fills your hearts with happiness"

GOD'S DELIVERY PEOPLE

Suppose you have something important you want delivered to someone who needs it. You wrap it up, address it, and hand it over to the delivery person.

What would you think if, instead of delivering the package, the driver took it home, opened it, and kept it?

Imagine confronting him and having him respond, "Well, if you didn't want me to keep it, why did you give it to me in the first place?"

You'd likely say something like, "You don't understand your job. Yes, I put it in your hands, but I didn't expect you to keep it! The package doesn't belong to you. You're just the middleman. Your job is to get the package from me and deliver it to the person I want to receive it. I'm counting on you to get it where I intend it to go!"

We need to stop thinking of ourselves as owners and instead see ourselves as God's couriers. His messengers. His delivery people.

(Acts 14:17, GNT, emphasis added). God's provision for our physical and emotional needs, as part of his common grace, showcases his generosity.

Some view Paul's command to "do good" as different from being rich in good deeds and being generous. But in fact, these commands all emphasize the theme of generosity.

"Doing good" can sound vague though. What does it really mean? Galatians 5:22-23 indicates that a fruit of the Spirit is "goodness." The word Paul used in 1 Timothy 6:18 that's translated "to do good" is the verb form of this same word. In other words, God wants us to bear the fruit of his Spirit. Doing good goes far beyond simply doing no harm—it means actively reaching out to people through both small and large acts of generosity.

Many Greek scholars believe that "goodness," as listed in Galatians 5:22, specifically involves generosity: "'Goodness' is a rare word [that] conveys the idea of benevolence and generosity toward someone else, a going the second mile when such magnanimity is not required."[5]

Greek scholars Robert Mounce and J. B. Phillips, as well as the New American Bible and the New Revised Standard Version, all translate this word in Galatians 5:22 as "generosity" rather than "goodness." Renowned scholar F. F. Bruce is inclined to agree.[6]

Martin Luther was a Greek expert who translated the New Testament into German in 1522. In his commentary on Galatians, he describes the word translated "goodness" in English in Galatians 5:22. He says it refers to "when a man willingly helpeth others in their necessity [need] by giving, lending, and such other means."[7]

Louw and Nida's dictionary, widely used by Bible translators, defines this word often translated "goodness" as "to be generous, generosity . . . the act of generous giving."[8]

These definitions fit perfectly with the idea that the Holy Spirit's first indwelling of God's people resulted in widespread acts of radical generosity: "They sold property and possessions to give to anyone who had need" (Acts 2:45, NIV). We're told, "God's grace was so powerfully at work in them all that there were no needy persons among them. For from time to time those who owned land or houses sold them, brought the money from the sales and put it at the apostles' feet, and it was distributed to anyone who had need" (Acts 4:33-35, NIV).

A life characterized by greed and stinginess is neither Spirit-filled nor Christlike. If we know Jesus and the Holy Spirit is at work in our lives, we'll see the fruit of generosity.

We're to Desire a Different Kind of Riches

I have a friend who observes our adult daughters, our sons-in-law, and our grandchildren and tells me, "You are a rich man." He's absolutely right. I value that kind of wealth far more than financial riches.

By telling us to be rich in good deeds, God is likewise encouraging us to redefine our view of riches.

Being rich as the world defines it is merely an illusion. We fail to recognize true and lasting riches as compared to false and fleeting ones. Someone can have great earthly riches, as the rich fool did or as Ebenezer Scrooge did, and have a profoundly impoverished soul. And someone can have almost no earthly riches, like the poor widow and countless others, and have a vibrant, thriving soul.

When we give, we don't surrender riches. Rather, we trade one kind of riches for another. The first kind we can't take with us when we die. According to Jesus, the second kind of riches will go before us and await us in Heaven after we die (Matthew 6:19-20).

If I take Jesus seriously and choose a smaller house and less expensive cars here on Earth so I can invest the savings in God's Kingdom, my Lord will give me eternal treasures in Heaven that, in retrospect, will make a big house and nice cars seem utterly trivial.

But why not believe Jesus now rather than wait until Heaven—when it will be too late to reverse our choices—to believe what he said was true all along? We might ask ourselves, *Why settle for an expensive necklace or a deluxe entertainment system now when by giving away the money we could contribute to an imperishable treasure in eternity?*

God Rewards Good Works

We shouldn't be surprised that God speaks so favorably of our good works—including good things we do with his money. While good works certainly cannot save us, they are the result and manifestation of God saving us. In fact, we're told, "We are God's handiwork, created in Christ Jesus to do good works, which God prepared in advance for us to do" (Ephesians 2:10, NIV).

Notice that Paul doesn't say that God prepared doctrines for us to believe (as important as they are), but *works for us to accomplish*. In fact, God has a literal lifetime of good works laid out for us. Instead of burdening us, this should excite us. He has purposes, sometimes hidden, in every person and opportunity that crosses our paths.

Sadly, many Christians have come to think of *works* as a dirty

GOD'S BUSINESS

Esther Jiang, founder of Gendai Exhibition in Shanghai, China, prayed that "God would let me start my own company that was led by God and serving God." He answered her prayer. Esther says, "I use the money to support [Christian] brothers and sisters. I realized that my business can serve God and the church, and I share God's words with my employees." Esther is doing good work on several levels—providing employment, sharing generously, and giving profits to accomplish God's purposes.*

* "Three Lessons from Esther and Caspar Jiang, China," JoyGiving.org, accessed January 24, 2019, https://joygiving .org/esther-and-caspar/.

word. It isn't! True, God condemns works done to try to earn salvation or to impress others (Isaiah 64:6; Hebrews 9:14). But our Lord enthusiastically commends good works done for the right reasons (Matthew 6:4). James wrote, "Faith by itself isn't enough. Unless it produces good deeds, it is dead and useless. . . . If you are wise and understand God's ways, prove it by living an honorable life, doing good works with the humility that comes from wisdom" (James 2:17; 3:13, NLT).

Where we spend eternity, whether Heaven or Hell, depends on the object of our faith. But our works demonstrate the authenticity of our faith. One of the mental hurdles some of us must get past is understanding the difference between salvation by faith and serving God by works. Let me be clear: *Salvation is 100 percent about God's work for us.* No work can save us except the work Christ did on the cross on our behalf. But because he has endowed us with Christ's righteousness (2 Corinthians 5:21), we can now do works that please God and for which he is glad to reward us.

In fact, Jesus "will reward each person according to what they have done" (Matthew 16:27, NIV).

Scripture says of the church, Christ's bride, "'Fine linen, bright and clean, was given her to wear.' (Fine linen stands for the righteous acts of God's holy people.)" (Revelation 19:8, NIV). In a book I wrote years ago, one of my editors deleted that parenthetical statement about righteous acts, thinking I'd made it up and it was bad theology. He had no idea he was deleting God's inerrant words!

God would not promise us rewards if he didn't want us to have or desire them. And he wouldn't promise to reward our works unless he truly valued them. (We'll talk more about rewards in chapter 18.)

Because God created us in his likeness, we follow his example when we do good works. Christ-followers do good works out of a heart of love but also "so that in every way they will make the teaching about God our Savior attractive" (Titus 2:10, NIV). Our goodness and generosity point others to the goodness and generosity of our God.

Christ's People Are Created for Good Works

God has given us the gifts, opportunities, and resources we need to do everything he has planned. We were "created in Christ Jesus" (Ephesians 2:10)—not to do random or insignificant good works, but to do works prepared for us from eternity past. But God doesn't only prepare works for us to do; he also continually prepares us to do those works. What a thrilling concept!

Thirty-eight years ago, when I was still a pastor, Nanci and I opened our home to Diane, a pregnant teenager who had previously had an abortion. While she lived with us, she gave birth and placed her baby for adoption. There were many tough times for

Diane and for us, including late nights when I drove through town trying to find her. We had a two-year-old daughter at the time, and our second daughter was born shortly after Diane delivered, so our own stresses were multiplied.

But we had the joy of seeing Diane come to Christ and later become a terrific wife and mother. Over the years she has also had a powerful ministry to others. We are still close to her, and we regularly reap a harvest of joy that vastly outweighs the initial trials.

Diane once told me, "Abortion filled me with grief and regret. But when I think of the child I placed for adoption, I'm filled with joy, because I know he's being raised by a wonderful family that wanted him." We had the privilege of being with Diane when she was joyfully reunited with the son she surrendered for adoption thirty-three years earlier.

As I write these words, nearly forty years after Diane lived with us, she is driving nearly an hour to bring us dinner because our family has been in the midst of a difficult season. I'm sure the meal will be great, but the real payoff, both now and forever, is in our precious relationship, which will outlive this world and be our treasure in the next.

Does doing good and ministering to others involve sacrifice? Absolutely. Often we see payoffs in this life, though sometimes it takes a while. But even when we don't see the return on our investments now, Jesus promised we *will* see them in the next life, when he will make sure we "will be repaid at the resurrection of the righteous" (Luke 14:14, NIV).

Joy Is Found in Being Rich in Good Works

Why has God made us rich compared to much of the world we live in? There is a direct biblical answer: "Your plenty will supply what they need. . . . You will be made rich in every way so that you can be generous on every occasion" (2 Corinthians 8:14; 9:11). Don't assume that God prospers you beyond what you need just to raise your standard of living. It's more likely, according to these verses, that he prospers you to raise your standard of *giving*. He provides in excess not for us to live excessively, but so we can become rich in good works.

As thoughtful Christ-followers, we should never assume that financial abundance is God's provision for us to live in luxury. We should assume that God entrusts us with his money not to build our kingdom on Earth, but to build *his* Kingdom in Heaven. A good question to ask God is, "Lord, whose kingdom am I focused on building: yours or mine?"

Tom Hsieh worked for a successful network and communications provider, and he later became CEO and co-owner of a telecom consulting firm. Tom and his wife, Bree, chose to live in Pomona, California, then the fourth-largest city in LA County— and the second poorest. They decided to live at or below the median household income there in order to fit in with the neighbors they wanted to reach. (At one point, this was $45,000 a year, while they were making far more and giving away the rest.)[9]

When the company Tom worked for, EarthLink, went public, Tom's stock options suddenly made him a millionaire several times over. By then he and his family had discovered that God took care of them quite well on $45,000, allowing them to experience the joy of generosity. So when his subordinates showed up driving brand-new luxury cars and high-end SUVs, he continued to drive his used three-cylinder Geo Metro, and it made him smile. Why? Because his car was fine, and he had the far greater joy of giving away most of his income to Kingdom causes.

Intentionally living in the inner city has given Tom and Bree unique ministry experiences. When they were on a walk one day, two boys stopped and asked if they knew the Bible and would teach it to them. The next Wednesday, the boys showed up with several of their friends, and they continued to come each week. "I've never had that happen to me before in the suburbs," Tom says. He goes on to add, "We get to be a part . . . of shining God's light here in this neighborhood."

Another time Tom and Bree invited a troubled young girl to live with them. "We saw [her] life completely changed in twelve weeks," Bree says. "I think we have to just believe, as people who follow Jesus, that our lives can make a difference when we follow him."

The Hsiehs also opened their home to neighbors who had lost their apartment and were living in substandard conditions with

GIVING IS CONTAGIOUS

When our missions pastor in Oregon returned from Sudan, he told his church about a desperate need and opportunities to make a difference. People responded wholeheartedly. A group of fourth graders raised thousands of dollars through work projects. A sixth-grade girl took the $50 she had saved up to play on a basketball team and gave it to help Sudanese believers. One family had saved hundreds of dollars to go to Disneyland, but after hearing about the persecuted Christians in Sudan, the children asked if they could give the money to help these believers instead. Before long, people had given $60,000 to help in Sudan. There was never even an offering. It was a spontaneous outbreak of giving, from the grass roots. When people told their giving stories, it thrilled and encouraged the congregation to give more. The joy was palpable.

their children. Having so many people under one roof was some-times stressful, but overall they say it was "amazing." Tom and Bree knew this arrangement presented some challenges for their daughter, Cadence, who lost some of her space and toys. When Bree asked her what she learned, Cadence said, "It was hard, but if you let it happen your heart gets bigger and there's room for more people. So it's really worth it."[10]

The Hsieh family knows the joy of being rich in good works. In the process, they have stored up not only future eternal treasures but also present treasured relationships. By some people's defini-tions, they have turned away from the good life they could easily afford. But by giving what they could have kept, they have taken hold of the truly good life, which is both priceless and enduring.

CHAPTER 14

THE ADVENTURE OF GIVING

....

When a man becomes a Christian, he becomes industrious,
trustworthy and prosperous. Now, if that man, when he gets all
he can and saves all he can, does not give all he can, I have
more hope for Judas Iscariot than for that man!

JOHN WESLEY

Be generous, and you will be prosperous.
Help others, and you will be helped.

PROVERBS 11:25, GNT

Mary Clayton Wood, a dear friend, tells a story about God teaching her what it means to be ready and willing to share. One year during Lent, M. C. challenged her Bible study group to give away something spontaneously, without replacing the item. After issuing the challenge, she thought, *This is going to be so easy!*

M. C. says, "I walk into my kids' school the next day . . . with my favorite white blouse on. And I do love clothes!" She continues, "The secretary looks at me . . . [and says,] 'That is the most beautiful blouse I've ever seen.'"

M. C. had another shirt on underneath, and she asked the Lord if he wanted her to take off the blouse and give it to the secretary. M. C. says, "Well, he did want me to take it off right then, but I didn't!"

She couldn't sleep that night, thinking about what the secretary had said and wondering, *Why do I care so much about this blouse?*

The next morning M. C. wrapped up the blouse and gave it to the secretary, saying, "I just want to bless you . . . and tell you how much God loves you." The woman opened the gift and started weeping.

About a week later, M. C. received a note from the secretary that said, "This was the most meaningful gift I've ever gotten in my entire life. . . . You must really know God." Reflecting on the note, M. C. says, "This taught me that when I give extravagantly, even though it seems like a small gift monetarily . . . it opens the door for the gospel." Mary adds that some time later, upon speaking with the woman again, the woman said to her, "I will listen to anything you have to say, because you are so giving."[1]

At first, Mary Clayton thought she would be happier keeping the blouse. But once she gifted it, everything changed. Her experience reminds us that our greatest happiness arises when we willingly give up what we would rather have kept. Eventually, at death, we must part with every prized material possession we have, so why not joyfully and eagerly give it sooner, when it can glorify God, help others, and bring us joy now and everlasting rewards later?

Giving Is Actual, Not Theoretical

The third command of 1 Timothy 6:18, "Be generous," is really our central subject, and nearly everything in this book connects to it. The Greek word translated "generous" here means to be a liberal giver, quick to part with money and possessions in order to help others.[2] It corresponds to the idea of holding things loosely. This means unclenching our grip on things, so that God and others don't need to pry open our hands. It means giving "not reluctantly or under compulsion," and experiencing in our own lives what it means that "God loves a cheerful giver" (2 Corinthians 9:7, NIV).

Some versions translate the last of the four commands in 1 Timothy 6:18 as "be *willing* to share" (emphasis added). I much prefer the translations, such as the English Standard Version and the New Living Translation, that render it "*ready* to share." "Willing," as we commonly use the term, is theoretical. Paul was not speaking of theory, but practice.

Recently my neighbor Mike, seeing that I was unable to start my lawn mower, pushed his over for me to use. Had Mike been simply *willing* to share, he might have waited for me to ask to borrow his mower after I'd spent another fruitless hour trying to get mine started. Instead, Mike was ready and eager to share, and took the initiative to do so. *This* is what Paul had in mind.

When I'm in stores, I sometimes look for people who need help or appear to be short on cash. I may notice an elderly person looking confused or staring at an item that's out of reach. It might seem noble to think, *I'd be glad to help if they asked*, but in most cases that willingness would do them no good because they are too embarrassed to request help. But when I offer my help, they usually say yes. Often this interaction leads me to give away one of my small books that I usually carry with me, but even when it doesn't, it's still a gospel-inspired act of sharing.

According to 1 Timothy 6:18, being willing to share isn't about waiting for someone to approach us or saying, "If you ever need help, let me know." As well intentioned as that offer is, most people are hesitant to impose, and they never go back to the person who offered help. Being ready to share means saying, "I want to help.

May I work in your garden Saturday?" or "I'd like to bring you dinner on Tuesday—would that work for you, or would another night be better?" Instead of making people feel like beggars, we should pray for opportunities to be generous—and then proactively look for them.

A few days ago, while on a bike ride, I had a God-ordained flat tire forty feet from a homeless man sitting on a bench. I was ten miles from home, and while I waited for a friend to pick me up (he was willing and eager to do so), the homeless man and I talked about where we grew up and discovered that we both enjoy coffee. I also shared the gospel with him. He was somewhat resistant, but God often uses conversations even when there's initial defensiveness.

I handed the man three dollars. He put up his hand to say no, but I said, "Look, you didn't ask me for this. I just want you to buy yourself a cup of coffee."

Had I said, "Do you want some money?" his answer would have been no. He accepted my gift because I wasn't just willing but ready and eager to share. I pray he will accept God's infinitely greater gift of salvation in Christ. And if he does, perhaps that cup of coffee will have played a small role.

Debt Can Choke Out Generosity

Being able and ready to give requires being good stewards and living within our means, spending and saving money wisely. In particular, it means doing all we can to remain free of unnecessary debt. How often do we have nothing to give because we spent or precommitted the abundance God entrusted to us?

Debt warrants deeper study, and I've written extensively about

A STRANGER IN THE AIRPORT

A soldier who had served for seven and a half months in Iraq was granted fifteen days at home with his wife and children. While waiting for his flight, the soldier told a man named Brad that he was taking his family to a water park, Great Wolf Lodge, for four days, partly to celebrate his son's ninth birthday. Brad asked him for his address so he could drop him a note. Brad met the soldier's wife after they landed, and he thanked her for their service.

When the family arrived at Great Wolf Lodge, the front desk attendant said, "You have a message on your account . . . from Brad."

The soldier said he didn't know anyone named Brad. The attendant told them, "Brad from Atlanta said have a good time."

When the soldier and his wife tried to pay, they were told, "It's paid in full."

"Paid in full by who?"

"Brad."

Recounting what happened and the deep impact it made on them, the soldier's wife says she was speechless. "For somebody to do that for us is just unreal."

The soldier says, "It takes a lot to get me. It got me."*

* "I Like Military," Vimeo video, 5:00, posted by I Like Giving, January 4, 2016, https://vimeo.com/150728073.

it in other books.[3] But it's important to briefly mention it here. If we take God's Word seriously, we should avoid debt when we can, since "the borrower is servant to the lender" (Proverbs 22:7, NLT). And since Jesus tells us we cannot serve both God and money, we should ask ourselves, before undertaking any debt, *How will this affect my capacity to give generously?*

In rare cases where we must accumulate debt—for instance, to buy a reasonably priced house that may be a good long-term investment—we should borrow a small enough amount to allow us to make affordable payments and pay off the debt as early as possible. Countless people set their real estate budget, only to end up spending way more on a house than they can afford, and then for years regret that they "can't afford to give." We must learn to say no to many of our wants in order to say yes to obedience, freedom, and generosity—and the happiness God brings to us through them.

People have told me, "I need to wait until I'm out of debt before I start giving." But postponing obedience is never wise. Since God commands and encourages us to be ready and eager to give, we dare not wait until we're out of debt to obey. Debt reduction is important, but not as important as giving to God and to the needy.

When we give, God is pleased and will honor our efforts to pay off our debts. God says that when his people give him tithes and freewill offerings, he will "throw open the floodgates of heaven and pour out so much blessing that there will not be room enough to store it" (Malachi 3:10, NIV). Even if you don't believe this passage applies to New Testament Christians, surely these words of Jesus do: "Give, and it will be given to you" (Luke 6:38). Isn't that exactly what people who want to get out of debt need?

So give generously to the Lord—not instead of striving to eliminate debt, but in concert with it.

Both Time and Money Are Part of Giving

The fourfold expression of generosity in 1 Timothy 6:18 doesn't have to be exclusively financial. However, it wouldn't be true to this passage to say, as some have, that it's as much about giving time as it is about giving money. Paul's terminology relates to money. It's a series of commands specifically to "those who are rich" (verse 17, NIV), not to "those with time on their hands." The person who says, "I can't afford to give to my church, so instead I teach Sunday school" is embracing one important sphere of service while neglecting another.

We should not choose one area of obedience instead of another. We are to freely give to God and others of our time, energy, skills, wisdom, *and* money and possessions.

Of course, our giving of all these resources need not and will not be perfectly balanced all the time. Sometimes we'll give more time—and with it more energy and wisdom and skills—than money and possessions. On other occasions, and especially when we live far from the people in need, we will give more money than time. We all need to grow in the areas where we struggle. Whenever I've given of my time and neglected work I "need to do" so I can help people, I've felt God's pleasure.

No Act of Kindness Is Wasted

I was at a high school reunion where a woman told the group a story in which, to my surprise, she mentioned my name. She said that fifteen years earlier, she was working as a supermarket checker, and one particular day I had taken the time to encourage her and give her a book. She then said something that silenced the room: her plan had been to go home and take her life. She changed her mind when she sensed that I loved her and that God did too.

This revelation stunned me. While I vaguely remembered talking to her, I had no idea how God used that conversation in her life. Since she was on the job, I don't think our interaction could have lasted more than three minutes. Likewise, there are countless people who have been generous to me and who I'm certain have forgotten it, but I still remember . . . and obviously God does too.

This corresponds to the question of the righteous, who will ask when Jesus credits them for giving to him, "Lord, when did we see you hungry and feed you, or thirsty and give you something to drink? When did we see you a stranger and invite you in, or needing clothes and clothe you? When did we see you sick or in prison and go to visit you?" (Matthew 25:37-39, NIV). Christ will say to them, "Truly I tell you, whatever you did for one of the least of these brothers and sisters of mine, you did for me" (verse 40, NIV).

While part of their confusion is due to not understanding how they gave to Jesus by giving to others, I think it's likely that they also fail to remember many of the times they gave. Those who give generously only a handful of times are likely to remember those instances. But someone who gives generously every week, in big and small ways, won't remember most of them in a few months, much less decades.

I love the picture of Jesus rewarding us someday for things he will have to remind us we did! I also love the thought that when we see people in Heaven, some will thank us for giving to them, including those we never met directly. Certainly God sees, values, and remembers our every act of generosity, even when we don't.

Thirty-year-old Ana Harris, who has struggled with debilitating Lyme disease for years, writes:

Take heart friends, you may have less energy and health to work with but you can still give what little you can. And in the eyes of Jesus, your feeble expression of gratitude to your caregivers can be more significant than someone else's founding a non-profit. Just give what you have to give.

The sick mom heating up canned soup for her family in the microwave may be giving more than the mom who is cooking an all organic meal from scratch.

The sick wife who takes three hours to write a simple birthday card in between waves of pain may be giving more than the healthy wife who organizes a big birthday party. . . .

The sick believer who fights to concentrate enough to say a two-sentence prayer for a person in need may be giving more than the healthy ones who are leading Bible studies and starting ministries.

The people we love may not always realize this, but we can rest assured that Christ is watching and he knows. He knows our hearts. He knows that what a suffering person has to give looks different than what a healthy person has to give.

And he's a God who counts two copper coins a priceless gift [Mark 12:41-44].[4]

God's Sovereignty Means Our Giving Isn't Random

The popular expression "random acts of kindness" is catchy and good hearted, but as believers in a sovereign God, we should see how he orchestrates our lives, including the people we know and the needs he brings across our path.

Cathy Osbun, a friend of EPM (our ministry), told me she knew someone whose husband was going to college, so grocery money was tight. She said, "The Holy Spirit prompted me to gather up some food, including the ham I'd just bought with my $300 monthly grocery budget. I struggled with that ham, thinking we'd have no more grocery money for the month. Thankfully the Holy Spirit won. I had my sister quietly place the bags of groceries on my friend's porch."

While Cathy didn't expect it, what happened next seemed like God's way of showing his approval. "I shopped at a grocery store that drew a signed receipt weekly for that amount in free groceries. The next week my receipt for over $300 was drawn. As far as I know, my friend never knew who provided the groceries, but God sure did."

I believe that while it's wise to do most of our major giving in a thoughtful, planned way, there's certainly a place for spontaneous giving. But even unanticipated giving is not ultimately random. If you believe in a sovereign God, then being somewhere at a certain time and place when a particular person is also there is not random, but providentially orchestrated by God.

Acts 17:26 says, "From one human being he created all races of people and made them live throughout the whole earth. He himself fixed beforehand the exact times and the limits of the places where they would live" (GNT). Since God fixes the exact times and limits of where people live, doesn't this suggest he also fixes the times and places we will be on any particular day? Sure, people have free will, but that doesn't mean God can't take into account your free will and mine (and everyone else's), so he can schedule us for divine appointments with people at certain times and places.

The next verse tells us the beautiful purpose God has for fixing our exact times and places: "He did this *so that they would look for him, and perhaps find him* as they felt around for him. Yet God is actually not far from any one of us" (Acts 17:27, GNT, emphasis added). Part of our role in divine appointments is helping people look for and find the grace of Jesus. Perhaps having his followers everywhere is part of the way God is not far even from unbelievers. He touches others through us.

Too many of us are bored with our Christian lives, and the reason for that is largely because we don't see life in terms of the daily opportunities for adventure granted us by our sovereign God.

One afternoon, I bought a stranger lunch at a pizza place (I left my credit card with the cashier while I ate, and told her to use it for whoever came in next). As I saw the stranger smile, this thought came to me: *God had me here today, not for a random act*

SLEEP ON IT FOR SEVENTY-TWO HOURS

Lijo Mathew, founder and CEO of Slingshot Holding in Dubai, United Arab Emirates, grew up wanting to be a billionaire. But then he had a radical experience with God. He says, "God's blessed me with the ability to make money, so we're going to give."

He believes some people are naturally smarter or more talented or stronger than some, and there's not much that can be done about that. But when it comes to generosity, that's in our hands! He says, "This is one thing we have control over that makes us genuinely like Christ."

Knowing they can't always give to every need, Lijo and his wife ask God to lead them as they consider what to say yes to. Lijo says he is learning to act on what the Holy Spirit tells him as opposed to how he feels. To help him discern this, he says, "I sleep on it for seventy-two hours."

But he adds that when he and his wife know a family who's struggling, they don't need to pray about buying their groceries for a month; they just do it.*

* "Three Lessons from Lijo Mathew, United Arab Emirates," JoyGiving.org, accessed January 25, 2019, https://joy giving.org/lijo/.

of kindness, but to fulfill his ancient plan and purpose. He prepared in advance for me to buy lunch for this man at this place and time.

I couldn't have put that particular man on my schedule. What I *can* put on my schedule is a giving adventure—a day of giving, where I don't buy anything for myself without giving something to someone else.

After spending two bucks at a dollar store on work gloves and a pair of giant plastic spiders to scare my grandsons (both purchases proved to be good investments), I kept my eyes open for a giving opportunity. Leaving the store, I saw an energetic and raggedly dressed little boy peering into every window. From the look on his face and the way he ran ahead of his mom and grabbed the door, he thought he'd arrived in paradise.

I approached the young mom with three dollar bills and asked if she would buy some things for her son. She looked at me, incredulous. "Are you sure?" Smiling broadly, she walked in to share the good news with him.

I didn't have one of my booklets, and I didn't have the opportunity to tell her I'm a Christ-follower. But I didn't waste money that day. Jesus was behind the whole thing. I prayed he would use this tiny event somehow in their lives.

Jesus said that where your treasure goes, your heart will follow. Three dollars isn't much of a treasure, but I can still picture that woman and her son, and even as I write this, I'm praying for them again.

That's what giving does—it takes us on an adventure and ties our hearts to people we otherwise would never have noticed or connected with. And some of them we will see again on a redeemed Earth filled with endless adventures.

CHAPTER 15

TREASURES DEPOSITED IN HEAVEN

....

*Crowns to give I have none, but what thou hast given I return,
content to feel that everything is mine when it is thine, and
the more fully mine when I have yielded it to thee.*

PURITAN PRAYER

*Sell your possessions and give to the poor. Make money-bags for yourselves
that won't grow old, an inexhaustible treasure in heaven.*

LUKE 12:33, CSB

Gary Bergh grew up working at his family's business, Bergh Machinery, half a mile from my home.

When Gary was dating Deanne, she was pursuing overseas missions. He told me, "I pictured all missionaries as outgoing people who preached on street corners, and I didn't see myself in that role."

Gary said,

After we were married, we participated in weekly prayer meetings for missionary families from our church. The Spirit touched me one night, and as we were driving home, I told Deanne that I thought God was calling us into missions. She was surprised. Not knowing where or when or what he was calling us to, I left my family

business and went through a one-year Bible college
program.

Gary and Deanne prayed for direction. Meanwhile, in 1991,
shortly after serving as missions pastor at their church, I traveled
in Russia and Ukraine, where Bill Kapitaniuk of Slavic Gospel
Association brought in Bibles by the truckload and gave them to
people, many of whom had never seen one before.

I also visited France, where Bill and his family printed tens of
thousands of Bibles for Eastern Europe and what was then still
the Soviet Union. Bill earnestly explained the mission's biggest
obstacle: printing press malfunctions and breakdowns. He said,
"What we need isn't an evangelist or a Bible teacher; we need
someone who knows how to keep the printer running!"

Knowing Gary's mechanical background and gifting, I immediately thought of him. I came home and told him and Deanne
what Bill had said. Gary continues his story:

Within a year, we left with our two children for France,
not knowing the language or what the work would be
like. But I was mechanically inclined and loved serving
and using my hands. I had never seen a printer before—
let alone repaired one—but I learned quickly. One thing
I especially enjoyed was working on the machine that
stitched the Bible pages together. I would put the loose
pages in one end of the machine and pull the sewn pages
out the other end, and during the process, I would pray
for the people who would receive those Bibles. I thanked
God for the joy I experienced in being able to use my
mechanical talents for his Kingdom.

Gary explained, "There were challenges, and we missed our family and friends, but we knew we were exactly where God wanted us. He used these difficulties to draw us into a deeper dependency on him. Those two years changed us, and now we serve in our work, in our neighborhood, and at home in the ways God has gifted us."

By faith Gary and Deanne uprooted their lives to become even richer in good works, serving Christ in an unfamiliar place. They didn't give up the good life; they embraced it, storing up treasures in Heaven in the process. When they later returned to the United States, they kept hold of that life. To this day, whenever I see them at church, I praise God for how they used their unique gifts to do just what was needed to faithfully invest in the world to come.

Our Giving Sends Treasures Ahead

Building on previous verses, Paul said: "In this way [being rich in good deeds, generous and ready to share] they will lay up treasure for themselves as a firm foundation for the coming age" (1 Timothy 6:19, NIV). Notice we store up eternal treasures in the *coming* age by giving away temporary treasures in the *present* age.

In this chapter we'll address laying up treasures, and in the next we'll see how doing so builds an eternal foundation.

Paul's language in 1 Timothy 6:19 unmistakably alludes to Christ's words about the kind of giving that transfers treasures to Heaven (Mark 10:21; Luke 12:33-34). Consider especially this passage:

Do not lay up for yourselves treasures on earth, where moth and rust destroy and where thieves break in and steal, but lay up for yourselves treasures in heaven, where neither moth nor rust destroys and where thieves do not break in and steal. For where your treasure is, there your heart will be also.

MATTHEW 6:19-21

Note that Jesus used the same word, "treasures," for both the things people value on Earth (for instance, money and possessions) *and* the things we will one day value in Heaven. This doesn't mean the treasures are the same, but it does mean they are parallel. The same way we value certain material treasures now, we should learn to value eternal treasures that mean a great deal to God. It's clear from many passages in Scripture that God plans to reward us in Heaven for our acts of faithfulness on Earth. Hence, the most natural understanding is that the treasures awaiting us in Heaven will be God's eternal rewards for our faithful giving of earthly treasures for his purposes.[1]

When it comes to our money and possessions, the old sayings are true: "You'll never see a hearse pulling a U-Haul" and "You can't take it with you." People can put jewelry, prized possessions, and other treasures in their coffins or graves, but these items won't accompany them to the afterlife. Many of the beautiful treasures at the National Museum of Egyptian Civilization had been buried with the pharaohs, with the idea that these belongings would go to the afterlife with them. The souls of the pharaohs are long gone, but their treasures didn't move an inch until the grave robbers arrived.

In his words about storing up treasures in Heaven, Jesus added a stunning corollary. He essentially said this, in what I call the Treasure Principle: "You can't take it with you, but you *can* send it on ahead."[2]

A FAMILY'S LAST SUPPER

A South African pastor stood in line at a convenience store in New Orleans and noticed a family who didn't have enough to pay for their few items. He touched the father's shoulder and asked him not to turn around, then handed him money to pay his bill.

Nine years later, that same pastor was in New Orleans again as a guest speaker. Afterward a man walked up to him and shared how he'd come to know Christ.

Years ago he, his wife, and their child were completely destitute. Intending to take their lives together, they drove to a cliff. But they decided they wanted to give their child one last meal before they all died. Standing in the store line, he realized the items for the meal cost more than they had.

The man behind him said to please take the money from his hand but not turn to look at him. Then he said, "Jesus loves you."

They drove back to the cliff and wept for hours before driving away. They couldn't go through with suicide. The next Sunday they attended a church displaying a "Jesus loves you" sign.

Nearly a decade later, the man told the South African pastor that when he heard him speak that day, he immediately recognized his distinctive voice and accent.

Through a small act of kindness in that store and the words "Jesus loves you," God used that pastor to save three lives and draw the family to a church where they surrendered their lives to Christ.*

* Ilene Wright, "A Very Touching Story of the Power of Giving," City-Data.com Forum, January 26, 2009, http://www.city-data.com/forum/christianity/549297-very-touching-story-power-giving.html#ixzz25hoJvQk2.

Paul's point in 1 Timothy 6:19 aligns precisely with Christ's galaxy-tilting message—one that should radically change our perspective on our current lives and how we view money and material things.

Jesus promised us treasures in Heaven as a direct result of selling our possessions and giving them to the needy. What a trade: we can transfer wealth from Earth's precarious paper bags to Heaven's safe, secure, and unassailable vaults, where it will never be lost!

Just what are these treasures? Jesus is our first and principal eternal treasure. All else pales in comparison to him (Philippians 3:7-11). Heaven is our second treasure—a place where Christ lives and where we are to set our minds (Colossians 3:1-2). Eternal rewards, our third treasure, seem to center primarily around the positions of service we'll be granted and the friends we will enjoy forever in Heaven because of what we have done with the money God entrusted to us on Earth (Luke 16:9).

Your role in that Kingdom is not only as a son or daughter of the King but also as an investor, an asset manager, and an eternal beneficiary. Your reward may include the privilege of being a ruler in that Kingdom—a king or queen serving under the King of kings (Daniel 7:18, 27; Luke 19:17).

Who would dare to think such a thing possible—that we creatures of dust can make choices in this life that result in eternal gain? If it were our idea, it would be heresy! But it's not. Jesus said it, and Paul, in words inspired by the Holy Spirit, concurred: we give away treasures we would otherwise lose and invest them instead in eternal causes, yielding heavenly treasures that will be ours forever.

We all want our assets to be safe—that's why we lock our houses and cars and try to make wise investments. But Matthew 6 and 1 Timothy 6 tell us there's only one truly safe place: God's Kingdom. Even if the world's most sincere and brilliant investment guru promises fantastic returns, that money still could be lost because no one but God is omniscient and omnipotent. (Even if the investment advisers got it all right and there were huge returns, we're going to leave them all behind the moment we die!)

Financial managers think in terms of ROI: return on investment. There is nothing in the history of the universe that has had such a staggering and everlasting ROI as God's Kingdom. Consider the guarantees: "The LORD Almighty has purposed, and who can thwart him? His hand is stretched out, and who can turn it back?" (Isaiah 14:27, NIV). Job described God's power this way: "I know that you can do anything, and no one can stop you" (Job 42:2, NLT). "The LORD . . . does not fail" (Zephaniah 3:5). Since God's promises of eternal returns on investment are based on his character, there is no greater assurance of lasting provision and security. This is why my friend Mart Green, as he chooses what to support financially, thinks in terms of EROI: *eternal* return on investment.[3]

Our Hearts Follow Our Money

After telling his disciples to store up treasures in Heaven, Jesus said, "Where your treasure is, there your heart will be also" (Matthew 6:21). If you invest in stocks, bonds, annuities, or real estate, your affections are more likely to be tied to the market. You will naturally pay close attention to the companies in which you are a substantial shareholder.

Likewise, if you give to help the poor and reach the lost, then your heart will connect with them—and their Creator in Heaven. Your long-term vested interests will no longer be in a perishable earthly kingdom but in God's eternal Kingdom. The more you give, the more that will be true, just as the less you give, the less it will be true.

While you may observe differing returns when you give, you can have confidence in the sovereign and loving God, who promises he will accomplish his eternal purposes.

When we relocate our treasures from Earth to Heaven, we also relocate our hearts. Giving shifts our center of gravity away from our earthly kingdoms to God and his Kingdom.

We might think that if we become godly, we will become better givers. That's true to a degree, but while a godly choice may precede giving, giving actually moves our hearts toward whatever we've given to. If it's a God-honoring cause, our hearts will be drawn closer to God through the giving.

We shouldn't underestimate the power of generous actions, even when our hearts aren't there yet. Act in a loving way toward someone you don't love or who has hurt you, and over time you will likely find that you love and forgive them. Do you want a greater heart for God? For his Kingdom? For the poor? For mission work? For your church? Then the answer is clear: give more to God, his Kingdom, the poor, missions, and your church. In each case, your heart will follow your treasure and you will care more about each of them. If you want a heart for something, give to it and your heart will go there!

When we give, our thoughts become increasingly fixed on Christ, the person we were made for, and Heaven, the place we were made for. This means that giving is not merely a spiritual thermometer that indicates our heart's condition (though to a degree it does that). It's something much more: a spiritual thermostat that has the power to *change* our heart's condition. Just as in setting a thermostat we don't simply measure temperature but actually change it, giving changes our hearts toward God, others, and Heaven.

Giving moves our hearts to places they otherwise would never go. I have seen conservative church women in their seventies give their time and money to help teen prostitutes and drug addicts, and in doing so, the older women have become the younger women's deep personal friends and advocates. That is the power of love, which is not only the inspiration for giving but also the outcome of it.

I saw this transformation happen in my own life after I'd been a Christian just a few months and read Richard Wurmbrand's *Tortured for Christ*. Immediately I looked for a way to give my summer job money to help persecuted believers. To my delight, I discovered a ministry serving the persecuted church. Ever since I started supporting this ministry forty-five years ago, my heart has been aligned with such believers. And when I give to persecuted Christians today, my heart is reinvested in them and their Lord, and my vested interests just keep growing.

Giving is not simply the indication of a changed life. It's a God-ordained means of changing our lives!

Shifting the location of our treasures, and thereby the location of our hearts, redirects the trajectory of our lives from Earth's dead-end streets to Heaven's unending thoroughfares.

We Can Use Money to Serve Both God and People

Jesus said, "Make friends for yourselves by means of the wealth of unrighteousness, so that when it fails, they will receive you into the eternal dwellings" (Luke 16:9, NASB). At first glance, "the wealth of unrighteousness" may appear to imply all money is bad. But since Scripture is clear elsewhere that money can be used in ways that please God, it can't be inherently evil. Through giving we can use it righteously, for God's glory.

Our Lord doesn't tell us to stay away from "worldly" wealth but to make strategic use of it by investing in helping people. When we give our riches away, God transforms our money and all our earthly valuables into something precious that will infinitely outlast this world. We are to use money in this life to "make friends" with others by caring for them physically and spiritually. This won't earn our entrance into Heaven, but according to Luke 16:9 it will result in our being welcomed into these friends' heavenly homes (that's what dwelling places are). These people, I think, are an important part of the treasures or "crowns" we can anticipate in Heaven (1 Thessalonians 2:19).

Do I believe Jesus is suggesting we'll actually share lodging, meals, and fellowship with friends in God's Kingdom? Yes, I think this is the clear teaching of the passage. To some this sounds far fetched, only because when they think of Heaven, they don't think of resurrected people living on a resurrected Earth. They can't imagine living in dwelling places and eating and fellowshipping together. But that's *exactly* what Scripture teaches us. Jesus himself, in his resurrection body, ate food and insisted he had flesh and bones (Luke 24:39-40). Since we're told that our bodies will be like his in the resurrection (Philippians 3:21), we, too, should expect to one day, on the New Earth, joyfully eat and drink and talk with each other, just as he did after his resurrection.

Sometimes I ponder the people I will welcome into my living place on the redeemed Earth, including those who gave of their love, prayers, time, and money to disciple me. There are those who helped me attend Bible college and seminary, and those who helped send me on mission trips and gave to the church to help me serve as a pastor, and others who have faithfully supported our ministry. I also ponder what it will be like to be invited into the homes of people whom, by God's grace, I was able to touch for eternity through the life I lived, the things I taught and wrote, and the money I gave.

When that time comes, will any of us wish we had given less?

Wealth We Give Really Can Last Forever

A. W. Tozer said, "Any temporal possession can be turned into everlasting wealth. Whatever is given to Christ is immediately touched with immortality."[4] That profound statement is worthy of repeating: *Whatever is given to Christ is immediately touched with immortality.* Like Matthew 6:20 ("Lay up for yourselves treasures in heaven"), 1 Timothy 6:19 emphatically supports this idea. We store up treasures in Heaven when we serve God and others. While we don't know exactly what our heavenly treasures will be, we do know that God is the greatest giver in the universe, so whatever treasures (also called "rewards") he bestows on us will surely be magnificent.

God, who had no beginning, will last forever. We, who had a beginning, will also last forever, and so will our relationship with Jesus and other people who love him. The meager flame of this life will appear to be snuffed at our deaths, but on the other side, it will rage to sudden and eternal intensity. In light of this knowledge, we should learn to "fix our eyes not on what is seen, but on what is unseen" (2 Corinthians 4:18, NIV), living each short day in the light of the long tomorrow.

We can choose where to fix our eyes. Instead of locking them on the short-term treasures we can see, we are called to turn our gaze, by faith, to the eternal treasures of Heaven, where Jesus is. We should ask ourselves whether we are learning to focus on what's most eternally important.

Tozer helps us ask four questions to uncover what our hearts treasure:

1. What do we value most?
2. What would we most hate to lose?
3. What do our thoughts turn to most frequently when we are free to think of whatever we want to?
4. What affords us the greatest pleasure?[5]

Based on these four questions, each of us should ask, *What's my treasure?* Is it a car, a boat, jewelry, a library, or a gun collection? Is it art, coins, or gold? Is it savings, a retirement program, the stock market, or real estate? Or is it God's gifts to us of our families, churches, and coworkers? (Of course, we are right to treasure our family members and the people in our lives, as long as we see them as God's gifts to us and don't make them his substitutes or competitors.) Or is our treasure the God we should love with all our hearts, and people in desperate need of our love?

What we treasure most will be clearly demonstrated in what we fix our eyes on. The same material things we enjoy as God's gifts can also become unhealthy objects of our attention and devotion. Giving generously goes a long way toward keeping this from happening, since it not only gives us more vested interests in Heaven but also reduces the number of earthly treasures that could distract us from God and others.

If we live the good life by generously living for Jesus now, what is truly important will await us when we get to Heaven. Of course, the most important thing is that we will be with Jesus. But what is also important to him, and therefore should be to us, is this final affirmation: "Well done, good and faithful servant" (Matthew 25:21).

As C. T. Studd, missionary to China and later to Africa, said, "Only one life, 'twill soon be past, only what's done for Christ will last."

Either Wealth Leaves Us, or We Leave It

Note that Matthew 6 and 1 Timothy 6 do not tell us to *renounce* our earthly treasures. Rather, these passages tell us to *relocate* our treasures to Heaven. The point is not to belittle earthly treasures—some of them are necessary, and others are helpful or at least harmless. However, we are to recognize their value as currency that can be strategically placed into Heaven's economy.

Jesus warns us not to store up treasures on Earth, not because that wealth *might* be lost, but because it *definitely will* be lost. Moths destroy fabric, rust corrodes metal, and thieves can steal anything. Jesus could have gone on—fires consume, floods wash away, governments seize, investments fail. No earthly treasure is safe.

In fact, God says this present Earth will be consumed by fire (2 Peter 3:10). The only way to fireproof our treasures on Earth is to give them away, thereby relocating them to Heaven. Paul said the fire of God's holiness will consume whatever we've done that amounts to wood, hay, and straw—in other words, things that won't last into eternity (1 Corinthians 3:12-14).

Since God, his Word, and people are eternal, what will last is what's used wisely for God, his Word, and his people. Jesus invites us to choose our treasury. Will we invest most of our treasures on Earth and lose them when we die? Or will we invest most of our treasures in Heaven, where they will be ours for eternity?

If you think about it, there's only one smart choice.

Giving Is Actually Investing

The scriptural command to store up treasures in Heaven proves that giving isn't simply parting with wealth—it's actually transferring wealth to another location, where it will never be lost. In fact, giving to God's Kingdom is the most dependable and profitable investment there has ever been!

Paul said the rich can give in such a way as to store up treasures that will become a firm foundation in Heaven. Jesus told his disciples that at the resurrection, God will personally reward them for helping the poor (Luke 14:13-14).

We will either use up our money or lose it to the government or to death. But there's a third alternative: we can give it away now. Giving gives us the greatest control, and also the greatest security, because once we give it away, it can never be lost or taken from us. The moment we give, God is pleased. While we should seek to be wise givers, once we place our money in God's hands, it's up to him to determine how it will make a difference.

I believe one reason many of us fear death is because our treasures are predominantly here on Earth. We've put them in the wrong place. Since every day brings us closer to our death, every day takes us further from our riches. We end up backing into eternity, not wanting to let go of our stuff.

If we spend our lives storing up treasures on Earth, then every day of our lives, as we get closer to our deaths, we're headed away from our treasures. But if we store up our riches in Heaven, which we get closer to every day, we're always headed toward—not away—from them. This knowledge brings happiness and hope as we face the future. That's why Jesus wants us to let go of many of our things and walk with arms wide open toward eternity.

Copernicus sparked a revolution when he proposed that the sun doesn't revolve around Earth. Giving sparks a Copernican revolution for Christians who understand that life doesn't revolve around the things of Earth. It revolves around God and his Kingdom in Heaven.

Think of treasures as having mass and, therefore, gravity. Gravity holds things in orbit around that mass. The larger the mass we accumulate—the more treasures we store up on Earth—the greater its gravitational pull on us.

But consider how this changes when we give. The more we part with to invest in eternal interests, the less mass our treasures on Earth have, and therefore the less power they have to hold us in their orbit.

Giving multiplies the mass of our treasures in Heaven. This corresponding increase in Heaven's gravitational pull places us more in orbit around God and his Kingdom and his values. The more we give, the more our center of gravity shifts away from our own temporary earthly kingdoms to Christ's eternal Kingdom.

When Jesus warns against greed and says how hard it is for the rich to enter God's Kingdom (for example, Mark 10:25), he is recognizing that unless drastic measures are taken to prevent it, our earthly money and possessions will acquire such critical mass that we will be held captive by them. This is also evident in 1 Timothy 6:9-10 and other passages, and is observed to be true by all who are wise.

However, generosity diminishes our possessions' hold over us while increasing the hold of the causes we give to. Every time we give, we subtract mass and gravity on Earth and add mass and gravity in Heaven. As always, Jesus was exactly right: our hearts really do follow our treasures!

Giving, then, not only brings life change to those we give to, though that would be reason enough to do it. It also beautifully enriches our own lives by refocusing our hearts and investing us in Heaven. In doing so, giving empowers us to take hold of the good life God intends for us.

Is It Wrong to Seek Rewards or Treasures in Heaven?

Despite the fact that 1 Timothy 6:17-19 and many other passages clearly teach that God rewards us when we honor and obey

THE DOCTRINE OF ETERNAL REWARDS

- **God rewards us generously.** Jesus promises "a hundred times" return (Matthew 19:29, NIV)—a return far out of proportion to the amount originally invested.
- **God rewards us fairly.** God has "set a day when he will judge the world *with justice*" (Acts 17:31, NIV, emphasis added). The Lord will "search the heart and examine the mind, to reward each person according to their conduct, *according to what their deeds deserve*" (Jeremiah 17:10, NIV, emphasis added).
- **God rewards us in his perfect knowledge.** "Nothing in all creation is hidden from God's sight. Everything is uncovered and laid bare before the eyes of him to whom we must give account" (Hebrews 4:13, NIV). The Lord will "bring to light what is hidden in darkness" (1 Corinthians 4:5, NIV).
- **God knows and will reward us for our intentions.** "He will . . . expose the motives of men's hearts" (1 Corinthians 4:5, BSB). His Word "judges the thoughts and attitudes of the heart" (Hebrews 4:12, NIV). If our giving has been done for our own glory or as an attempt to control others, God won't reward us.
- **God won't overlook anyone or anything as he gives rewards.** "The Lord will reward each one for whatever good they do" (Ephesians 6:8, NIV). In dispensing rewards, Jesus will not neglect

him, I know from observing resistance to this doctrine that many Christians bristle at the idea that we should ever be motivated by rewards—whether for giving or anything else.

But before we discount the idea of rewards as a motivator, we need to look at what Scripture actually says about it. According to Jesus, God's two most important commandments are to love him and to love other people (Matthew 22:36-40). If you told your

our smallest acts of thoughtfulness (Mark 9:41). When we extend hospitality or give a meal to those unable to pay us back, Jesus promises, "although they cannot repay you, you will be repaid at the resurrection of the righteous" (Luke 14:12-14, NIV).

- **God will reward us for showing kindness to the undeserving.** If we "love [our] enemies, do good to them, and lend to them without expecting to get anything back," Jesus promises that our "reward will be great" (Luke 6:35, NIV).
- **God will reward us for wise stewardship.** He gives us resources and opportunities, and then gives us more if we manage them well (Matthew 25:14-23).
- **God will reward us for our endurance.** If we endure difficult circumstances because we've placed our trust in God, we will be "richly rewarded" (Hebrews 10:34-36, NIV). To those who persevere under persecution for their faith, Jesus promises, "Great is your reward in heaven" (Luke 6:22-23, NIV).
- **God will reward us for identifying with those suffering for Christ.** "You suffered along with those in prison and joyfully accepted the confiscation of your property, because you knew that you yourselves had better and lasting possessions. So do not throw away your confidence; it will be richly rewarded" (Hebrews 10:34-35, NIV).

children there were two things more important than anything else that you were asking them to do, and they did it, would you want to reward them through your praise and other gifts of appreciation? Certainly you would. Does God love his children less than you love yours? Certainly not.

Giving is not only God's command—it's also an act of love for him and our neighbors, fulfilling his two greatest mandates. He therefore considers it especially worthy of commendation and reward. Jesus pointed out that even ordinary humans don't give their children stones and snakes when they ask for bread and fish (Matthew 7:9-10). He said, "If you, then, though you are evil, know how to give good gifts to your children, how much more will your Father in heaven give good gifts to those who ask him!" (verse 11, NIV).

In his kindness and common grace, God sometimes gives to us even when we don't honor him. But certainly he always grants special rewards to his faithful children. His rewards don't contradict his love; they express it.

When a father rewards his child, demonstrating his love, it's a way of saying "Well done," and it draws the child's heart toward him. Since we know this to be true, whether we've experienced the love of a good father firsthand or not, I'm baffled that we would be surprised or resistant to the idea that God the Father delights in rewarding his children—or that his children should look forward to being rewarded by their Father.

God explicitly promises us rewards for giving, including the present rewards of happiness (Acts 20:35) and true abundant life, as well as the eternal rewards of treasures in Heaven (Matthew 6:19-20). What honors Christ is always best for us, and therefore what's best for us is always what truly honors Christ.

Our Father offers us rewards to honor us and enrich our relationship with him, and also to reinforce our desire to obey him and to experience the abundant life. Clearly he intends that his children would value the rewards he promises. God rewards what makes him happy, and when we, his beloved children, gratefully receive his rewards, it makes *us* happy. (Anything that doesn't ultimately bring us joy isn't a reward.)

Many see generosity as virtuous because our giving helps others come out ahead while putting ourselves behind. But that's not how God's economy works. As we've seen in 1 Timothy 6 and Matthew 6, when we give we are storing up treasure for ourselves. We serve God for his glory, yes, but what is for God's glory is always for our good. There is no conflict whatsoever between serving God and people out of love, and realizing that doing so enriches our own lives. Selfish people pursue personal gain *at the expense of others*. If others aren't hurt by what we do in our self-interest, that's good. But giving goes far beyond that. Others aren't simply "not hurt"; they are helped. And for helping them, God rewards us!

It's no more selfish to desire the rewards our Father offers us than it is to want to receive approval from a human parent or mentor, or a bonus from a gracious employer, or a tip from a customer. Rewards are not a zero-sum game. There's not a finite number of rewards that God can't go beyond. One person storing up treasures for themselves in Heaven doesn't reduce the number of treasures available to others. When God rewards our service for Christ, everyone gains and no one loses.

Of course, God doesn't *have* to reward anyone for anything. He does so because he *wants* to. And regardless of what you and I think about it, that's exactly what he's going to do!

Why does God reward us? Because he is pleased by what we've done. A child who wants to be rewarded by his parents realizes they will be pleased by his good deeds. Hence, his desire for their approval isn't mercenary—it's just a built-in part of his love for them.

Naturally, reward should never be our *only* motivation. We should be motivated by gratitude to serve God (Hebrews 12:28). We should be motivated by our ambition "to please him" (2 Corinthians 5:9). But these motives aren't in conflict with the motive of reward. The same Bible that calls us to obey out of our love for God as Father and Redeemer (Deuteronomy 7:9; 11:1; 30:20) also calls us to obey out of our fear of him as Creator and Judge (Genesis 2:17; Deuteronomy 28:58-67; Hebrews 10:30-31) and out of our hope in him as Rewarder (Deuteronomy 28:2-9; Hebrews 11:6). Each motivation coexists with and complements the others.

We want to enjoy the work we do for a living. Hopefully we also want to please our boss and help the company thrive. But these motivations for working in no way invalidate the fact that we also look forward to our employer paying us for the work we do! And if we're given a bonus, we don't refuse to accept it because we have no right to desire or value being rewarded for a job well done. Instead, we gratefully receive it and say a heartfelt thanks. God graciously promises us fantastic riches that he doesn't owe us and also commends and rewards us for our faithful service. Should that make us happy? Of course!

Sometimes we need the combined persuasiveness of several incentives to do what's pleasing to the Lord. This isn't a matter of mixed motives (some good, some bad). Rather, it's about *multiple* motives—each of them good, and each wired into us by God himself. In concert, these multiple motives reinforce one another and encourage us to obey and gladly serve our Father.

God Loves Rewarding His Children

Suppose I told my grandsons, "If you work in my yard a full day, I'll pay you sixty dollars and take you out to your favorite burger place." Would it be appropriate for them to want to earn the money and look forward to eating out? Of course! I made the offer, and I *want* them to want those things. When I reward them for their hard work, I'll be every bit as happy as they are!

But suppose my grandsons did the yard work joylessly, then said, "It's just our duty, Pops, so we refuse the money and we don't want to go out to eat with you." That might sound noble and virtuous, but in fact I wouldn't like it at all. And God doesn't either. Why? Because warm personal relationships matter to us, and life isn't only about duty.

If human beings invented the idea that God should reward those who serve him, it would be audacious and presumptuous. After all, he saves us purely by his grace. Who are we to demand or even expect him to reward us? But in fact, rewards are not our idea; they are God's—just as in my analogy, it was my idea to reward my grandsons, not theirs. God is the one who has revealed his perfect plan to reward us. Who are we to downplay what pleases God and what he has gladly promised us? When someone says to me, "I don't care about rewards," my response is, "God clearly cares—why shouldn't you?"

Despite what many people say, being motivated by the prospect of reward is not wrong. Indeed, something is wrong if we're *not* motivated by reward.

"God is not unjust. He will not forget how hard you have worked for him and how you have shown your love to him by caring for other believers, as you still do" (Hebrews 6:10, NLT). God is always watching and will always reward, both forever and here and now. "The eyes of the Lord search the whole earth in order to strengthen those whose hearts are fully committed to him" (2 Chronicles 16:9, NLT).

He'll always reward the child who gives to the offering the money she saved for a softball mitt.

He'll always reward the teenager who kept himself pure despite temptations.

He'll always reward the man who tenderly cared for his wife with Alzheimer's, the mother who patiently raised the child with cerebral palsy, the child who rejoiced in God despite his disability.

He'll always reward the couple who downsized, selling their large house to live in a small one and give the difference to those in need.

He'll always reward the unskilled who were faithful and the skilled who were meek and servant hearted.

He'll always reward the parents who modeled Christ to their children and the children who followed him despite their parents' mistakes.

He'll always reward those who suffered while trusting him and those who comforted the suffering.

Why? Because that's who he is. It's his nature, his pleasure, and his promise. "The Son of Man is going to come in his Father's glory with his angels, and then he will reward each person according to what they have done" (Matthew 16:27, NIV).

God desires you to want what he has offered—not only the gift of your salvation, but also the abundant rewards and treasures in Heaven he kindly volunteers to give us for serving him faithfully. Your service for him includes giving generously, which is close to his heart and at the very heart of the gospel. He's the same one who promises to make your giving pay off, both now and forever.

CHAPTER 16

KINGDOM PRIORITIES

....

*The world is poor because her fortune is buried in the sky
and all her treasure maps are of the earth.*
CALVIN MILLER

*[Abraham] was looking forward to the city with foundations,
whose architect and builder is God.*
HEBREWS 11:10, NIV

Rosemary Khamati was raised in Uganda and led to Christ by her aunt. Five years after she got married, her husband became abusive and unfaithful. Finally she had to leave with her four daughters and try to rebuild their lives.

Rosemary oversaw the building of a school in Sudan and helped train the community to farm. She later founded PEACE International in response to the flight of a million South Sudanese from their homes when civil war broke out in 2013. Many ended up in camps in northern Uganda. "They had nothing," Rosemary says. "For their houses they had a piece of cloth tied on four sticks."[1]

This woman, who had once lost her dreams, including her marriage and her home, gave these refugees hope that they, too, could start over. PEACE International built a school that quickly filled with children.

Rosemary says, "If Jesus came today, I'll be glad that I'm going to Heaven after I have touched the life of a child of South Sudan, of a man and a woman of South Sudan."[2]

Rosemary is one of those faithful believers who has experienced great difficulty, of whom God says "the world was not worthy of them" (Hebrews 11:38, NIV). Such people are said to "desire a better country, that is, a heavenly one" (Hebrews 11:16). Like many faithful servants of God over the millennia, Rosemary has seen the things promised and "welcomed them from a distance." She recognizes that she is among the "foreigners and strangers on earth" who are "looking for a country of their own." We're told of these people, "God is not ashamed to be called their God, for he has prepared a city for them" (Hebrews 11:13-16).

But this isn't simply the work of Rosemary and her co-laborers. Behind them stand (and kneel) prayer warriors and giving warriors. These faithful supporters financially back Rosemary's work, even though most of them have never been to Sudan. Without them, she wouldn't have the resources to be rich in good works, sharing with the destitute people she serves.

Behind every ministry there are countless faithful givers who say no to certain earthly treasures in order to say yes to reaching the physically and spiritually needy all over the world. For every Rosemary there must be multiple partners in generosity.

I often tell those who pray for and give to our ministry (Eternal Perspective Ministries) that they have a crucial role in helping every hungry, disabled, or suffering person; every prisoner; and every Bibleless person God uses us to reach. In fact, this book you are reading has been faithfully prayed over by members of our prayer team, who generously give their time behind the scenes to ask God to empower and direct me when I'm writing.

Our ministry recently received a large contribution from Brenda, a new donor. When a staff member called her to say thanks, Brenda explained that she'd just turned seventy and was required to make withdrawals from her IRA. Instead of spending the money on something for herself, she decided to give it all away to ministries she believed in, and ours was one of them. Investor-donors like Brenda give because they desire a better country. They are also storing up treasures that will be theirs in that city with foundations that will never be shaken.

Through praying and giving to Christ-exalting, people-helping work, we anticipate hearing the audience of one say, "Well done, good and faithful servant! . . . Come and share your master's happiness" (Matthew 25:23, NIV). And in that better country, Jesus will lavish upon us the glories of his goodness, including those treasures that, through giving, we transferred from Earth to Heaven.

Giving Builds an Eternal Foundation

Speaking through Paul, God says, "Command them to do good, to be rich in good deeds, and to be generous and willing to share. In this way they will lay up treasure for themselves *as a firm foundation for the coming age*" (1 Timothy 6:18-19, NIV, emphasis added).

Some commentators think Paul's reference to treasure in Heaven as a "firm foundation" is a mixed metaphor. After all, how do treasures relate to foundations?

But since Paul's mention of storing up treasures in Heaven mirrors Jesus' words in Matthew 6:19-21, from the Sermon on the Mount, his reference to a firm foundation was likely inspired by the end of that same message. Shortly after instructing his disciples to store up heavenly treasures (verses 19-21) and to serve God, not money (verse 24), Jesus said, "Everyone who hears these words of mine and puts them into practice is like a wise man who built his house on the rock. The rain came down, the streams rose, and the winds blew and beat against that house; yet it did not fall, because it had its foundation on the rock" (Matthew 7:24-25, NIV).

Jesus followed that graphic word picture with this commentary: "Everyone who hears these words of mine and does not do them will be like a foolish man who built his house on the sand. And the rain fell, and the floods came, and the winds blew and beat against that house, and it fell, and great was the fall of it" (Matthew 7:26-27).

Eternal gain, with its infusion of present contentment and happiness, can't be built on what's rickety, transient, and unstable. A life constructed on money and possessions is a life built on sand. A life built on Jesus and obedience to God's Word is a good life, built on bedrock. Only when our foundation is solid are we secure.

It's critical to understand that "these words of mine" certainly include what Jesus said perhaps four minutes earlier in his teaching, about giving away earthly treasures to store up treasures in Heaven (Matthew 6:19-21). Directly following is Christ's statement that his disciples could not serve both God and money (verse 24), then the encouragement not to worry about whether God would provide for their material needs (verses 25-34) and the assurance that God always gives good gifts to his children who ask him (Matthew 7:11).

The world's wisdom is, "Do what you can with your wealth today to build a firm foundation for your future years." Is there any parent or financial counselor, secular or Christian, who would disagree with that? But Scripture tells us we need a far larger perspective concerning our "future years."

A SMALL ACT OF LOVE

Our friend Tami periodically takes a leave from her job at a high school to serve refugees in Egypt. But when you have a heart for people, when you're living the good life, it shows up close to home just as it does overseas.

One day Tami recognized a young woman outside a grocery store in Oregon, where she lives. Tami says, "She wasn't the energetic young girl I once knew. She looked like she hadn't slept in days. I asked God how I could help her."

Aware of trauma and pain in the girl's past, Tami went into the store and got her a gift card to buy dinner and clothes. Tami says, "When I handed her the gift, she wrapped her thin arms tightly around my neck. But I was given the greatest gift—loving this broken young girl even in this small way."

We tend to be extremely shortsighted, envisioning our future as limited to this life only. God's Word encourages us to use our present wealth so it will keep yielding dividends forever on his New Earth (Revelation 21–22). In contrast to those who think forty years ahead, we should think forty *billion* years ahead. We are to plan for the eternal life that began in this world, the fullness of which awaits us after death. Only when we think with that perspective can we, with eyes wide open, choose present actions that will pay off in our eternal futures.

An Eternal Foundation Is Both Strong and Beautiful

Kalos, the Greek word describing the foundation in 1 Timothy 6:19, is translated "good" in most other passages, but in this verse, various versions render it "strong," "solid," or "firm." These adjectives are understandable choices, since strength, solidity, and firmness obviously make a foundation good.

Though *kalos* is rarely translated "beautiful" in 1 Timothy 6:19, four Greek lexicons I consulted cite "beautiful" as the first or primary possible meaning. It's rendered "beautiful" in various passages in most translations.

We don't typically think of foundations as attractive. However, John's description of the New Jerusalem gives us a different perspective on the world to come, where foundations are not just solid and functional but startlingly beautiful:

> The foundations of the city walls were decorated with every kind of precious stone. The first foundation was jasper, the second sapphire, the third agate, the fourth emerald, the fifth onyx, the sixth ruby, the seventh chrysolite, the eighth beryl, the ninth topaz, the tenth turquoise, the eleventh jacinth, and the twelfth amethyst.
>
> REVELATION 21:19-20, NIV

The next verses speak of gates made of pearls and streets of transparent gold. Clearly, when it comes to foundations and physical structures in the next life, God highly prizes beauty! He is the inventor of beauty and aesthetics, and his redemptive plan for his children is to give them "a crown of beauty instead of ashes" (Isaiah 61:3, CSB).

A precious stone, a diamond necklace, or a gold bracelet on Earth, beautiful though it may be, is but a fading glimpse of the beauty of the precious stones that will surround us on the New Earth. Imagine this: diamonds, gold, and pearls on Earth may be traded in now for God's expression of "Well done" and might foreshadow infinitely more beautiful treasures in Heaven. Hence, we need not deny the beauty of precious stones and jewelry and art, but we should consider that while they are real treasures now, they are merely faint reflections of far greater treasures.

How might the value of liquidated diamonds and gold and paintings secure safety and justice for orphans, child slaves, and prostitutes? How might that money provide health and new life for people living on the streets?

At the conclusion of the movie *Schindler's List*, Oskar Schindler—who saved many Jews from the Nazis—looks at his car and his gold pin and regrets that he didn't give more of his money and possessions to save more lives. Schindler uses his opportunity far better than most. But in the end, he longs for a chance to go back and choose human lives over material possessions.

Just as unbelievers have no second chance to relive their lives and choose Christ, Christians get no second chance to do more to help the needy and invest in God's Kingdom. We have one brief opportunity—our lifetime on Earth—to use our resources to make a difference.

John Wesley said, "I value all things only by the price they shall gain in eternity."[3] If we truly understood that both the present and the eternal results of giving are far more beautiful than any earthly treasure we could possess, we'd never hesitate or wonder whether it's worthwhile to give. Our sacred and joyful opportunity here on Earth, picking up on Paul's words in 1 Timothy 6:19, is to use our lives, which are built on the foundation of Christ, to help build a magnificent foundation for the world to come.

Five minutes after we die, we'll know exactly how we should have lived. But then it will be too late to rewind and live this life over. Fortunately, God has given us his Word so we don't have to wait until we die to find out how we should have lived. Moreover, he's given us his Spirit to empower us to live how he tells us to live.

In this light, we should ask ourselves, *What will I one day wish I had given away while I still had the chance?* When you come up with the answer, why not give it away now?

Candace Dorsett shared this story with me that I think speaks powerfully of the strong and beautiful foundation of love demonstrated in giving:

> My mother's cancer diagnosis was worse than the doctors believed, and she was sent home with not much time. My brother was getting married in three weeks. He and his bride-to-be canceled everything—venue, meal, and cruise—and decided to be married at our home in two days so Mom could be there. Overnight the word went out about my mom and brother. People were so eager to do anything for this meek and generous woman who had lived her whole life as a testimony to the Lord.
>
> Friends, family, church members, and neighbors showed up the next morning. They came with lawn mowers, cleaning supplies, and pizzas. They worked all day to get the house and family farm ready for a wedding. Cleaning, catering, flowers, photographer, preacher, decorations, bow ties, and suspenders—it was beautiful. All generously given for a woman who only asked for prayers to "finish well."

Do you imagine this young couple who changed their grand wedding plans for the sake of a dying mother will look back and regret that sacrifice? No! And those who volunteered their time, energy, and money to make that wedding happen stored up for themselves treasures as a firm foundation—and a *beautiful* foundation, one full of as much joy for them as the family they helped.

Our Treasure Includes Our Personal Relationships

The Message paraphrases Luke 12:33-34 this way: "Be generous. Give to the poor. Get yourselves a bank that can't go bankrupt, a bank in heaven far from bank robbers . . . a bank you can bank on. It's obvious, isn't it? The place where your treasure is, is the place you will most want to be, and end up being."

Treasures in Heaven include godly power (Luke 19:15-19), possessions (Matthew 6:20), and pleasures (Psalm 16:11). Jesus promises that those who sacrifice on Earth will receive "a hundred times as much" in Heaven (Matthew 19:29). That's 10,000 percent—an impressive return!

But generous givers will also find *people* among their heavenly treasures. Paul called the Thessalonians he ministered to his "joy" and his "crown" (1 Thessalonians 2:19). Likewise, when they ministered to Paul through their giving, they invested in him in such a way that *he* could be their joy and crown.

When Stacey's husband learned he would be losing his job, their family agreed to live on a strict budget, using cash only. Stacey took two hundred dollars out of the bank for groceries but ended up having to use it to fix their car instead. The following week, a friend who knew nothing of their need gave Stacey several gift cards for their local grocery store, which added up to exactly two hundred dollars. Stacey says, "I cried—and I'll never forget how utterly clear the Lord's provision was to us through her."

Stacey's friend was used by God to meet her grocery needs right down to the dollar. She didn't know the exact amount, but God did. This friend will find other rewards in Heaven, but one of her rewards will be an eternal, God-stamped relationship with Stacey herself.

When I started Eternal Perspective Ministries in 1990, I never anticipated God would use our organization to reach many prisoners with the gospel or help disciple believers in prison. The key to this part of our ministry is our staff member Sharon. With her great heart for prisoners, she handles their correspondence and sends requested books without charge.

Recently Sharon reported that in just one week we received 375 letters and 331 orders from prisoners, to whom we shipped 498 books. We're a small ministry, and reaching prisoners isn't our main focus. Yet more than 30,000 inmates have contacted us. We've sent them 70,000 books, a great investment because in prisons each book is typically read by many.

Heartfelt letters from inmates tell us of conversions, profound life changes, and gratitude for our help. These letters reflect the deeply personal nature of Sharon's ministry. God has forged precious relationships with many—very few of whom we will meet in this world.

Sharon is both a giver and a gift, not only to us but to thousands of prisoners. Our ministry to prisoners wouldn't exist without her faithful and diligent follow-up with people in need who are often forgotten.

Others, moved by Sharon's example, have invested in this ministry. Some visit prisoners and write letters bringing gospel hope. Others financially support Christ-exalting prison ministries.[4]

Imagine hearing someone say to you on the New Earth, "Thank you for giving and praying for me when I was hopeless, lonely, and wracked with guilt. The letters you wrote and the books you sent changed my life. Let's sit down and share our stories!"

"THEY ARE MY FAMILY"

In Ethiopia, three-year-old Sameson hardly knew his father and was given up by his mother. He was left with his aunt and had to work long hours alone in terrible conditions.

"I was always sad when I was younger," he says. "I would just sit there crying, watching the cattle. I would sometimes hear other children talk about the love of their mothers and fathers and I would get very depressed."

After becoming a sponsored child, he felt as though he'd moved from one world to another. He began seeing other children his age happily playing together at the Compassion center. Over the years, he moved from being an angry young man to a very caring one.

Through the sponsor's support, Sameson was able to enroll in a two-year training course in woodworking, which has become his main source of income as an adult. Not only does his business provide income for five other workers, but he also teaches woodworking and mentors children who are sponsored just as he was.

There is a touching video about Sameson in which he shares what his life used to be like and how he has been transformed. The video shows him doing woodworking, employing others in his business, and being a big brother to young boys who are part of the same program that changed his life. He shows the letters from his sponsors, which he has kept all these years. "I love them. . . . They are like my family . . . to me, they are my family."*

* "Sameson's Story," YouTube video, 4:10, posted by Compassion UK, December 23, 2015, https://www.youtube.com/watch?v=HompyAhEEE8#action=share.

Do You Have an Eternal Investment Portfolio?

A wonderful ten-minute video by World Team captures the historic day when the Kimyal tribe of Papua, Indonesia, celebrated the completed translation of God's Word into their language.[5] I've watched this several times, and I still weep with joy as I see their intense emotions, ranging from amazed silence to heartfelt sobbing to joyous praise.

"Our hearts are no longer heavy; they are light," one of the Kimyal elders remarks.[6]

"This . . . is a very important year," another man says. "It's a year of rejoicing. . . . Today, through God's Son, Jesus Christ, God has brought us His Word. So today, we are living in the light."[7]

In their beautiful language, they sing, "To Him who sits on the throne, and to the Lamb, be blessing and honor and glory and dominion forever and ever."

This is the pastor's prayer upon receiving the New Testament:

The month that you had set, the day that you had set, has come to pass today. Oh my Father, my Father, the promise that you gave Simeon that he would see Jesus Christ and hold Him in his arms before he died. I also have been waiting under that same promise, O God. You looked at all the different languages and chose which ones will be put into Your Word. You thought that we should see Your Word in our language. Today, the day you had chosen for this to be fulfilled, has come to pass. . . . You have placed it here in our land. And for all this, O God, I give You praise.[8]

Though Nanci and I didn't help get Bibles to that particular tribe, by God's grace, we have helped get God's Word to other tribes in different parts of the world. That knowledge enhances my joy as I watch the Kimyal people. Can you think of anything better, and more lasting, that you could do with money God has entrusted to you than invest in translation of Scripture into the language of a Bibleless people? It's financially possible for a church or even a family to fund Bible translation for an entire people group!

Compare that investment to buying an RV, a larger TV, or a high-end vacation, or putting more money into an already ample retirement plan. It's not that those things are inherently bad. It's that getting God's Word to those who long for it is so inherently good, so superior, so much longer lasting, and so eternally beautiful! What will become of that new car or bigger home or better phone? Compare their temporal nature to the eternal impact of money given to reach the unreached, get clean water to a remote village, feed hungry children, or educate young people so they can get good jobs and thrive.

There's an old joke that says, "The two happiest days of a man's life are the day he buys his boat and the day he sells it." Sometimes the things we think we want most take up the most time and work and financial resources. But what if the funds from that boat— or anything else we liquidate—were given to God's Kingdom to build what 1 Timothy 6:19 calls our eternal foundation? How much greater would our happiness be?

As of this writing, there are still about four thousand languages without any Scripture translations.[9] In Nanci's and my eternal investment portfolio, one of our top priorities is helping fund translations of Scripture for the remaining unreached people groups. It is sheer joy for us to have a part in what will outlive this world and forever endure in the next, where people of every tribe, nation, and language will forever exalt Jesus as King (Revelation 5:9; 7:9-10).

Imagine the privilege that is ours: God lets us exchange temporal and fading treasures that we cannot keep for eternal treasures that we cannot lose. This is a vital part of the good life, the abundant life—with the ultimate payoff. It's the only surefire investment we can't afford to pass up.

The life God calls us to is not as much about denying lesser pleasures as embracing greater ones. The highest pleasure is in following Christ, glorifying him, loving others, caring for them, and finding joy in the God who gives us all good things.

How incredible to know that what we do for the good of others and for God's glory is also, in God's amazing plan, the foundation for our own happiness, both now and forever.

CHAPTER 17

ETERNAL LIFE STARTS BEFORE WE DIE

....

Eternal life is not a peculiar feeling inside! It is not your
ultimate destination, to which you will go when you are dead.
If you are born again, eternal life is that quality of life
that you possess right now.

W. IAN THOMAS

This is how God loved the world: He gave his one and only Son, so
that everyone who believes in him will not perish but have eternal life.

JOHN 3:16, NLT

While eating with friends at Chick-fil-A, fifteen-year-old Drew Formsma saw an older man sitting by himself. The boys decided to talk with him, and then each contributed five dollars to buy him a gift card.

The man was deeply moved, as was everyone who saw it happen. The kids won't remember what they ate that day, but they'll never forget that man or the joy their gift brought him and them.[1]

Another time Drew saw a boy and his grandfather sitting in a restaurant. The boy wasn't talking or listening—he was preoccupied with his phone. Drew approached him and asked, "Hey, bud, is this your grandpa?"

"Yeah, it's my grandpa."

"I bet your grandpa's got some great stories about his childhood."

"Yeah."

"But you're going to have to get off that phone to hear those stories."

Drew watched the boy put his phone in his pocket. Then as he left the restaurant, he saw the two talking face to face. Drew says, "I could have changed their relationship forever."[2]

Giving comes in different forms—not just money and gift cards, but the gift of time and the gift of a bold action to speak into someone else's life, even someone we don't know.

Did Drew and his friends have to wait until Heaven to experience any rewards? No. They experienced an immediate payoff of gladness and satisfaction. By investing in others' lives, they were taking hold of the good life, "the life that is truly life."

What Kind of Life Will You Grab Hold Of?

All we've been studying in 1 Timothy 6 has built up to these God-breathed words: "In this way [through generous giving] they will lay up treasure for themselves as a firm foundation for the coming age, *so that they may take hold of the life that is truly life*" (1 Timothy 6:19, NIV, emphasis added).

When will we take hold of that abundant life? Not after we die, but after we give! In fact, after each time we give. While the treasures Jesus and Paul spoke of await us in Heaven, attaining the authentic life happens here and now.

Our investments that result in treasures in Heaven have an expressly stated purpose: "so that" we can take hold of the abundant life Jesus came to give us. Of course, that's not the *only*

WHEN GIVING BECOMES PERSONAL

Matt and Tiffany Loeffler were praying about starting a family. They felt the Lord leading them to adoption as "Plan A." After taking a trip to an orphanage in Haiti, they began the process of international adoption but soon learned the orphanage was a human-trafficking ring aided by corrupt Haitian officials.

Tiffany says, "While reason told us to walk away, our hearts were committed as soon as we signed our first home study document. These were our kids, and there was nothing we would not do, no amount of money we would not spend, or time we would not wait to bring them into our family."

Haitian authorities stopped all international adoptions, but Matt went to Haiti to search for their kids, who had been kidnapped by the traffickers. Matt and Tiffany drained their savings and made a total of sixty-six trips to Haiti. Along the way, Matt even faced death threats, and others urged them to give up. But they persevered, and the Lord not only rescued their children but transformed their lives as well.

While waiting more than six years to bring their kids home, Matt gave up his well-paying job to lead mission teams and start a microfinance foundation in Haiti. The Loefflers also developed an orphan-care ministry that equips people in their church to mentor, foster, or adopt children. Tiffany later quit her job to build a regional alliance of agencies, nonprofits, and church ministries that work together to protect kids and strengthen families.

Tiffany says, "In addition to the immense blessing of parenting two incredible kids, we also have a deeper understanding of God's heart for all His children who are lost or separated from Him. We watched God do the impossible, and the lessons of faith we've learned along the way are truly irreplaceable."*

---

* Tiffany Loeffler, "Faith for the Impossible," Defending the Cause Regional Alliance, November 1, 2018, https://www.defendingthecause.org/single-post/2018/11/01/Faith-for-the-Impossible?fb_comment_id=1521813431201869_1521815581201654.

purpose. We give because we love God and people. But we are also told to give in order to grab hold of the good life now.

I believe we can take hold of only one kind of life at a time. In order to take hold of the life that is truly life, we must say no to a life of pride, self-deification, sex-obsession, and money-love. We must say no to the pathetic "life" spent craving Facebook and Instagram likes and viewing the world through the lens of a selfie. We must reject what our world calls the good life and embrace what God tells us is the *true* good life.

We simply cannot say yes to God's promises of overflowing abundant life without simultaneously and consciously saying no to the false claims of the one whom Jesus called "a liar and the father of lies" (John 8:44). Giving helps us do exactly that.

The Message paraphrases Ecclesiastes 8:12-13 well:

> Even though a person sins and gets by with it hundreds of times throughout a long life, I'm still convinced that the good life is reserved for the person who fears God, who lives reverently in his presence, and that the evil person will not experience a "good" life. No matter how many days he lives, they'll all be as flat and colorless as a shadow—because he doesn't fear God.

In other words, the good life is reserved for those who love God and worship him in reverence, in both this life and the next.

Jesus Uses Giving to Bring Us Abundant Life

Here's how different teams of Greek scholars render the last phrase in 1 Timothy 6:19:

- life indeed (RSV)
- what true life is like (CEV)
- the real life (CJB)
- true life (NLT)
- the life which is permanent (PHILLIPS)

All of these expressions speak of the good life. This authentic and contented, vibrant and superior life is granted to us by Jesus who is "*the* Life" (John 14:6, emphasis added). We're told, "In him was life, and the life was the light of men" (John 1:4). Jesus says, "I have come so they may have life. I want them to have it in the fullest possible way" (John 10:10, NIRV). J. B. Phillips renders the verse this way: "I came to bring them life, and far more life than before." *The Message* paraphrases it, "I came so they can have real and eternal life, more and better life than they ever dreamed of."

Jesus says that whoever "believes him who sent me has eternal life and will not be judged but has crossed over from death to life" (John 5:24, NIV). Jesus makes two points about this kind of life: it's the life that's eternal, and it's the life that once and for all leaves death behind.

Knowing Jesus, the source of all life, is vital to taking hold of true life instead of the pseudolife alternatives that riddle our fallen world.

Note that in 1 Timothy 6:17-19, giving is not just a result of sanctification but a cause of it. Four times Paul told the wealthy to give. He didn't say, "Wait until you feel your motives are right, then give." Rather, he said to just go ahead and do good, be rich in good deeds, be generous, and be ready to share, and then look forward to future rewards while experiencing the good life now.

While Paul said elsewhere that "God loves a cheerful giver" (2 Corinthians 9:7), he wasn't suggesting we wait to feel cheerful before we give. God also loves a cheerful Bible student, but we don't postpone Bible study until we're feeling happy about doing it. Cheerfulness sometimes precedes and sometimes follows giving, as it does Bible study and prayer and evangelism. When we start with obeying Jesus and giving our treasure, our hearts will follow with peace and joy. Just as the habit of saying thank you will eventually make us feel more thankful, the practice of giving will eventually make us feel more generous.

Under divine inspiration, Paul commanded God's people to give, and obedience brings life-transforming results. Giving can deliver us from the plague of ruin, destruction, and grief that comes with money-love (1 Timothy 6:9-10). Giving is the safety valve that releases the excess pressure of wealth, keeping it from destroying us. On top of that, by relocating our treasures to Heaven, giving also relocates our hearts there. That's how it ushers in the abundant life, increasing both our holiness *and* our happiness.

Giving has a redemptive quality for the giver. We can redeem money, just as we can redeem time (Ephesians 5:16). Of course, Christ is the only Redeemer, but he works redemptive miracles of grace through us when we give. Then, when we learn of the redemptive effects of our giving, we enter further into the true and good life.

Strategic Living and Giving Brings Gladness and Purpose

Because he is the blessed (happy) God who has given us all things to enjoy, God offers us a happy life (1 Timothy 6:15, 17). Psalm 16:11 testifies to this truth: "You will make known to me the path of life; in Your presence is fullness of joy; in Your right hand there are pleasures forever" (NASB). Pleasure comes in serving God and others in a spirit of humble thanks.

Remarkably, 1 Timothy 6:18 offers a clear formula for taking hold of the abundant and happy life: be rich in good deeds, be generous, and be quick to share with those in need.

When I asked my Facebook followers to share their giving stories, Clyde Powers wrote this:

> Since learning we're stewards of what God has poured into our hands, we've been privileged to help a single mom pay off her car loan, help a woman with airfare so she could visit her hospitalized husband, buy half a mobile unit for a pro-life clinic, join with others to repair a washed-out road to a Christian conference grounds, and provide funds for parents to travel for medical care for their child. The list goes on, and we praise God for all of it!

Does this sound like someone who has turned away from the good life . . . or someone who has grabbed hold of it?

Notice that Paul's command was "Be generous," not "Live simply." It's sometimes said, "Live simply so that others may simply live." But while living simply certainly has many benefits, it doesn't *automatically* do anything good for others. In *A Christmas Carol*, Scrooge lives simply, as misers often do, but his austere living doesn't help anyone. You could simplify your life by quitting your job, withdrawing from society, and living in the woods. But who would benefit?

A better statement would be "Give generously so that others may live." For example, I could live more simply if I didn't have a computer. Instead, I use a computer to serve God. It's a tool that allows me to create books that reach people and also generate royalties to help fund God's Kingdom. Simpler living can fight materialism and free up assets to help others, but our goal should be strategic and generous living.

God's counsel to former thieves is not just to make enough money so they can pay their own way, but "Be honest and work hard, so you will have something to give to people in need" (Ephesians 4:28, CEV).

If we're asked, "Why do you work for a living?" our answer should not just be so we can provide for ourselves and our families, but also so we can help people in need.

Let's Take Hold of the Good Life

We are not merely to wait for the good life and hope that someday it will come to us. Rather, we are to *take hold of* it here and now (1 Timothy 6:19). We don't need to wonder how to do this. God directly tells us it's by generous giving.

The word meaning "take hold of" indicates a present-tense action that brings results now. In the English Standard Version, it's rendered "seized" in Acts 16:19, 18:17, and 21:30, in contexts where believers are grabbed and dragged away or beaten. This aggressive word implies that we must vigorously, tenaciously clutch the true life. If we don't, it will slip away from us.

Sometimes God asks us to give radically in order to let go of a mediocre Christian life and grab hold of an abundant one. When he does so, we need to listen carefully. And when others sense that God is leading them to radical giving, we need to be careful not to hinder the Holy Spirit.

Years ago I knew a single man who came to Christ in his twenties. After growing in his faith for several years, he read the

Scriptures and sensed God leading him to sell his beautiful house and give away the money for God's Kingdom.

I'll never forget the excitement on his face when he told me this. But when I saw him a month later, he looked sad. I asked him if he was okay. He told me that he'd shared this plan to sell his house with his Bible study group, and they told him it was unwise. They talked him out of it.

Over the years, when I've told that story, I've had a number of people say they believe the group's counsel saved this young man from a poor decision. I heartily disagree. I knew his circumstances, the depth of his conviction, and his joy at the prospect of selling his house. He was a skilled carpenter with a high-paying job. If he'd followed through on his decision, he still would have been in the top one or two percent of the world's wealthiest people. But he also would have had eternal rewards and the joy of knowing he had followed the Lord's prompting. And who knows how God might have led him next?

If he'd listened to God's leading through his Word and not to the counsel of his well-meaning Christian friends, he likely would have set his life on a trajectory of trust in God. Instead, the last I heard, this now middle-aged man doesn't have the heart for God he once did.

To this day, I wonder what great things God might have done in and through him if he'd said yes to God, no to his culture (including, sadly, his church culture), and grabbed hold of the life that is truly life.

Don't Wait to Embrace an Eternal Perspective

In my book *The Treasure Principle*, I use an analogy that many tell me has helped them understand money's transitory nature and the importance of adopting an eternal perspective *now*.[3]

Imagine you're alive during the Civil War. Your home is in the North, but while staying in the South, you've accumulated a good deal of Confederate currency. Suppose you know for a fact the North is about to win the war. What will you do with your Confederate money?

If you're smart, there's only one answer. You'll cash in your soon-to-be-worthless Confederate currency for US currency—the only money that will have value the moment the war ends. You'll keep only enough Confederate currency to meet your basic needs for that short period until the money loses all its value.

As believers, we have insider knowledge of a coming social and economic upheaval. For us to accumulate vast earthly treasures in the face of the inevitable is equivalent to stockpiling Confederate money. It's not only wrong—it's just plain stupid! This world's currency will be worthless at our death or Christ's return, both of which are imminent. Those who want to live the true and abundant life must recognize and embrace this reality.

All our currency and possessions are essentially Confederate money. God encourages us to make good use of this temporary currency while we still can, both to live on and to give in order to purchase eternal assets. We can provide for our families and also put the money to work for the love of God and for the good of others, storing up eternal treasures. (Remember, salvation is totally unearned, independent of what we do, while God promises to reward us specifically for what we do.)

Jesus said explicitly in Matthew 6:19-21 what Paul clearly assumed in 1 Timothy 6:9-10: all earthly treasures are doomed. When the Lord returns, money and possessions that could have been used to feed the hungry and fulfill the great commission will go up in smoke.

How much valueless money will you have left when you die or when Christ returns? Why waste it? Why not trade it in now for what will have eternal worth? Why not invest in eternity what you cannot keep and what will not satisfy your heart even if you do keep it?

Have you ever played one of those card games where the winner is the one who runs out of cards first? At the end of the game, every card left counts against you. The American dream is to die with as many cards in our hands as possible. But we're playing the wrong game. Shouldn't our goal be to have no cards at life's end since we can no longer invest them in God's Kingdom?

When the classic Dickens story *A Christmas Carol* begins, we meet Ebenezer Scrooge. This wealthy miser is caustic, complaining, horrendously greedy . . . and profoundly unhappy. After Scrooge's radical transformation from his three supernatural visions, he walks through the streets of London, freely distributing his wealth to the needy. He's giddy with delight. The man who only one day earlier scoffed at charity now takes his greatest pleasure in giving! He is a timeless picture of how God forgives our core sin of selfishness and replaces it with the sanctifying grace of giving.

What caused Scrooge's joy-filled transformation? Gaining an eternal perspective. Through supernatural intervention, he was allowed to see his past, present, and still-changeable future through the eyes of eternity.

God can give us that same life-changing eternal perspective. We can learn the vital importance of giving while we're still living. He has given his Word and his indwelling Holy Spirit to teach and guide us, and to liberate us to experience the real life that pours itself out in generous giving.

There's Significance and Pleasure in Giving

Giving is more than a noble and compassionate act. It's a giant lever positioned on the fulcrum of this world, allowing us to move mountains in the next world. When we die, we will see at last the incredible, eternal results of our giving.

Because we give, eternity will be different—for others and for

NINETEEN QUESTIONS TO ASK BEFORE GIVING TO ANY ORGANIZATION

1. Am I fulfilling my first giving responsibility—to my local church?
2. Are there aspects of this ministry that make it uniquely worth investing in?
3. Have I not only read the literature from this ministry but also talked with others who know it close up and have no vested interest in it?
4. Have I considered taking a ministry or vision trip to see and participate in what this ministry is doing on the field?
5. Does the ministry's staff demonstrate a servant-hearted concern for those they minister to?
6. Do the organization's workers demonstrate a sense of unity, camaraderie, and mutual respect?
7. Have I talked directly with people at the "lower levels" of this ministry? How do they feel about the organization?
8. Is this ministry biblically sound and Christ centered? Do people call on the Lord Jesus to ask his guidance and seek the Holy Spirit's empowerment to do their work?
9. What kind of character, integrity, purity, and humility is demonstrated by the ministry leaders?
10. What kind of accountability structures does the organization have?

us. Giving away our money, possessions, time, and talents is a sacred opportunity to make a great and eternal difference. And it's also our opportunity to enter into living the good life *now*.

When he was young, Matt McPherson sought the Lord's direction for his life. Matt built archery bows and asked God for the wisdom to build the best bows in the world. He developed the

11. If this is a secular organization, why would I give to it rather than to one that is distinctively Christian?
12. How clear are this organization's goals, objectives, strategies, and tactics, and how effectively are they being carried out?
13. Is this organization teachable and open to improvement to become more strategic?
14. Am I certain I have an objective view of this ministry, or have I seen the positives without the negatives?
15. What ethics and what view of God and people are demonstrated in this organization's fund-raising techniques?
16. How much money does the organization spend on overhead expenses and fund-raising, and how much in actual ministry to people?
17. Does this ministry show a clear understanding of cross-cultural ministry factors and local conditions and how the flow of money may affect those conditions?
18. Does this organization speak well of others and cooperate with them?
19. Is this ministry permeated by a distinctly eternal perspective?*

* For the full article, see Randy Alcorn, "Nineteen Questions to Ask Before You Give to Any Organization," Eternal Perspective Ministries, December 26, 2012, https://www.epm.org/resources/2012/Dec/26/nineteen-questions-ask-you-give-any-organization..

single cam bow and now owns one of the world's largest archery bow companies.

Matt started other business ventures, including McPherson Guitars, which he began with his father. Their goal is to make money to impact the world. They now fully support more than seven hundred missionaries worldwide.

Matt's story is another one that makes me thank God for furthering his Kingdom by *not* calling some people to spend their lives as pastors or missionaries—people such as Stanley Tam, R. G. LeTourneau, Art DeMoss, David Green, Alan and Katherine Barnhart, and a number of others in this book. There are millions of faithful business and professional people, including musicians, artists, and athletes, spread across the world. If Matt has fully funded seven hundred missionaries, how many tens of thousands of other missionaries have been able to go do their work because believers in secular vocations have faithfully used their gifts and passions to build businesses that generously send and support them? And while supporting missionaries, they themselves serve Christ in the unique mission fields of their businesses and neighborhoods.

Matt McPherson says, "When I'm dying, I'm not going to be wishing I'd bought myself something else. I'm going to be thinking, 'I wish I would have done more for Christ.'"[4]

I think Matt is exactly right. When we enter Christ's presence, we'll see with eternity's clarity.

So while we still have our earthly lives to live, why not sharpen our long-distance vision and grab hold of the good life now?

Why not make what will be most important to us when we die most important to us now?

Why not spend the rest of our lives closing the gap between what we are giving and what we will one day *wish* we'd given?

CHAPTER 18

WHEN GOD KEEPS OUTGIVING US

....

[God] gives by cartloads to those who give by bushels.
CHARLES SPURGEON

Give away your life; you'll find life given back, but
not merely given back—given back with bonus and blessing.
Giving, not getting, is the way. Generosity begets generosity.
LUKE 6:38, MSG

Cliff Benson Sr. and Cliff Benson Jr. say that at one time they congratulated themselves for giving 10 percent of their incomes, as if that were the ultimate standard. But eventually they realized the biblical view of generosity required them to look at what to do with the other 90 percent.

They pioneered a homebuilding company with the intent of giving away half the earnings. Cliff Sr. says, "I think that's what excites us. . . . Starting a business, we're making money so we can give it away."[1]

"Generosity is fun! There is no way you can know how much fun it is until you're there," Cliff Jr. says. "When you're spending on yourself, the joy part passes quickly, but the joy of giving and its eternal rewards—that lasts a long time."[2]

Do You Have the Gift of Giving?

It may surprise you to hear it, but I believe God has likely given you the gift of giving. How can I say that without even knowing you?

If you are pondering these words, that means you have access to this book, are able to read, and probably are above the 95th percentile when it comes to wealth on a worldwide scale. Very likely you are closer to the 99th percentile (making $15 an hour would put you at the 98th). Just as it makes sense for God to provide access to books and training for someone with the gift of teaching or medical knowledge and resources for those with the gift of mercy, it makes sense that God would provide abundant material resources to those he entrusts with the gift of giving.

In Romans 12:6-8, Paul lists seven spiritual gifts, including prophesying, serving, teaching, showing mercy, and giving. I'm convinced that of all these gifts, giving is the one least thought about and discussed in Christian circles today. It's the gift buried deepest in the Western church.

We regularly see the gift of teaching, and we know what it looks like. We hear testimonies about miraculous healings, restored marriages, successful parenting, dramatic conversions, and nearly everything else except giving. We know about Bible students and prayer warriors, but rarely do we hear stories of giving warriors, some of whom give most of their incomes away. To whom do young people look for encouragement or an example if they think they might have the gift of giving and wonder what it might look like to steward that gift?

Of course, all of us are called to serve, show mercy, and give, even if we don't have those gifts. But in different times of history, God may sovereignly distribute certain gifts among his people more widely according to the current needs and opportunities. (For example, I believe God gave the gift of mercy during plagues.)

Now suppose God wanted to fulfill his plan of world evangelization and help an unprecedented number of suffering people around the planet. What cultural developments might he inspire? The technology to make people more reachable is practically at our fingertips. What else might we expect God to provide? It makes sense to me that he would raise up willing servants all over the globe who are eager to do the labor of physical and spiritual need-meeting. I think he would also likely provide unprecedented wealth to meet all those needs and further his Kingdom.

Look around. Isn't that exactly what God is doing? Now is the time for an army of giving warriors to rise up and cheerfully underwrite the great costs of sending people to reach others in the name of Jesus!

So if you've never asked God, "Have you given me the gift of giving?" now would be a good time. Perhaps that's why, of all the books in the world, God has put this one in your hands right now. And perhaps, just like he did with Queen Esther, God has raised you up and provided you with your particular gifts and opportunities and material resources "for just such a time as this" (Esther 4:14, NLT).

Does Giving Create More or Less Reason to Worry?

There are people who reason, *If I give generously, I'll have to worry about where the money will come from to replace what I've given.* But Jesus actually says the opposite. Immediately after he commands us not to store up treasures on Earth but store them in Heaven (Matthew 6:19-21), he says we are to adopt the right perspective (verses 22-23) and serve the right master—God, not money (verse 24).

Our Lord immediately follows this statement by saying three times, "Do not worry" (Matthew 6:25, 31, 34, NIV). The "therefore" of verse 25 tells us that his command not to worry must be understood in light of what he has just stated. In other words, anyone who is investing in the right treasury, adopting the right perspective, and serving the right master has nothing to worry about. In contrast, those who invest in the wrong treasury (Earth, not Heaven), adopt the wrong perspective (the temporal, not the eternal), and serve the wrong master (money, not God) have every reason to worry.

Jesus specifically tells us not to worry about life's necessities—food, drink, and clothes. Then he says "But seek first the kingdom of God and his righteousness, and all these things will be added to you" (Matthew 6:33). According to our Lord, giving isn't the problem that will leave us short of material provision. In fact, it's part of the solution to our material needs, since God promises to provide for givers, just as he did in Old Testament times (Malachi 3:8-11). Jesus promises the same (Luke 6:38). When we give away our treasures, we are seeking God's Kingdom first. This is the very thing Jesus says fulfills the condition for his promise to provide the material goods we need.

In this affluent society, we have come to a place of self-deception about how much we need to live on. One wealthy widow told me of other widows she knows who are sitting on large fortunes. She said, "Whenever we discuss whether we should give more, we get into the 'bag lady syndrome'—talking as if unless we have millions of dollars stashed away, we're going to end up out on the streets!"

The truth is, generous giving isn't a cause for insecurity and worry. It's a cure for it.

A SURE WAY TO BRING RUIN ON YOUR HOUSE

Charles Spurgeon made these comments about giving 150 years ago:

> Churlish souls stint their contributions to the ministry and missionary operations, and call such saving good economy; little do they dream that they are thus impoverishing themselves. Their excuse is, that they must care for their own families, and they forget that to neglect the house of God is the sure way to bring ruin upon their own houses. . . . In a very wide sphere of observation, I have noticed that the most generous Christians of my acquaintance have been always the most happy, and almost invariably the most prosperous. I have seen the liberal giver rise to wealth of which he never dreamed; and I have as often seen the mean, ungenerous churl descend to poverty by the very parsimony by which he thought to rise. Men trust good stewards with larger and larger sums; and so it frequently is with the Lord; He gives by cartloads to those who give by bushels. Where wealth is not bestowed, the Lord makes the little much by the contentment which the sanctified heart feels in a portion of which the tithe has been dedicated to the Lord.*

* Charles H. Spurgeon, *Morning and Evening: Daily Readings*, October 26 (morning).

Giving Has a Boomerang Effect

Scripture is full of God's words to generous givers: "Honor the LORD with your wealth and with the firstfruits of all your produce; then your barns will be filled with plenty" (Proverbs 3:9-10). But God doesn't intend for us to keep everything he brings into our barns! We are to distribute it generously. We give to him, he gives to us, and we keep giving it back to him, recognizing that it belongs to him anyway. Jesus says, "Give, and you will receive. Your gift will return to you in full—pressed down, shaken together to make room for more, running over, and poured into your lap. The amount you give will determine the amount you get back" (Luke 6:38, NLT).

Recalling the words of one of his customers, R. G. LeTourneau put it this way: "I try to shovel out more for God than He can for me, but He always wins. He's got a bigger shovel."[3] As many others have, he lived out the proverb: "Give freely and become more wealthy; be stingy and lose everything. The generous will prosper; those who refresh others will themselves be refreshed" (Proverbs 11:24-25, NLT).

In some cases God's extra provision is obvious—we get an unexpected check in the mail or are given something we thought we'd have to buy. One time Nanci and I discovered an error we'd made in our bank balance, finding we had significantly more money than we realized.

In other cases, God's provision is less obvious but equally generous. A washing machine that should have broken down a decade ago keeps working. A car with more than two hundred thousand miles runs for three years needing no repairs. A checking account that should have dried up long before the end of the month somehow makes it through. As God miraculously stretched the widow's oil supply in Elisha's day (2 Kings 4:1-7), and as he made the Israelites' clothes and sandals last forty years in the wilderness (Deuteronomy 8:4), I'm convinced he sometimes graciously extends the life of things that would normally need replacement.

Consider Bob, who decided he wanted to give sacrificially when his church started a building campaign to expand their crowded sanctuary. Every morning he'd made a Suisse Mocha coffee. He calculated that if he gave up this habit for three years, he'd be able to give an additional $780.

As part of his church's financial campaign, Bob gave a short speech at church, mentioning his plan to forgo his coffee.

Two days later, he received a call from a woman asking if he was the Mr. Hodgdon who spoke at church. That evening she delivered a box to him, introducing herself as a General Foods employee. Inside were several months' worth of Suisse Mocha, the same product Bob had given up. Bob added, "The strange thing is, I've never seen or heard from her since. I've looked for her at every church service, but maybe it was one of God's angels. You just cannot out-give God."[4]

This small thing wasn't small to Bob. It showed his Father's gracious kindness to him and prompted him, in a childlike way, to trust and give even more.

This is not health-and-wealth gospel or prosperity theology. I'm certainly not saying that God must always give back to us exactly what we give up, or ten or a hundred times more, in some kind of karma-like transaction or misapplication of Mark 10:30. Sometimes he gives us joy or patience or endurance as we make real sacrifices for him—and such intangible gifts are considerably more precious than a stash of morning coffee. But aren't you glad God sometimes rewards us with little things to remind us of his love and approval?

Don't Postpone Your Giving

There's a difference between giving your money to a worthy cause and leaving your money to that ministry after you die. By all means,

I recommend that you designate substantial gifts in your will to your church and favorite ministries. In fact, if your remaining family members are financially secure, you may well leave the bulk of your estate to God's work. Nanci and I have made arrangements to do this. But having someone else dispose of your estate when you die requires no faith in God and no sacrifice on your part. You have no choice but to leave your money and possessions to someone.

The point is, give generously and substantially *now*, when you can see your faith at work and benefit from God's favor. Delayed giving is delayed obedience.

Many people hesitate to give because they think they are supposed to hang on to their wealth to pass it on to their children and grandchildren. I would encourage you to rethink that assumption.

In Old Testament times, many people were too poor to buy land. It was essential that parents pass land ownership to their children and grandchildren. With no inheritance, they would end up enslaved or unable to care for their parents, who normally lived on the property with them. As a result, they were told, "A good person leaves an inheritance for their children's children" (Proverbs 13:22, NIV).

Today in the United States and many other affluent countries, inheritances are often radically different from those in ancient Israel. They are usually windfalls coming to grown people who

- live separately from their parents;
- are not (and shouldn't be) dependent on them;
- have regular incomes generated by their own work, skills, saving, and investing; and
- have far more than they need.

When such people inherit a house, a farm, or other real estate, what becomes of it? It doesn't go to children who need it in order to do their work and produce an income. Rather, it's usually sold. The inheritance just increases their already high standard of living—sometimes dramatically.

Well-meaning parents have caused serious marital conflicts by leaving money to their grown children. Money that's "his" because it came from his parents and "hers" because it came from her parents divides the marriage and fosters unhealthy independence.

Many studies and personal observations confirm that inherited wealth, which is unearned income, can be a corrupting influence. It can lead to financial irresponsibility, waste, and laziness, and often feeds addictions.

For many years I've had the opportunity to speak to and interact with wealthy believers, and I've been struck by heartbreaking stories about the devastating effects of receiving a large inheritance. In *The Legacy of Inherited Wealth*, two wealthy heiresses share their interviews of seventeen adult heirs, who recount the blessings and curses of their inherited wealth. Their stories suggest that the curses far outweigh the blessings. Although these people tried to find the bright side of inherited wealth, they were much more convincing when talking about the dark side. They experienced frustration, anger, doubt, insecurity, and resentment—all tied to growing up wealthy or becoming wealthy through inheritance.[5]

People often testify of the character, discipline, self-control, and trust in God they developed when they were younger and had less to live on. How ironic that these same people pass on large amounts of money to their children, robbing them of similar blessings.

Certainly we should not transfer wealth to adult children unless we've witnessed a track record of wisdom in their financial choices. Without wisdom, wealth would not only be wasted but also damage children by subsidizing bad habits and sabotaging discipline and self-control. Surely there are better things we can do with God's money than provide additional temptations for beloved children who have yet to demonstrate that they can steward wealth wisely.

Many parents have adult children who are already making more money than the parents themselves did, or who are poised to do so. I have asked people, "What do you hope your children, who are already extremely wealthy by global standards, will do with the inheritance you plan to leave them?"

"Well, it would be great if they gave it away to those who really need it."

The obvious response is, "But if God has entrusted the money to you, then why don't *you* do that?"

Consider this question: What would you think if your money manager died and left all your money to *his* children? Well, if our money really belongs to God and we are his money managers, what makes us think that when we die it should all go to *our* adult children, especially if we believe God is their primary provider and will take care of them just as he has taken care of us?

Nanci and I have been generous to our children and grandchildren and plan to continue to be generous with them. We helped them early in their marriages to make down payments on their houses. Now both families have good incomes, and like us, being middle-class Americans, they are among the world's wealthy. We told them years ago that we'll leave them only a modest amount of money—enough to help our grandchildren without hurting them. But the larger portion of our estate will go to our church and worthy ministries. Meanwhile, we're not waiting until we die to support those ministries. The great bulk of our giving will have been done in our lifetimes.

God Invites You to Test His Provision by Giving

Gerard and Geraldine Low of Singapore believe that God wants us to test his promises to provide and trust him to show his greatness and sufficiency (Malachi 3:10; Luke 6:38).

WHEN YOU HAVE NOTHING LEFT TO GIVE

During the 2008 recession, our friends Mike and Doreen, like many others, saw their paychecks shrivel. One month there was no paycheck at all.

Concerned they wouldn't be able to pay their mortgage and give to ministries and missionaries who were counting on them, Doreen called their mortgage loan officer. It was a Saturday, but not knowing what else to do, she left a message. Though he never went to his office on Saturdays, he did, and signed them up for free refinancing through a government program ending that day. The refinance eliminated two months of mortgage payments and reduced future payments. Fulfilling their giving commitments took priority over paying the mortgage, and suddenly they were able to do both!

During this same time, Doreen was offered a fulfilling job that allowed her to work from home and fill in the financial gaps. Gradually their income returned, and they had not missed a single gift or payment. She considers these "coincidences" a miracle of God's grace.

Imagine how differently this story would have ended if they had chosen to "solve" their problem by eliminating giving. At the very least, they would have missed out on watching God provide day after day, not to mention missing out on the eternal rewards from gifts withheld.

Every year the Lows pray and decide how much they are going to give. But almost without fail, crises arise, bringing financial instability, to the point that they have wondered if they could—or should—give at the level they've determined.

Still, they have stuck to their commitment, even when it has meant dipping into their savings. "We're accountants by training," Gerard says, "so we started a spreadsheet of what we've promised to give to God. Each time we almost run out of money to give to God, God restores our lost income and provides the means for us to continue giving."[6] They are taking God at his word when he invites us to test him in this area. "If you don't let go, you're not giving Him a test," Geraldine says.[7]

Because God is the greatest giver in the universe, he won't let you outgive him. Go ahead and try. See what happens. Nanci and I, like the Lows and countless others, have been amazed and thankful to see God come through again and again. The more you experience this, the greater your joy and delight and trust in God.

When more comes back, whatever you do, don't hold it tightly. Remember God has told us exactly why he provides for us so abundantly: "You will be made rich in every way so that you can be generous in every way" (2 Corinthians 9:11, CEB). The verse continues, "Such generosity produces thanksgiving to God."

Keep joyfully giving it back to God by meeting the physical and spiritual needs of others. Don't wait for your treasures to follow your heart; instead, give away your treasures freely and then watch your heart follow them to what will matter when this life is done. You can do so trusting that God is using your giving as part of his preparations for your eternal future, which will be wonderful beyond all anticipation.

It's incredible, but true. We will certainly outlive our present lives, and we can also outgive them. We can reach beyond our deaths and into eternity, transferring our treasures from Earth to Heaven.

This is the good life, the adventure of trusting God and seeing him work in us and through us and around us. This is the abundant life of excitement and happiness, to be followed by the unending pleasures of eternal life with God and his people in a renewed and vastly improved universe. In that world awaiting us, we will join Jesus, our greatest treasure, and be reunited with beloved family and friends who know him. In addition, we will meet many people for the first time, including those forever touched by our investments in their lives. All these people—old acquaintances and new ones—will be our joy and our crowns (Philippians 4:1; 1 Thessalonians 2:19).

Keep in mind EROI—*eternal* return on investment. At the end of this brief life and the beginning of the next and unending one, can you imagine anything better than hearing Jesus say to you: "Well done, you good and faithful servant! . . . You have been faithful in managing small amounts, so I will put you in charge of large amounts. Come on in and share my happiness!" (Matthew 25:23, GNT).

NOW IS YOUR WINDOW OF OPPORTUNITY

....

In May 2000, John Piper preached a message to forty thousand college students at a conference. The reaction was so strong that it resulted in his book *Don't Waste Your Life*.

John shared with the students the story of two women—both about eighty years old—whom his church supported. Ruby was a missionary nurse in Cameroon. Laura, a doctor, was visiting her. While they were traveling to Cameroon villages, the brakes in their car went out. They crashed and died.

Ruby had spent most of her life serving Christ among the poor and needy, and she was still doing so twenty years after most of her American counterparts had retired to sunshine states.

Speaking of the two women who died, Piper asked, "Is this a tragedy?"[1] Though it was certainly a heartbreaking story, his answer was no, it wasn't a tragedy.

Piper then read to the students from a *Reader's Digest* article, telling of what he called a real tragedy. The article portrayed "the good life": a couple in their fifties who retired early to spend time cruising on their thirty-foot trawler, playing softball, and collecting seashells.

"Don't buy that dream," Piper said. "The American dream, a nice house, a nice car, a nice job, a nice family, a nice retirement, *collecting shells* as the last chapter before you stand before the Creator of the universe to give an account of what you did: 'Here it is, Lord, my shell collection! . . . And I've got a good swing, and look at my boat.' . . . Don't waste your life."[2]

Sure, there's a time for picking up shells or playing golf, because, as 1 Timothy 6:17 tells us, God "gives us everything to enjoy" (NCV). And no, we won't all spend our lives working with Africa's poorest like Ruby did.

What we do need is to look for people like Ruby and help support them. We should say, "Whether I go or whether I stay here and serve Christ in my neighborhood, community, workplace, and church, I resolve not to waste my life. I will give generously to further God's Kingdom around the globe. I, too, commit myself to living the good life, the abundant life, a life forever invested in Jesus, his gospel, and his people."

What Do You Believe about Giving and the Good Life?

In the early chapters of this book, we saw how Jesus turns society's view of the good life on its head. He warns us to watch out for greed and insists that our lives aren't about how much money we earn and how many things we own (Luke 12:15). He reveals something that is counterintuitive to those who lack perspective but is obvious to all who have experienced it: there's greater happiness to be found in giving than receiving (Acts 20:35).

Not only *shouldn't* we be satisfied by hoarding or overspending; we *can't* be. Generosity really is the good life.

We've seen that once our basic needs are met and some reasonable wants are fulfilled, money stops helping us and starts hurting us. Wealth easily becomes an idol, a false god. Jesus says we can't serve both God and money. But the good news is that Jesus came to set us free from money-love so that we can serve God *with* money.

Jesus makes it clear that the abundant life consists not in material abundance but in the life-giving spiritual abundance found only in him. Eternal and abundant life begins in this world when we come to Jesus, the ultimate giver, and continues as we become more like him. The gospel itself centers on the single greatest act of giving in the history of the universe.

In 1 Timothy 6:18-19 we discovered that there is one central way to grab hold of the life that is truly life. We might have expected a list of spiritual disciplines or any number of God-honoring practices. Instead, God says we can experience the abundant and authentic life in Christ by being generous and eager to share. In giving, we gain a life-infusing foretaste of the infinite happiness of the world where Jesus will forever be the unchallenged King of kings. Generosity simultaneously stores up eternal treasures in Heaven, gives vital help to the needy, and front-loads eternal joy into our present lives.

But all those are just words, and they will make no difference to you *unless you believe them.* Even if you accept them in theory but don't ask, "Lord, what do you want me to do with your money and possessions?" there won't be any lasting difference in your life. Is God telling you it's time to raise the bar of your giving and grab hold of the good life? Based on the Scriptures we've studied, I believe he is.

Understand that giving is putting into God's hands what belongs to him anyway. It's an investment in eternity, in what will forever outlive this life. But please don't overlook the added incentive that it's also an immediate investment in the abundant life. We give both to honor Jesus and to benefit others. And in the process, amazingly, we benefit ourselves and our families, both now and forever. Let's not disregard any of the motives God gives us for serving him.

What Happens Next?

No sooner will you put down this book than you'll be tempted to forget it or how God might have spoken to you as you read. Don't let the devil whisper rationalizations to keep you from a transformed life. Don't listen when he says, "If your heart isn't in giving, you shouldn't do it." Don't let him convince you, "All those stories about people's happiness in giving are exaggerated; it's better to hold tight to what you have." And don't let him tempt you to think, *Sure, someday when I make a lot more money, then I'll start giving.* If you buy into that, it will simply never happen.

While the devil lies to us, saying that giving will rob us of the good life, Jesus tells us the truth: that giving generates the good life. Now the only question is, who will we believe?

Jesus tells us to be generous and eager to share. If you wait until you have no doubts or worries, you'll probably never take

FINAL QUESTIONS TO ASK

Since God owns it all, shouldn't we stop acting as if *we* do? Shouldn't we ask him,

- What do you want me to do with your money and possessions?
- What should I buy and not buy with your money?
- How much do you want me to keep, and how much do you want me to give?
- In light of all the needs globally and locally, where and to whom do you want me to give?

Since we are God's money managers, shouldn't we check with him regularly and ask how he wants us to invest what belongs to him?

Are we living with the daily conviction that at the end of our term of service—when we die or when he returns—we'll undergo a final and all-encompassing job performance evaluation? "Each of us will give an account of himself to God" (Romans 14:12).

Are we asking ourselves daily how Jesus wants us to serve him with all he's entrusted to us? Are we aware that he wants to reward our faithful service to him on Earth with treasures that will last forever in Heaven? "Whatever you do, work at it with all your heart, as working for the Lord, not for human masters, since you know that you will receive an inheritance from the Lord as a reward. It is the Lord Christ you are serving" (Colossians 3:23-24, NIV).

that next step. But if you do take that step by faith, you will find it exhilarating. Ultimately giving may become the healthiest and most joy-saturated addiction you've ever experienced.

It's critical that we take hold of the good life now and use the limited window of time God has entrusted to us to invest in eternity. After we leave this world, we will never have another chance to move the hand of God through prayer. Or heal a hurting soul.

Or share Christ with one who can be saved from hell. Or care for the sick. Or serve a meal to the starving. Or comfort the dying. Or rescue the unborn. Or translate the Scriptures into someone's heart language. Or bring the gospel to an unreached people group. Or open our homes. Or share our clothes and food with those in need.

What you do with your resources in this life is your autobiography. The story you will have written with the pen of faith and the ink of works will go into eternity unedited, to be seen and read as is by the angels, the redeemed, and God himself.

When we view today in light of the long and unending tomorrow, our choices become tremendously important. My choices to read my Bible, pray, go to church, share my faith, and give my money—actions graciously empowered not by my flesh but by God's Spirit—are of eternal consequence, not only for other souls, but for mine.

At death, we put the signature on our life's portrait. The paint dries. The portrait is permanently finished. No future renovation is possible. I have revised this book a number of times, but once I die, it will be too late to go back and revise my life, making different choices about what I do and say, whom I trust and serve, and how much I give. When the final buzzer sounds, no more points can be scored, and the outcome is permanent. This is our opportunity, right here and now, to grab hold of the good life and experience all that God has for us.

I can't tell you exactly what it will look like for you to embrace the abundant life Jesus offers you. I don't know what you've read in this book that the Holy Spirit might use to move these truths from theory to reality for you. But I can tell you with absolute certainty that committing to live the generous life to God's glory will please and honor him and infuse you with Christ-centered happiness. Someday, probably in this life but for sure in the next one, you will realize it was one of the most important decisions you ever made.

Perhaps this will require making some lifestyle changes to loosen the grip of material things and free up more money to invest in God's Kingdom. Maybe God is calling you to downsize your home, drive an older car, sell some jewelry, give away a portion of your savings, forgo an expensive vacation, or skip some lattes or dinners out so you can find more to give away. Perhaps you'll be led to invest your time and money in serving at a local ministry and reaching out to needy people in your city and neighborhood. Maybe you'll plan some giving adventures where you pay for people's groceries or meals and discover that what some call random acts of kindness are actually divine appointments.

I can assure you that once you experience the good life, the abundant life, the generous life, deep inside you will never want to settle for less. Life will never be the same—nor will you want it to be!

When it comes to giving, just start doing it. And never stop doing it. Then watch how God transforms you and those you give to.

God is the one who promised to give you "a rich and satisfying life" (John 10:10, NLT). So go ahead—ask him to help you, by the power of his Holy Spirit, to take hold of the life that's truly life.

That's a prayer he delights to answer.

Acknowledgments

Thanks to my dear friend Ron Beers, publisher at Tyndale House, who has been a great encouragement to me for decades. I am profoundly grateful for Stephanie Rische, my wonderful editor of this book and a number of my others.

Thanks also to Linda Howard, acquisitions director; Kara Leonino, acquisitions editor; Dean Renninger, designer; Brittany Bergman, copyeditor; Kristi Gravemann, marketer; Annette Taroli, product manager; Tim Wolf, buyer; and Katie Dodillet and Amanda Woods, publicists. Thanks to my friend Tim Green for his cover design.

Thanks also to the terrific staff members of Eternal Perspective Ministries, who each help me in their own way with my books, my life, and our ministry together. Special thanks to Chelsea Weber, my outstanding assistant, who does so much for me in countless areas. And as always, my heartfelt thanks to EPM's Stephanie Anderson, Doreen Button, and Kathy Norquist, who did a great job editing this book before I submitted it.

As always, heartfelt thanks to my wife, Nanci, who is my soul mate and deserves credit but not blame for whatever I do.

To all of the above, this fully applies: "As iron sharpens iron, so one person sharpens another" (Proverbs 27:17, NIV).

Notes

CHAPTER 1: WHAT IS THE GOOD LIFE?

1. Kristen Kuchar, "The Emotional Effects of Debt," The Simple Dollar, updated December 13, 2017, https://www.thesimpledollar.com/the-emotional-effects -of-debt/.

2. Christian Smith and Hilary Davidson, *The Paradox of Generosity: Giving We Receive, Grasping We Lose* (New York: Oxford University Press, 2014), 1.

3. Ibid., 44.

4. Jenny Santi, *The Giving Way to Happiness: Stories and Science behind the Life-Changing Power of Giving* (New York: Random House, 2015), xix.

CHAPTER 2: HAVING MONEY IS NOT THE GOOD LIFE

1. Karen S. Schneider and Bob Meadows, "Owen Wilson: What Happened?" *People*, September 10, 2007, https://people.com/archive/cover-story-owen-wilson-what -happened-vol-68-no-11/.

2. Kim Teller, letter to the editor, *People*, December 10, 2007, https://people.com /archive/mailbag-vol-68-no-24/.

3. "Global Health Observatory (GHO) Data: Suicide Rates (Per 100 000 Population)," World Health Organization, last updated July 17, 2018, http:// www.who.int/gho/mental_health/suicide_rates/en/.

4. Randy Alcorn, "Our Time aboard Operation Mobilization's Ship, *Logos Hope*," see "Story Onboard Ship," YouTube video, 0:27, Eternal Perspective Ministries, July 28, 2017, http://www.epm.org/blog/2017/Jul/28/ship-logos-hope.

5. Robert Powell, "The Good Life Is Not Only about Money," MarketWatch, July 30, 2010, https://www.marketwatch.com/story/the-good-life-is-not-only -about-money-2010-07-30.

6. Jesse Carey, "12 of DL Moody's Most Profound Quotes about Faith," *Relevant*, February 5, 2016, https://relevantmagazine.com/god/12-dl-moodys-most -profound-quotes-about-faith.

7. Christian Smith and Hilary Davidson, *The Paradox of Generosity: Giving We Receive, Grasping We Lose* (New York: Oxford University Press, 2014), 224.

8. Dr. and Mrs. Howard Taylor, *Hudson Taylor and the China Inland Mission: The Growth of a Work of God* (London: China Inland Mission, 1918), 384, https://archive.org/stream/hudsontaylorchin00tayl/hudsontaylorchin00tayl_djvu.txt.

9. Alice Gray, *Treasures for Women Who Hope* (Nashville: Thomas Nelson, 2005), xvii–xx.

10. Randy Alcorn, "Twelve Giving Stories," Eternal Perspective Ministries, February 16, 2010, https://www.epm.org/resources/2010/Feb/16/twelve-giving-stories/.

11. Ibid.

12. Ibid.

CHAPTER 3: A BETTER KIND OF ABUNDANCE

1. Renee Lockey, "Work like a Doctor, Live like a Nurse," *WDW Blog*, March 1, 2018, https://womendoingwell.org/work-like-a-doctor-live-like-a-nurse/.

2. Richard Wurmbrand, *Tortured for Christ* (Colorado Springs: David C. Cook, 2017), 58.

3. Aleksandr I. Solzhenitsyn, *The Gulag Archipelago: 1918–1956*, trans. Thomas P. Whitney and Harry Willetts, abridged by Edward E. Erickson Jr. (New York: HarperCollins, 2007), 313.

4. "Pete and Deb Ochs: Jailhouse Generosity," Vimeo video, 8:35, Generous Giving, https://generousgiving.org/media/videos/pete-and-deb-ochs-jailhouse-generosity.

CHAPTER 4: WHAT LOVE LOOKS LIKE

1. Trevor Hamaker, "What's the Difference between Love & Charity in the New Testament?" *Varsity Faith* (blog), July 14, 2010, http://www.varsityfaith.com/2010/07/whats-difference-between-love-charity.html.

2. "The Holy Man," LIFE International, July 9, 2016, https://www.lifeinternational.com/articles/holy-man.

3. Laura Bult, "Nobel Peace Prize Winner Elie Wiesel's Best Quotes on Survival, Activism and Humanity," *New York Daily News*, July 2, 2016, https://www.nydailynews.com/news/world/elie-wiesel-quotes-survival-spirituality-humanity-article-1.2697132.

4. John Wesley, "On Dress (Sermon 88)," Wesleyan-Holiness Digital Library, accessed April 11, 2019, https://whdl.org/dress-sermon-88.

5. This story originally appeared on the author's blog. See Randy Alcorn, "John Wesley's Example of Giving," Eternal Perspective Ministries, May 14, 2014, https://www.epm.org/blog/2014/May/14/john-wesley-giving. See also Charles Edward White, "Four Lessons on Money from One of the World's Richest Preachers," *Christian History* 19 (Summer 1988): 24, https://christianhistoryinstitute.org/uploaded/50cf76d05900d6.14390582.pdf.

6. Utpal Dholakia, "Why People Who Have Less Give More," *Psychology Today*, November 20, 2017, https://www.psychologytoday.com/us/blog/the-science -behind-behavior/201711/why-people-who-have-less-give-more.

7. Randy Alcorn, *Happiness* (Carol Stream, IL: Tyndale, 2015), 217–24.

8. Christian Smith and Hilary Davidson, *The Paradox of Generosity: Giving We Receive, Grasping We Lose* (New York: Oxford University Press, 2014), 11–12.

9. Arthur C. Brooks, as quoted in "Those Who Serve Others Are *Happier, Healthier,* and *More Prosperous,*" Spokane Cares, accessed January 8, 2019, http://www .spokanecares.org/index.php?c_ref=160.

CHAPTER 5: THE BEST INVESTMENT WE CAN MAKE

1. John Rinehart, "The Gospel Patron behind Sudan Interior Mission," Gospel Patrons, May 19, 2017, https://www.gospelpatrons.org/articles/the-gospel-patron -behind-sudan-interior-mission.

2. "Who We Are: About," SIM, accessed January 4, 2019, https://www.sim.org/en _US/about.

3. Rinehart, "Sudan Interior Mission," https://www.gospelpatrons.org/articles/the -gospel-patron-behind-sudan-interior-mission.

4. "I Like Foster Care," YouTube video, 3:44, posted by I Like Giving, August 31, 2017, https://www.youtube.com/watch?v=-h5yPCurnWE&sns=em.

5. Elisabeth Elliot, *Shadow of the Almighty: The Life and Testament of Jim Elliot* (Peabody, MA: Hendrickson, 2008), 11.

CHAPTER 6: THE DANGERS OF BEING RICH

1. Graham Noble, "The Life and Death of the Terrible Turk," *Eurozine*, May 23, 2003, https://www.eurozine.com/the-life-and-death-of-the-terrible-turk.

2. Lindsay Wissman, "2017 Federal Poverty Level Guidelines," PeopleKeep, February 7, 2017, https://www.peoplekeep.com/blog/2017-federal-poverty-level -guidelines.

3. "June 2018 Median Household Income," Seeking Alpha, August 1, 2018, https:// seekingalpha.com/article/4193310-june-2018-median-household-income.

4. Globalrichlist.com also allows you to calculate your relative wealth by entering the equity in your home and the total value of all your possessions and investments.

5. Paul Piff, "Does Money Make You Mean?" TED talk, October 2013, https:// www.ted.com/talks/paul_piff_does_money_make_you_mean/discussion?referrer =playlist-306.

6. Anne Manne, "The Age of Entitlement: How Wealth Breeds Narcissism," *Guardian*, July 7, 2014, https://www.theguardian.com/commentisfree/2014/jul /08/the-age-of-entitlement-how-wealth-breeds-narcissism. See also Jessica Gross, "Six Studies on How Money Affects the Mind," *TED Blog*, December 20, 2013, https://blog.ted.com/6-studies-of-money-and-the-mind/.

7. William Barclay, *William Barclay's Daily Study Bible*, Luke 18, StudyLight.org, https://www.studylight.org/commentaries/dsb/luke-18.html.

8. William F. High with Ashley B. McCauley, *The Generosity Bet: Secrets of Risk, Reward, and Real Joy* (Shippensburg, PA: Destiny Image, 2014), 71–72.

9. Ibid., 73–74.

CHAPTER 7: PUT YOUR TREASURE WHERE IT WILL LAST

1. "The Stanley Tam Story," YouTube video, 1:01:55, posted by U.S. Plastic Corporation, April 9, 2014, https://www.youtube.com/watch?v=QxPGFlxTSro.

2. Kate Gibson, "Nearly Half the Planet's Population Lives on Less than $5.50 a Day," CBS News, updated October 17, 2018, https://www.cbsnews.com/news /nearly-half-the-planets-population-lives-on-less-than-5-50-a-day-worlf-bank -reports/.

3. John Rinehart, *Gospel Patrons: People Whose Generosity Changed the World* (Reclaimed Publishing, 2014).

4. Ibid., 37–57.

5. Ibid., 61–92.

6. Ibid., 94–128.

CHAPTER 8: CONTENTMENT: WHEN ENOUGH IS ENOUGH

1. William F. High with Ashley B. McCauley, *The Generosity Bet: Secrets of Risk, Reward, and Real Joy* (Shippensburg, PA: Destiny Image, 2014), 35–36.

2. "The Decision That Led to 9 Million Downloads," *Life.Church Open Network Blog*, October 7, 2016, https://openblog.life.church/the-decision-that-led-to -9-million-downloads/.

3. "The Bible App," YouVersion, accessed January 7, 2018, https://www.youversion .com/the-bible-app/.

4. High with McCauley, *The Generosity Bet*, 37.

5. Tori DeAngelis, "Consumerism and Its Discontents," *Monitor on Psychology* 35, no. 6 (June 2004): 52, https://www.apa.org/monitor/jun04/discontents.

6. Ibid.

7. Gary G. Hoag, *Wealth in Ancient Ephesus and the First Letter to Timothy* (Winona Lake, IN: Eisenbrauns, 2015).

8. Jeremiah Burroughs, *Rare Jewel of Christian Contentment* (Lafayette, IN: Sovereign Grace, 2001), 2.

9. Jerry Bridges, *The Practice of Godliness* (Colorado Springs: NavPress, 1996), 85.

10. Steven J. Cole, "Lesson 27: The Secret for Contentment (Philippians 4:10-13)," Bible.org, July 30, 2013, https://bible.org/seriespage/lesson-27-secret-contentment -philippians-410-13.

11. Hoag, *Wealth in Ancient Ephesus*, 177.

12. C. S. Lewis, *The Weight of Glory* (New York: HarperCollins, 2001), 34.

13. Randy Alcorn, *If God Is Good: Faith in the Midst of Suffering and Evil* (Colorado Springs: Multnomah Books, 2014).

14. Mark and Jennifer Higinbotham, personal testimony, October 16, 2017.

CHAPTER 9: MONEY: A BLESSING OR A CURSE?

1. Journey of Generosity is an overnight event put on by Generous Giving, https://generousgiving.org/small-gatherings.
2. "Three Lessons from Esther and Caspar Jiang, China," JoyGiving.org, accessed January 8, 2019, https://joygiving.org/esther-and-caspar/.
3. Ibid.
4. Ibid.
5. Mark Cartwright, "Temple of Artemis at Ephesus," Ancient History Encyclopedia, July 26, 2018, https://www.ancient.eu/Temple_of_Artemis_at_Ephesus/.
6. Associated Press, "Hundreds of Coins Found in French Patient's Belly," NBC News, February 18, 2004, http://www.nbcnews.com/id/4304525/ns/health-health_care/t/hundreds-coins-foundin-french-patients-belly.
7. Charles R. Swindoll, *Strengthening Your Grip: How to Be Grounded in a Chaotic World* (Brentwood, TN: Worthy Books, 2015), 88.
8. Rich Duprey, "Maybe You Were Better Off Not Winning the Lottery Jackpot," Motley Fool, January 27, 2018, https://www.fool.com/retirement/2018/01/27/maybe-you-were-better-off-not-winning-the-lottery.aspx.
9. Derek Thompson, "Lotteries: America's $70 Billion Shame," *Atlantic*, May 11, 2015, https://www.theatlantic.com/business/archive/2015/05/lotteries-americas-70-billion-shame/392870/.
10. Jeff Rose, "6 Ways to Prevent Ruining Your Life If You Win the Lottery," *Forbes*, August 21, 2016, https://www.forbes.com/sites/jrose/2016/08/21/winning-the-lottery.
11. Motley Fool, "Maybe You Were Better Off."
12. Annie Gabillet, "Lottery Horror Stories That Will Make You Think Twice about Buying That Ticket," Popsugar, May 28, 2018, https://www.popsugar.com/smart-living/Lottery-Horror-Stories-33026559.
13. Nick Britten, "Lottery Winner Dies after Blowing Millions on Drink, Racehorses and Football," *Telegraph*, April 2, 2010, https://www.telegraph.co.uk/news/uknews/7547902/Lottery-winner-dies-after-blowing-millions-on-drink-racehorses-and-football.html.
14. Tony Dokoupil, "'The Drama Is Nonstop': Powerball Winner 'Wild' Willie Wants His Old Life Back," NBC News, September 25, 2013, http://usnews.nbcnews.com/_news/2013/09/25/20663854-the-drama-is-nonstop-powerball-winner-wild-willie-wants-his-old-life-back.
15. See Randy Alcorn, *Happiness* (Carol Stream, IL: Tyndale, 2015), 81–82.
16. John Wesley, *John Wesley*, ed. Albert C. Outler (New York: Oxford University Press, 1964), 241.
17. John Piper, "Is Love of Money Really the Root of All Evils?" Desiring God, February 7, 2017, https://www.desiringgod.org/articles/is-love-of-money-really-the-root-of-all-evils.
18. Ibid.

19. Tony Cimmarrusti, "Tony and Martha Cimmarrusti: 2017 Celebration of Generosity," Vimeo video, 16:13, Generous Giving, https://generousgiving.org/media/videos/cimmarrusti-2017.

CHAPTER 10: WHAT MONEY CAN DO TO YOUR SOUL

1. John Cortines and Gregory Baumer, *God and Money: How We Discovered True Riches at Harvard Business School* (Carson, CA: Rose Publishing, 2016), 120–21.
2. Gregory Baumer, "God and Money: An Interview with Gregory Baumer and John Cortines," YouTube video, 13:55, posted by Crossroads Church, March 11, 2018, https://www.youtube.com/watch?v=9bVrZTMZNgM.
3. Cyprian, *The Lapsed: The Unity of the Catholic Church*, chapters 9–11.
4. John Wesley, *John Wesley*, ed. Albert C. Outler (New York: Oxford University Press, 1964), 246.
5. John Chrysostom, as quoted in John C. Haughey, ed., *The Faith That Does Justice: Examining the Christian Sources for Social Change* (Eugene, OR: Wipf & Stock, 1977), 130.
6. Ray Bradbury, *Fahrenheit 451* (New York: Simon & Schuster, 2018), 149–50.

CHAPTER 11: THE GOOD NEWS ABOUT MONEY

1. Richard L. Pratt Jr., *1 & 2 Corinthians*, Holman New Testament Commentary (Nashville: B&H, 2000), 156.
2. Ibid.
3. Randy Alcorn, *The Apostle*, Kingstone Bible, vol. 10 (Leesburg, FL: Kingstone Comics, 2015).
4. Timothy Friberg, Barbara Friberg, and Neva F. Miller, *Analytical Lexicon of the Greek New Testament*, Baker's Greek New Testament, vol. 4 (Grand Rapids, MI: Baker Books, 2000), 165.
5. See Randy Alcorn, *Heaven* (Carol Stream, IL: Tyndale, 2004).
6. "Three Lessons from Raja B. and Shantha Singh, India," JoyGiving.org, accessed January 13, 2019, https://joygiving.org/raja-and-shantha/.
7. Ibid.
8. Ibid.
9. See Randy Alcorn, "Is God Happy, or Is He Blessed?" chapter 14 in *Happiness* (Carol Stream, IL: Tyndale, 2015).
10. Charles H. Spurgeon, "Adorning the Gospel" (Sermon #2416).
11. Archibald Thomas Robertson, *Word Pictures in the New Testament*, vol. 4.
12. John Phillips, *Exploring the Pastoral Epistles: An Expository Commentary* (Grand Rapids, MI: Kregel, 2004), 190.
13. Robert Jamieson, A. R. Fausset, and David Brown, *Commentary Critical and Explanatory on the Whole Bible*, 1 Timothy 1:11.
14. A. W. Pink, *Gleanings from Paul: Studies in the Prayers of the Apostle* (Bellingham, WA: Logos Research Systems, 2005), 344.

CHAPTER 12: THE SOURCE OF AUTHENTIC WEALTH

1. "Alan Barnhart: God Owns Our Business," Vimeo video, 16:58, Generous Giving, https://generousgiving.org/media/videos/alan-barnhart-god-owns-our-business.
2. Ibid.
3. Ibid.
4. Liz Essley Whyte, "Giving It All," *Philanthropy*, Spring 2014, https://www .philanthropyroundtable.org/philanthropy-magazine/article/spring-2014-giving -it-all.
5. Michael Douglass, "Here's How Many American Millionaires There Are," Motley Fool, January 23, 2017, https://www.fool.com/retirement/iras/2017/01/23/heres -how-many-american-millionaires-there-are.aspx.
6. See globalrichlist.com for more perspective on this topic.
7. Crown Financial Ministries offers a variety of stewardship resources and studies (https://www.crown.org). Good Sense Movement (https://goodsensemovement .org) offers printed and DVD resources by Dick Towner and others, including *Freed-Up Financial Living*. Dave Ramsey's Financial Peace University has helped many people get out of debt (https://www.daveramsey.com/fpu). See Howard Dayton's Compass—Finances God's Way at https://compass1.org. Many families have benefited from the practical financial advice of Ellie Kay (https://elliekay .com). See also Randy Alcorn, "Debt: Finding Freedom and Wisdom," chap. 16 in *Managing God's Money* (Carol Stream, IL: Tyndale, 2011).

CHAPTER 13: RICH IN GOOD DEEDS

1. William F. High with Ashley B. McCauley, *The Generosity Bet: Secrets of Risk, Reward, and Real Joy* (Shippensburg, PA: Destiny Image, 2014), 81.
2. Ibid.
3. Ibid., 82.
4. Ryan Scott, "Super Service Challenge Gamifies Giving for Businesses," *Forbes*, November 3, 2014, https://www.forbes.com/sites/causeintegration/2014/11/03 /super-service-challenge-gamifies-giving-for-businesses-3/#53da7564301b.
5. Timothy George, *Galatians: An Exegetical and Theological Exposition of Holy Scripture*, New American Commentary, vol. 30 (Nashville: B&H, 1994), 403.
6. F. F. Bruce, *The Epistle to the Galatians: A Commentary on the Greek Text* (Grand Rapids, MI: Eerdmans, 1982), 253–54.
7. Martin Luther, *A Commentary on Saint Paul's Epistle to the Galatians*, Galatians 5:22.
8. Johannes P. Louw and Eugene A. Nida, eds., *Greek-English Lexicon of the New Testament: Based on Semantic Domains*, 2nd ed., vol. 1 (New York: United Bible Societies, 1996), 569.
9. Lori Basheda, "Family Makes 200K a Year and Gives Most of It Away," *Orange County Register*, October 6, 2008, http://www.ocregister.com/2008/10/06/family -makes-200k-a-year-and-gives-most-of-it-away/.

10. "Tom and Bree Hsieh: Into the Neighborhood," Vimeo video, 7:44, Generous Giving, https://generousgiving.org/media/videos/tom-and-bree-hsieh-into-the-neighborhood.

CHAPTER 14: THE ADVENTURE OF GIVING

1. "Mary Clayton: Giving the Shirt off Your Back," Vimeo video, 5:10, Generous Giving, https://generousgiving.org/media/videos/mary-clayton-giving-the-shirt-off-your-back.
2. Johannes P. Louw and Eugene A. Nida, eds., *Greek-English Lexicon of the New Testament: Based on Semantic Domains*, 2nd ed., vol. 1 (New York: United Bible Societies, 1996), 568.
3. See Randy Alcorn, "Debt: Finding Freedom and Wisdom," chap. 16 and "Questions and Answers about Debt," chap. 17 in *Managing God's Money: A Biblical Guide* (Carol Stream, IL: Tyndale, 2011); "Debt: Borrowing and Lending," chap. 17 in *Money, Possessions, and Eternity* (Carol Stream, IL: Tyndale, 2003).
4. Ana Harris, "When You Don't Have Much to Offer," *Ana Harris Writes* (blog), January 10, 2018, http://anaharriswrites.com/when-you-dont-have-much-to-offer/.

CHAPTER 15: TREASURES DEPOSITED IN HEAVEN

1. I develop this in detail in my books *The Treasure Principle*, rev. ed. (Colorado Springs: Multnomah, 2017) and *The Law of Rewards* (Carol Stream, IL: Tyndale, 2003).
2. Alcorn, *The Treasure Principle*, 100.
3. Mart Green, "Mart Green on Life's Greatest Investment Opportunity," Eternal Perspective Ministries, December 28, 2018, https://www.epm.org/blog/2018/Dec/28/lifes-greatest-investment-opportunity.
4. A. W. Tozer, "The Transmutation of Wealth," in *Born after Midnight* (Harrisburg, PA: Christian Publications, 1959), 107.
5. Ibid., 106.

CHAPTER 16: KINGDOM PRIORITIES

1. "The Light and Life of Men," Vimeo video, 1:11:52, posted by Fellowship Bible Church, December 4, 2016, https://vimeo.com/194245357.
2. "Rosemary Khamati of PEACE International," Vimeo video, 2:15, posted by Fellowship Bible Church, December 2, 2016, https://vimeo.com/194067948.
3. John Wesley, *Wesley Gold*, comp. Ray Comfort (Orlando: Bridge-Logos, 2007), 107.
4. See https://www.prisonfellowship.org/action/ for opportunities to get involved with prison ministry.
5. "Dedication of the Kimyal New Testament," World Team, YouTube video, 10:50, https://us.worldteam.org/stories/video-details/dedication-of-the-kimyal-new-testament.

6. Ibid.
7. Ibid.
8. Ibid. See also Randy Alcorn, "The Word of God Entering a Tribe's Language in 2010," Eternal Perspective Ministries, December 31, 2010, https://www.epm.org/blog/2010/Dec/31/word-god-entering-tribes-language-2010.
9. Wycliffe Global Alliance, "2018 Bible Translation Statistics FAQs: Going Deeper," accessed January 21, 2019, http://resources.wycliffe.net/statistics/2018_Statistics_FAQs_EN.pdf.

CHAPTER 17: ETERNAL LIFE STARTS BEFORE WE DIE

1. "Drew Formsma at Ramsey Solutions," Vimeo video, 5:10, posted by I Like Giving, June 12, 2017, https://vimeo.com/221321916/1a2dd525a2.
2. Ibid.
3. Randy Alcorn, *The Treasure Principle*, rev. ed. (Colorado Springs: Multnomah, 2017), 7–8.
4. William F. High with Ashley B. McCauley, *The Generosity Bet: Secrets of Risk, Reward, and Real Joy* (Shippensburg, PA: Destiny Image, 2014), 196.

CHAPTER 18: WHEN GOD KEEPS OUTGIVING US

1. William F. High with Ashley B. McCauley, *The Generosity Bet: Secrets of Risk, Reward, and Real Joy* (Shippensburg, PA: Destiny Image, 2014), 154.
2. Ibid., 155.
3. R. G. LeTourneau, *Mover of Men and Mountains: The Autobiography of R. G. LeTourneau* (Chicago: Moody, 1972), 110.
4. High with McCauley, *The Generosity Bet*, 162.
5. Barbara Blouin and Katherine Gibson, eds., *The Legacy of Inherited Wealth: Interviews with Heirs*, rev. ed. (Blacksburg, VA: Trio Press, 1995).
6. Cameron Doolittle, "Three Lessons on Giving from Gerard and Geraldine Low," Generosity Path, December 12, 2016, http://www.generositypath.org/morestories/low?rq=gerard%20low.
7. Ibid.

CONCLUSION: NOW IS YOUR WINDOW OF OPPORTUNITY

1. "You Have One Life, Don't Waste It—John Piper," YouTube video, 7:28, posted by Desiring God, October 23, 2014, https://www.youtube.com/watch?v=mfpmbmsvu3A.
2. Ibid.

Discussion Questions

These questions are designed to give you the opportunity to consider and apply what you've read. They can be used for individual reflection or group discussion.

Chapter 1

1. Before you read this chapter, how would you have defined "the good life"? Does the idea that the good life is connected to generosity surprise you? In what ways does the connection make sense? In what ways might it not make sense?

2. According to the world's definition, do you feel you're currently living the good life? According to the Bible's definition, are you living the good life? In what ways?

3. Think of the people you know who are most generous with their love, time, money, and expertise. Overall, do they seem happier or unhappier than less generous people?

4. Randy writes, "One of the biggest misconceptions about giving is that the money we part with to help the needy or to spread the gospel just disappears and is gone forever" (p. 6). Can you relate? How might replacing this misconception with the concept of eternal investments affect your desire to give?

Chapter 2

1. Have you ever found yourself buying into the perception that celebrities (or people you know who have more money than you do) are automatically living "the good life"? Why do you think we often assume this to be true, despite the evidence to the contrary?

2. Have you ever asked God, "What do you want me to do with all your assets that you've put in my hands?" If you made that prayer a habit, in what ways might your outlook on money and giving change?

3. Take some time to read the following passages of Scripture, which speak of God's ownership: Leviticus 25:23; Deuteronomy 10:14; 1 Chronicles 29:11-12; Job 41:11; Psalm 24:1-2; Psalm 50:10-12; Haggai 2:8; 1 Corinthians 6:19-20. What do these passages say God owns? How is this biblical model countercultural?

4. If you began focusing on investments that will pay off twenty *million* years ahead instead of just twenty years,

how might your priorities and the way you spend your
money and time today change?

Chapter 3

1. What are some ways your money and possessions might
   be hindering you from the abundant life Jesus came to
   bring? In what ways have you believed Satan's lie that
   material goods will bring ultimate fulfillment in your
   own life?

2. After reading the illustration about the Sea of Galilee and
   the Dead Sea, which body of water do you think your
   present way of life more closely resembles? Why?

3. How could you use your money and possessions to
   demonstrate the abundant life Jesus has given you?
   What is something you could do today?

4. Read the following Scriptures about suffering for Christ:
   John 15:20; Acts 14:22; 2 Timothy 3:12; 1 Peter 4:16.
   How does understanding that God alone defines the good
   life change your perspective about difficulties and even
   persecution?

Chapter 4

1. Think back on Nanci's experience with the two elderly
   men at the grocery store. Have you had an unexpected
   opportunity to share a gift or an encouraging word with
   someone? What feelings did those experiences evoke?

2. What stood out to you most about John Wesley's story of giving? What do you think of his decision to set an amount to live on and give away the rest to help the needy?

3. Think of a time you planned a special gift for someone you love. How does that experience reflect the truth that Jesus affirmed, "There is more happiness in giving than in receiving" (Acts 20:35, GNT)? How can you make giving to others—and experiencing that God-given happiness—a more regular part of your life?

4. Randy reminds us, "If you love, you give. If you don't give, you don't love" (p. 48). Looking back at your choices over the last week, does your use of your money and time reflect love for God and others? What adjustments might you need to make in order to better honor Christ and experience the joy of giving?

Chapter 5

1. If Mary Jones had asked you about giving her inheritance to the three missionaries, what would you have advised? Would that advice have changed or been affirmed if you knew two of them would die? How do you think Christ would have viewed Mary's giving even if all three men had died without bringing the gospel to millions?

2. What do you think it will be like to meet someone in Heaven who is there because of missionaries or ministries you supported?

3. Of all the Christ-honoring causes you could support financially, which ones most excite you? Bible translation? Evangelism? Pro-life efforts? Missionary or pastoral care? Church planting? Fighting human trafficking? Caring for orphans? Feeding the hungry? Helping the homeless? How could you share these eternal investment opportunities with others?

4. What do you think might happen if you asked God to open your eyes to the needs surrounding you each day? What might be holding you back from the giving adventures right in front of you?

Chapter 6

1. Have you ever considered wealth a liability? In what ways do you think wealth could endanger you and those you love?

2. Jesus doesn't ask each of his followers to give up all their possessions. But if you had been in the rich young man's place and Jesus had told you to sell your possessions, give to the poor, and follow him, how do you think you would have responded? Which of your priorities need to be reordered so you can follow Jesus wholeheartedly?

3. Scripture says Jesus looked at the rich young man "and loved him" (Mark 10:21, NIV). How would grasping that God's warnings about wealth are given precisely because

of his love change the way you approach Scripture's warnings against loving money?

4. Do you see wealth as an automatic sign of God's blessing? How could studying what God has to say about the poor, particularly Jesus' words in the Beatitudes (Matthew 5:1-12), adjust your thinking?

Chapter 7

1. What stood out to you most about Stanley Tam's story? How is his approach to both business ownership and retirement different from what we typically see in our culture?

2. Randy acknowledges that not everyone owns a corporation or makes millions of dollars but emphasizes that all of us can cultivate hearts of generosity. In what practical ways could you express the belief, as Stanley Tam did, that God owns everything and has entrusted it to your care?

3. Read Colossians 3:23-24. How might your perspective about work change, knowing that God can use your job and your income to greatly impact eternity?

4. Think through the particular places of influence in which God has placed you. What are some ways you could use your role to share the good news about Jesus?

Chapter 8

1. Do you struggle with being content and happy with what God has provided for you? If so, what are some factors that contribute to your discontentment?

2. Since Paul tells us contentment can be learned (Philippians 4:10-13), think of one or two specific changes you can make in your thinking habits and practices that could lead to greater contentment.

3. List some ways you've seen God's tangible material care for you recently. Consider making this a regular practice—recording God's faithfulness in providing for you.

4. Identify at least one area (such as income, possessions, or achievements) in which you've caught yourself thinking, *If only I earned more/had more/did more* . . . Before reading this chapter, did you understand that this kind of thinking reflects a belief that God is not enough? Are you willing to present that area to God and ask him to correct your perspective for his glory and your good?

Chapter 9

1. List some evils you see in our world and communities today. What role does love of money play in perpetuating those evils?

2. Have you ever prayed Proverbs 30:8, "Give me neither poverty nor riches"? How might a prayer like this change

your perspective on money? What do you think might happen if you regularly prayed, "God, give me only as many riches as I can hold loosely and give freely out of love for God and others"?

3. Have you ever bought a lottery ticket? Were you surprised about the stories of what has happened to many who have won the big jackpots?

4. List ways you've used money for good. Now list ways you've misspent. How did you feel while using your money each of these ways, both at the time and as you look back?

Chapter 10

1. What stood out to you about the modern retelling of the parable of the rich fool (Luke 12:13-21)? Try writing your own version based on how money-love most tempts you.

2. Look over the list of the various translations of the phrase "pierced themselves with many pangs," from 1 Timothy 6:10. Which one stands out to you as the most somber warning against money-love?

3. What are some ways you could help your family pursue generosity and avoid money-love? Brainstorm some ideas for getting your loved ones excited about giving to meet the needs of others both near and far away.

4. Are there people in your life who help you by their example and words to avoid the dangers of materialism? If not, how could you develop that kind of relationship and accountability with a few key people?

Chapter 11

1. What do you think it would look like to flee materialism and money-love in our culture?

2. Read Galatians 5:16-26. What virtues should a Christian pursue, and how are these virtues similar to the ones Paul told Timothy to chase after in 1 Timothy 6:11-16?

3. If someone were to ask what you think eternity will be like, how would you describe it? How does a deeper understanding of eternal life in Heaven and on the New Earth change your view of money and possessions?

4. What do you consider to be the main advantages to turning away from materialism and pursuing God?

Chapter 12

1. Have you ever thought of yourself as rich? According to globalrichlist.com, where does your family's income or assets place you on the global scale? What would it look like if your family were to live beneath your means and give away more of what you don't need?

2. Take some time to think about the gifts and advantages the Lord has given you (for example, family, upbringing, education, financial resources, etc.). What do these suggest in relation to the words of Jesus: "From everyone who has been given much, much will be demanded; and from the one who has been entrusted with much, much more will be asked" (Luke 12:48, NIV)?

3. Consider taking a field trip to a landfill with your family or your small group. How does witnessing the temporary and throwaway nature of material possessions change your view of them?

4. As a family or with a group of friends, make a list of fun or enriching activities that don't cost much more than time. What could you do to replace expensive activities and give the money you've saved to Kingdom purposes?

Chapter 13

1. After reading about how the Lindseys creatively incorporated generous giving into their business environment, how might you be able to spread generosity in your spheres of influence: your family, workplace, church, or neighborhood? Or even on a national or global level?

2. The command to "do good" involves actively and generously reaching out to people. List three worthy ministries and three individuals or families you know of who would benefit from your generosity. Think of specific ways you could help them, and take at least one step to do so.

3. Based on what you read in this chapter, how would you respond to someone who says Christians shouldn't focus on doing good deeds since we're saved by faith, not works? What Scriptures from the chapter could you share with them?

4. What stood out to you in the story about the Hsiehs choosing to live on little while they gave large? What are some ways you could live on less?

Chapter 14

1. Who in your life right now could most use help—perhaps a meal or babysitting or housecleaning or assistance with a bill? Think of specific ways you could offer help and how you can word it so they know that you are *ready* to do it, not just that you're willing.

2. Is overspending on unnecessary things a temptation for you? What Internet sites or physical stores are most tempting to you? How could you change your habits in order to free up more money to be generous when others' needs arise?

3. Do you find it easier to give your time or your money? Why do you think that is? How could you grow in the area you find more difficult?

4. Before reading this chapter, had you ever thought about giving as an adventure? How could that perspective change your mind-set about generosity?

Chapter 15

1. Take some time to honestly answer A. W. Tozer's four questions on page 202. Based on your answers, what is your treasure? What adjustments might you need to make?

2. Have you ever thought about the fact that giving actually offers you the greatest control over your money? How could grasping this concept change your perceptions about giving?

3. Was there anything that surprised you about the idea of eternal rewards? How did this chapter challenge or influence your thoughts about God rewarding his children?

4. In a ninety-second video called "Live for the Line," Randy speaks about the fact that a person's life in this world is just a dot, which begins and ends and is very brief. But from that dot extends a line that goes on for eternity. If we are wise, while we live in the dot, we will live for the line. Consider watching this brief video and contemplating its significance in your own life. Scan the QR code below or type this link into your web browser: http://y2u.be/T2A9w2wU1Xw. What's your response to this message?

Chapter 16

1. How could the advice "Do what you can with your wealth today to build a firm foundation for your *eternal* years" change the way you budget, spend, and invest today?

2. What will you one day wish you had given away while you still had the chance? What possessions or money are you holding on to that will one day be useless to you?

3. Think through the eventual end of all possessions, including new cars, hot tubs, and entertainment systems (realizing there's nothing inherently wrong with any of them). From an eternal perspective, how might the money allocated for these items instead be invested in helping people and bringing them the gospel?

4. Have you ever thought about creating an eternal investment portfolio? What kinds of eternity-shaping projects or organizations or people would you include in yours?

Chapter 17

1. God offers us true, authentic, and abundant life in Jesus. What kind of pseudolife are you most tempted by? A life focused on money, possessions, popularity, relationships, abilities, appearance, or something else? What might you need to change or let go of so you can reject this pseudolife?

2. Since knowing Jesus is the key to taking hold of the true life, what are some ways you can daily invest in knowing him better and loving him more?

3. What would your initial advice have been to the young man with a great job who felt God wanted him to sell his house and give away the money? In light of what you see in Scripture, how do you think Jesus might have counseled him?

4. Can you imagine anyone saying on his or her deathbed, "I wish I'd bought more stuff"? What do you think dying people actually regret or wish they'd done differently in terms of their relationships, possessions, and choices?

Chapter 18

1. Have you ever asked God, "Do I have the gift of giving?" or asked him why he has given you so much? What causes has God put on your heart to support generously as part of the "army of giving warriors" Randy writes about?

2. Has there been a time when God provided for you and your family unexpectedly? How does remembering this experience encourage you to step out in faith as you give?

3. Have you ever thought that leaving money in your will takes no faith or sacrifice on your part? What are the pros and cons of giving substantially now instead of waiting until you die to leave money behind?

4. Read Malachi 3:8-12. Have you ever purposefully tested God's promise through generous giving? If not, what advantages would there be in doing so?

Conclusion

1. How has reading this book changed your ideas about what it means to live the good life?

2. As part of grabbing hold of eternal life here and now, what specific changes would you like to make when it comes to your relationships, money, possessions, and priorities? Ask God to empower you to make those changes so you can embrace the abundant and eternally minded life he intends for you.

3. Make a list of people you can share these life-changing truths about the good life with.

About the Author

RANDY ALCORN is the founder and director of Eternal Perspective Ministries (EPM), a nonprofit organization dedicated to teaching principles of God's Word and assisting the church in ministering to unreached, unfed, unborn, uneducated, unreconciled, and unsupported people around the world. His ministry focus is communicating the strategic importance of using our earthly time, money, possessions, and opportunities to invest in need-meeting ministries that count for eternity. He accomplishes this by analyzing, teaching, and applying biblical truth.

Before starting EPM in 1990, Randy served as a pastor for fourteen years. He has a bachelor of theology and a master of arts in biblical studies from Multnomah University and an honorary doctorate from Western Seminary in Portland, Oregon, and he has taught on the adjunct faculties of both institutions.

A *New York Times* bestselling author, Randy has written more than fifty books, including *Heaven*, *The Treasure Principle*, and the award-winning novel *Safely Home*. Over eleven million copies of his books have been sold, and his titles have been translated into more than seventy languages. All royalties from his books are given to the works of Christian ministries, including world missions and organizations that care for the poor.

Randy has written for many magazines, including EPM's *Eternal Perspectives*. He is active on Facebook and Twitter and has been a guest on more than eight hundred radio, television, and online programs, including *Focus on the Family*, *FamilyLife Today*, and *Revive Our Hearts*.

Randy resides in Gresham, Oregon, with his wife, Nanci. They have two married daughters and are the proud grandparents of five grandsons. Randy enjoys spending time with his family, biking, researching, reading, and underwater photography.

CONTACT ETERNAL PERSPECTIVE MINISTRIES:

www.epm.org

39085 Pioneer Blvd., Suite 206, Sandy, OR 97055

503-668-5200

FOLLOW RANDY ALCORN:

Facebook: www.facebook.com/randyalcorn

Twitter: www.twitter.com/randyalcorn

Instagram: www.instagram.com/randyalcorn_epm

EPM website: www.epm.org

Blog: www.epm.org/blog

Friends Around the World Activity Book

This activity book includes recipes, puzzles, crafts, and games that introduce kids to the joys and struggles of friends from far away. As they interact with the activities in the book and learn about life in other countries, kids will connect with and develop a heart of compassion for people around the world.

The Philippines: An Interactive Family Experience

Walk through the everyday life of kids and young adults living in poverty in the Philippines as they share their hopes, dreams, and joys. Vibrant illustrations and panoramic videos bring you into the Philippines, and the crafts, recipes, prayers, and devotions build kinship with families across the ocean. See the world through God's eyes—no passport required.

Friends Around the World Atlas

Colorfully illustrated maps and interesting facts introduce children to 25 countries where Compassion International is releasing babies, children, and young adults from poverty in Jesus' name.

CP1502

BOOKS BY RANDY ALCORN

FICTION

Deadline

Dominion

Deception

Edge of Eternity

Eternity

Lord Foulgrin's Letters

The Ishbane Conspiracy

Safely Home

Courageous

The Chasm

CHILDREN'S

Heaven for Kids

Wait Until Then

Tell Me About Heaven

STUDY GUIDES

The Grace and Truth Paradox Study Guide

The Treasure Principle Study Guide

The Treasure Principle Bible Study

The Purity Principle Study Guide

If God Is Good Study Guide

The Heaven Small Group Discussion Guide

The Heaven Workbook

NONFICTION

Happiness

God's Promise of Happiness

Does God Want Us to Be Happy?

Heaven

Touchpoints: Heaven

50 Days of Heaven

In Light of Eternity

Managing God's Money

Money, Possessions, and Eternity

The Law of Rewards

ProLife Answers to ProChoice Arguments

Sexual Temptation: Guardrails for the Road to Purity

The Goodness of God

The Grace and Truth Paradox

The Purity Principle

The Treasure Principle

Why ProLife?

If God Is Good . . .

The Promise of Heaven

We Shall See God

90 Days of God's Goodness

Life Promises for Eternity

Eternal Perspectives

Everything You Always Wanted to Know about Heaven

hand in Hand

Help for Women Under Stress

The Resolution for Men

Seeing the Unseen

Does the Birth Control Pill Cause Abortions?